TEXT BOOK OF PHARMACOLOGY - II

[According to latest syllabus of B. Pharm – V semester (BP – 503T) of Pharmacy Council of India]

Ms. Nidhi Mittal

Associate Professor

S R College of Pharmacy

Ambabai, Gwalior Road, Jhansi (U. P.)

Ms. Kalpana Purohit

Ph. D. Scholar

Department of Pharmaceutical Science

Mangalayatan University

Aligarh (U. P.)

Prof. (Dr.) Biswaranjan Ray

Professor

Department of Pharmacology

College of Pharmaceutical Science

Puri (Odisha)

Mrs. Prashansa Tripathi

Lecturer

Shanti College of Pharmacy

Nowgong, Chhatarpur (M. P.)

Mrs. Priyanka Ahirwar

Assistant Professor

Shanti College of Pharmacy

Nowgong, Chhatarpur (M. P.)

Notion Press

TEXT BOOK OF

PHARMACOLOGY - II

@Copyright Reserved with Publisher and Authors

First Edition 2024

Published by:

NOTION PRESS

Publisher and distributor

Head office: Notion press Media Pvt. Ltd.

7, Red cross Road,

Egmore, Chennai, Tamil Nadu 60008

Website: www.notionpress.com

TEXT BOOK OF PHARMACOLOGY - II
ABOUT THE BOOK

The Text Book of Pharmacology - II provides an extensive overview of drugs acting on the cardiovascular, urinary, and endocrine systems, along with a detailed exploration of autocoids and bioassay principles. It begins with an in-depth discussion on the Pharmacology of Drugs Acting on the Cardiovascular System. This section is divided into three parts. The first part introduces the electrophysiology of the heart and explains the pharmacological management of conditions like congestive heart failure, hypertension, angina, arrhythmias, and hyperlipidemia, highlighting the different drug classes used to manage these conditions.

The second part of the cardiovascular section focuses on the pharmacological management of shock, and includes a discussion on hematinics, coagulants, anticoagulants, fibrinolytics, antiplatelet drugs, and plasma volume expanders, which are vital for conditions affecting blood volume and clotting mechanisms. The third part further elaborates on advanced cardiovascular drug therapies.

Following the cardiovascular system, the book discusses the Pharmacology of Drugs Acting on the Urinary System, focusing primarily on diuretics and antidiuretics, which are essential for managing fluid balance and electrolyte homeostasis in the body.

The next major section covers Autocoids and Related Drugs, split into two parts. This section explores biologically active substances, such as histamine, serotonin (5-HT), and other autocoids, which play a crucial role in inflammation, allergy, and vascular functions, and the drugs that target these pathways.

The book also offers an extensive exploration of Pharmacology of Drugs Acting on the Endocrine System, detailing the function and pharmacology of pituitary hormones, thyroid hormones, calcium-regulating hormones, and drugs like insulin, oral hypoglycemic agents, glucagon, ACTH, and corticosteroids. Additionally, it covers androgens, anabolic steroids, estrogens, progesterone, and oral contraceptives, as well as drugs that affect uterine function.

Finally, the book includes a comprehensive section on Bioassay, discussing its principles, applications, and different types. It covers the bioassay of various hormones and drugs, including insulin, oxytocin, vasopressin, ACTH, d-tubocurarine, digitalis, histamine, and serotonin (5-HT), explaining how these assays are used to measure the potency and efficacy of drugs.

TEXT BOOK OF PHARMACOLOGY - II
NOTION PRESS
PREFACE

The authors feel great pleasure in presenting the first edition of the book **"Text Book of Pharmacology - II"** for graduate and post graduate students. The present book on **Text Book of Pharmacology - II** has been written according to the syllabus of M. Pharm of Pharmacy Council of India and covers full course of the subject.

THE SALIENT FEATURES OF THE BOOK ARE: -

- *Easy to understand style of writing* which makes the book a self-study material.

- *Each new concept has been introduced through day-today problem of interest* to the students which makes the subject matter interesting.

- *The language of the book, on the whole, is lucid and easy to understand.*

- Wherever needed *neatly labeled figures have been drawn*?

The authors hope that the students, teachers and other readers will find the book interesting and to the point covering the course. We hope that the students will receive the book warmly.

I express a sincere thank you to the Management of S R College of Pharmacy, Department of Pharmaceutical Science, Mangalayatan University, Department of Pharmacology, College of Pharmaceutical Science and Shanti College of pharmacy for their support during the writing of this book.

Every effort is made to keep the book error free. The author will gratefully acknowledge the suggestions to improve the book to make it more useful.

Wishing our readers success in examination and life ahead. The authors feel that their efforts will be fully rewarded if the book serves the purpose for which it is written.

TEXT BOOK OF PHARMACOLOGY - II
CONTENTS

CHAPTER – 1

PHARMACOLOGY OF DRUGS ACTING ON CARDIO VASCULAR SYSTEM – I

INTRODUCTION:

The pharmacology of drugs acting on the cardiovascular system is a vast and critical area of study, given the central role the heart and blood vessels play in maintaining homeostasis. Cardiovascular drugs are designed to treat a wide range of conditions affecting the heart and vascular system, including hypertension, heart failure, arrhythmias, and ischemic heart disease.

1. Overview of the Cardiovascular System

The cardiovascular system consists of the heart, blood vessels (arteries, veins, and capillaries), and blood. It is responsible for transporting oxygen, nutrients, hormones, and waste products throughout the body. The heart functions as a pump to circulate blood, and the blood vessels serve as conduits for blood flow. Key physiological aspects relevant to cardiovascular pharmacology include:

a. **Cardiac output (CO):** The amount of blood the heart pumps per minute.

b. **Peripheral resistance (PR):** The resistance offered by the systemic blood vessels to the flow of blood.

c. **Blood pressure (BP):** A product of cardiac output and peripheral resistance, regulated by neural, hormonal, and renal mechanisms.

2. Classes of Cardiovascular Drugs

The major classes of drugs used to treat cardiovascular diseases include:

a. Antihypertensive Agents

i. **Diuretics:** Reduce blood volume by promoting the excretion of sodium and water, leading to a decrease in blood pressure.

ii. **Beta-adrenergic blockers (Beta-blockers):** Decrease heart rate and contractility, reducing cardiac output and lowering blood pressure.

iii. **Calcium channel blockers (CCBs):** Inhibit calcium ion entry into vascular smooth muscle and cardiac cells, leading to vasodilation and decreased cardiac workload.

iv. **Angiotensin-converting enzyme (ACE) inhibitors:** Prevent the conversion of angiotensin I to angiotensin II, a potent vasoconstrictor, thus lowering blood pressure.

v. **Angiotensin II receptor blockers (ARBs):** Block the effects of angiotensin II, reducing vasoconstriction and lowering blood pressure.

vi. **Vasodilators:** Directly relax vascular smooth muscle, leading to vasodilation and a reduction in blood pressure.

b. Antianginal Agents

i. **Nitrates:** Dilate coronary arteries and veins, improving blood flow to the heart and reducing myocardial oxygen demand.

ii. **Beta-blockers:** Reduce myocardial oxygen demand by decreasing heart rate and contractility.

iii. **Calcium channel blockers:** Reduce myocardial oxygen demand and improve coronary blood flow.

c. Antiarrhythmic Agents

i. **Class I (Sodium channel blockers):** Modify the action potential duration and affect the conduction velocity in cardiac tissue.

ii. **Class II (Beta-blockers):** Decrease sympathetic stimulation of the heart, reducing heart rate and conduction velocity.

iii. **Class III (Potassium channel blockers):** Prolong the action potential duration and refractory period, reducing the likelihood of arrhythmias.

iv. **Class IV (Calcium channel blockers):** Slow the conduction through the AV node, reducing heart rate and preventing arrhythmias.

d. Drugs for Heart Failure

i. **Diuretics:** Reduce fluid overload, decreasing the workload on the heart.

ii. **ACE inhibitors/ARBs:** Reduce afterload by decreasing vascular resistance, making it easier for the heart to pump blood.

iii. **Beta-blockers:** Improve survival by reducing the adverse effects of chronic sympathetic activation on the heart.

iv. **Digitalis glycosides:** Increase the force of cardiac contractions (positive inotropic effect) and slow the heart rate.

e. Anticoagulants and Antiplatelet Agents

i. **Anticoagulants:** Prevent the formation of blood clots by inhibiting various factors in the coagulation cascade (e.g., warfarin, heparin).

ii. **Antiplatelet agents:** Prevent platelet aggregation, reducing the risk of arterial thrombosis (e.g., aspirin, clopidogrel).

3. Mechanisms of Action

Cardiovascular drugs work through various mechanisms to achieve therapeutic effects:

a. **Modulating autonomic nervous system activity** (e.g., beta-blockers).

b. **Influencing the renin-angiotensin-aldosterone system** (e.g., ACE inhibitors, ARBs).

c. **Affecting ion channels in cardiac and vascular smooth muscle cells** (e.g., calcium channel blockers).

d. **Directly affecting vascular tone** (e.g., nitrates, vasodilators).

e. **Modifying blood volume and composition** (e.g., diuretics, anticoagulants).

4. Clinical Uses

Cardiovascular drugs are prescribed based on the specific condition:

a. **Hypertension:** ACE inhibitors, ARBs, beta-blockers, diuretics.

b. **Angina pectoris:** Nitrates, beta-blockers, calcium channel blockers.

c. **Arrhythmias:** Antiarrhythmic drugs like sodium channel blockers, beta-blockers, potassium channel blockers.

d. **Heart failure:** Diuretics, ACE inhibitors, beta-blockers, digitalis glycosides.

e. **Thromboembolic disorders:** Anticoagulants, antiplatelet agents.

5. Side Effects and Considerations

The use of cardiovascular drugs requires careful monitoring due to potential side effects such as:

a. **Hypotension:** Excessive lowering of blood pressure.

b. **Bradycardia or tachycardia:** Abnormally slow or fast heart rate.

c. **Electrolyte imbalances:** Particularly with diuretics.

d. **Renal impairment:** Can be exacerbated by ACE inhibitors and ARBs.

e. **Bleeding:** With anticoagulants and antiplatelet agents.

6. Structure-Activity Relationship (SAR)

Understanding the SAR of cardiovascular drugs is crucial in predicting their efficacy, potency, and side effect profiles. Small changes in the chemical structure can significantly impact the drug's interaction with its target receptors or enzymes.

INTRODUCTION TO ELECTROPHYSIOLOGY OF HEART

Electrophysiology is the study of the electrical properties of biological cells and tissues, particularly their electrical activity. In the context of the heart, it involves understanding how electrical signals regulate heartbeats, the initiation of heart contractions, and the coordination of the heart's rhythm. This knowledge is crucial for understanding how cardiovascular drugs affect heart function and for managing arrhythmias (irregular heartbeats).

1. Basic Principles of Cardiac Electrophysiology

The heart's electrical activity originates from specialized cardiac cells capable of generating and conducting electrical impulses. These impulses coordinate the heart's contractions, ensuring efficient blood pumping. The main components of cardiac electrophysiology include:

a. **Resting Membrane Potential:** The difference in electrical charge across the cell membrane when the cell is at rest. For cardiac cells, this is typically around -80 to -90 millivolts (mV).

b. **Action Potential:** A rapid change in membrane potential that propagates along the cardiac muscle cells. It consists of several phases:

   i. **Phase 0:** Rapid depolarization due to the influx of sodium ions (Na+) through fast sodium channels.

   ii. **Phase 1:** Initial repolarization caused by the inactivation of sodium channels and the opening of potassium channels.

   iii. **Phase 2:** Plateau phase, characterized by a balance between the influx of calcium ions (Ca2+) and the efflux of potassium ions (K+), which prolongs depolarization.

   iv. **Phase 3:** Rapid repolarization due to the continued efflux of potassium ions and the closure of calcium channels.

   v. **Phase 4:** Resting phase where the cell returns to its resting membrane potential.

2. Cardiac Conduction System

The heart's conduction system ensures the synchronized contraction of the atria and ventricles. It includes:

a. **Sinoatrial (SA) Node:** The natural pacemaker of the heart located in the right atrium. It generates electrical impulses that initiate each heartbeat and set the pace for the heart rate.

b. **Atrioventricular (AV) Node:** Located at the junction between the atria and ventricles, the AV node delays the electrical impulse, allowing the ventricles to fill with blood from the atria before contracting.

c. **Bundle of His:** A collection of specialized fibers that conduct the electrical impulse from the AV node to the ventricles.

d. **Purkinje Fibers:** Fibers that distribute the electrical impulse throughout the ventricles, leading to coordinated ventricular contraction.

3. Cardiac Electrical Properties

   a. **Automaticity:** The ability of cardiac pacemaker cells to spontaneously generate electrical impulses. This is crucial for initiating and maintaining the heart's rhythm.

   b. **Conductivity:** The ability of cardiac cells to conduct electrical impulses from one cell to another. This ensures that the electrical signal spreads efficiently throughout the heart.

   c. **Excitability:** The ability of cardiac cells to respond to electrical impulses. This property ensures that the heart responds appropriately to the electrical signals.

   d. **Refractory Period:** The period following an action potential during which the heart muscle cannot be re-excited. It prevents the occurrence of additional impulses too soon, allowing the heart to refill with blood before the next contraction.

4. Electrocardiogram (ECG or EKG)

An ECG is a diagnostic tool used to record the electrical activity of the heart. It provides information about:

   a. **Heart Rate:** The number of heartbeats per minute.

   b. **Heart Rhythm:** The regularity of heartbeats.

   c. **Conduction Intervals:** Time intervals between different phases of the cardiac cycle.

   d. **Electrical Axis:** The general direction of the heart's electrical activity.

The ECG waveform includes:

   a. **P Wave:** Represents atrial depolarization.

   b. **QRS Complex:** Represents ventricular depolarization.

   c. **T Wave:** Represents ventricular repolarization.

5. Drug Effects on Cardiac Electrophysiology

Understanding cardiac electrophysiology is essential for predicting how drugs affect heart function. Drugs that influence electrophysiology can be classified based on their effects on various phases of the cardiac action potential and conduction system:

a. **Antiarrhythmic Drugs:** Modify the duration of the action potential and the conduction velocity, affecting heart rhythm. Examples include sodium channel blockers (Class I), beta-blockers (Class II), potassium channel blockers (Class III), and calcium channel blockers (Class IV).

b. **Beta-Blockers:** Decrease the heart rate and reduce the force of contraction by blocking beta-adrenergic receptors, which decreases sympathetic stimulation.

c. **Calcium Channel Blockers:** Affect the plateau phase of the action potential, reducing the influx of calcium and slowing conduction through the AV node.

d. **Digitalis Glycosides:** Increase the force of cardiac contractions and slow the heart rate by affecting the sodium-potassium ATPase pump.

6. Clinical Implications

A thorough understanding of cardiac electrophysiology is crucial for the effective use of cardiovascular drugs:

a. **Arrhythmias:** Drugs that affect electrophysiology are used to restore normal rhythm and prevent abnormal rhythms.

b. **Heart Failure:** Drugs that modulate cardiac output and heart rate can improve symptoms and outcomes.

c. **Hypertension and Ischemic Heart Disease:** Drugs that influence cardiac function can help manage these conditions.

INTRODUCTION TO ELECTROPHYSIOLOGY OF HEART

Electrophysiology of the heart involves the study of the electrical properties and activities of cardiac cells that govern the heart's rhythm and contraction. This field is crucial in pharmacology, as many cardiovascular drugs target these electrical processes to treat various heart conditions. Understanding these principles helps in comprehending how drugs affect heart function and can be used to manage arrhythmias, heart failure, and other cardiovascular disorders.

1. Fundamental Concepts

a. Resting Membrane Potential:

    i.   Cardiac cells maintain a resting membrane potential typically around -80 to -90 millivolts (mV). This potential is due to the differential distribution of ions across the cell membrane, primarily sodium ($Na+$), potassium ($K+$), and chloride ($Cl-$).

b. Action Potential:

    i.   The action potential is a brief, rapid change in membrane potential that leads to muscle contraction. It has several phases:

        1. **Phase 0:** Depolarization – Rapid influx of $Na+$ through voltage-gated sodium channels.

        2. **Phase 1:** Initial Repolarization – Closure of sodium channels and opening of potassium channels.

        3. **Phase 2:** Plateau – Balance between inward $Ca2+$ and outward $K+$ currents, contributing to prolonged depolarization.

        4. **Phase 3:** Repolarization – Outflow of $K+$ predominates, restoring the resting membrane potential.

        5. **Phase 4:** Resting Phase – The cell is ready to respond to the next stimulus.

c. Refractory Periods:

    i.   The refractory period is the time following an action potential during which the cell cannot be re-excited. It includes:

        1. **Absolute Refractory Period:** The time during which no new action potential can be generated, regardless of the strength of the stimulus.

        2. **Relative Refractory Period:** The time when a stronger-than-normal stimulus can initiate a new action potential.

2. Cardiac Conduction System

The heart's conduction system ensures coordinated heartbeats. It consists of specialized cells that generate and propagate electrical impulses:

a. **Sinoatrial (SA) Node:** Located in the right atrium, this node is the heart's primary pacemaker, initiating electrical impulses that set the pace of the heartbeat.

b. **Atrioventricular (AV) Node:** Located at the junction of the atria and ventricles, it delays the impulse, allowing the ventricles to fill with blood before contraction.

c. **Bundle of His:** Conducts impulses from the AV node to the ventricles.

d. **Purkinje Fibers:** Distribute the electrical impulse throughout the ventricles, leading to coordinated ventricular contraction.

3. Electrocardiogram (ECG or EKG)

An ECG records the heart's electrical activity and provides information about:

a. **P Wave:** Represents atrial depolarization.

b. **QRS Complex:** Represents ventricular depolarization.

c. **T Wave:** Represents ventricular repolarization.

d. **PR Interval:** Time between atrial depolarization and ventricular depolarization.

e. **QT Interval:** Duration of ventricular depolarization and repolarization.

4. Electrophysiological Properties

a. Automaticity:

i. The ability of certain cardiac cells to spontaneously generate electrical impulses without external stimuli. This is a key feature of pacemaker cells.

b. Conductivity:

i. The ability of cardiac cells to conduct electrical impulses from one cell to another, ensuring the electrical signal spreads throughout the heart.

c. Excitability:

i. The ability of cardiac cells to respond to electrical impulses. This property is crucial for the heart's ability to contract in response to stimulation.

5. Drug Interactions with Electrophysiology

Drugs that influence cardiac electrophysiology are essential for managing various cardiovascular conditions. They can affect:

a. **Heart Rate:** Drugs like beta-blockers reduce heart rate by blocking sympathetic stimulation.

b. **Conduction Velocity:** Calcium channel blockers and certain antiarrhythmics slow conduction through the AV node.

c. **Action Potential Duration:** Antiarrhythmic drugs such as potassium channel blockers can prolong the action potential, influencing the refractory period.

a. Antiarrhythmic Drugs:

i. **Class I (Sodium Channel Blockers):** Alter the phase 0 depolarization of the action potential, affecting conduction speed and excitability.

ii. **Class II (Beta-Blockers):** Reduce sympathetic stimulation, slowing heart rate and conduction.

iii. **Class III (Potassium Channel Blockers):** Prolong repolarization, thereby lengthening the action potential duration and refractory period.

iv. **Class IV (Calcium Channel Blockers):** Affect the plateau phase of the action potential and reduce conduction through the AV node.

b. Other Cardiovascular Drugs:

i. **Digitalis Glycosides:** Increase the force of cardiac contraction and modulate heart rate by affecting ion transport.

6. Clinical Implications

A detailed understanding of cardiac electrophysiology is crucial for:

a. **Diagnosing Arrhythmias:** Identifying abnormal electrical activity and tailoring treatment.

b. **Managing Heart Failure:** Adjusting treatment to balance cardiac output and avoid exacerbating arrhythmias.

c. **Controlling Hypertension and Ischemic Heart Disease:** Using drugs that influence heart rate and contractility to manage symptoms.

DRUGS USED IN CONGESTIVE HEART FAILURE

Congestive heart failure (CHF) is a condition where the heart is unable to pump sufficient blood to meet the body's needs. It can result from various underlying conditions, including coronary artery disease, hypertension, and cardiomyopathy. The management of CHF involves a combination of lifestyle modifications, medications, and sometimes surgical interventions. The pharmacological treatment aims to improve symptoms, enhance quality of life, and reduce mortality.

1. Diuretics

a. Mechanism of Action:

i. Diuretics reduce fluid overload by increasing urine production, which decreases blood volume and venous pressure, thereby reducing the workload on the heart.

b. Types and Examples:

i. **Loop Diuretics:**

1. **Furosemide:** Acts on the ascending loop of Henle, inhibiting the reabsorption of sodium and chloride.

2. **Bumetanide:** Similar to furosemide but more potent.

3. **Torsemide:** Has a longer duration of action compared to furosemide.

ii. **Thiazide Diuretics:**

1. **Hydrochlorothiazide:** Acts on the distal convoluted tubule, less potent than loop diuretics but useful for mild fluid retention.

iii. **Potassium-Sparing Diuretics:**

    1. **Spironolactone:** Aldosterone antagonist that helps retain potassium while excreting sodium.

    2. **Eplerenone:** Similar to spironolactone but with fewer side effects related to hormonal changes.

c. Clinical Use:

i. Diuretics are used to manage symptoms such as edema and pulmonary congestion in CHF. They are particularly effective in reducing symptoms of fluid overload.

2. Angiotensin-Converting Enzyme (ACE) Inhibitors

a. Mechanism of Action:

i. ACE inhibitors block the conversion of angiotensin I to angiotensin II, a potent vasoconstrictor. This leads to vasodilation, reduced blood pressure, and decreased workload on the heart. They also reduce the secretion of aldosterone, which decreases fluid retention.

b. Examples:

i. Enalapril

ii. Lisinopril

iii. Ramipril

iv. Captopril

c. Clinical Use:

i. ACE inhibitors are essential in managing CHF as they improve symptoms, reduce hospitalization, and enhance survival by decreasing the progression of heart failure and preventing worsening renal function.

3. Angiotensin II Receptor Blockers (ARBs)

a. Mechanism of Action:

i. ARBs block the action of angiotensin II at its receptor sites, leading to vasodilation and reduced secretion of aldosterone. They offer similar benefits to ACE inhibitors but without some of the common side effects like cough.

b. Examples:

i.   Losartan

ii. Valsartan

iii. Candesartan

c. Clinical Use:

i.   ARBs are used in patients who cannot tolerate ACE inhibitors due to cough or angioedema. They are effective in managing CHF and can be used as an alternative or in combination with ACE inhibitors.

4. Beta-Blockers

a. Mechanism of Action:

i.   Beta-blockers reduce heart rate and myocardial contractility by blocking beta-adrenergic receptors. This decreases the workload on the heart and improves symptoms over time.

b. Examples:

i.   **Carvedilol:** Non-selective beta-blocker with additional alpha-blocking properties.

ii. **Metoprolol:** Selective beta-1 blocker that reduces heart rate and contractility.

iii. **Bisoprolol:** Selective beta-1 blocker with proven efficacy in CHF.

c. Clinical Use:

i.   Beta-blockers are used to improve symptoms, reduce hospitalizations, and enhance survival in CHF patients. They are particularly beneficial in reducing the adverse effects of chronic sympathetic activation.

5. Aldosterone Antagonists

a. Mechanism of Action:

i.   These drugs block the effects of aldosterone, leading to reduced fluid retention and decreased potassium loss.

b. Examples:

i.   **Spironolactone:** Also has anti-androgenic effects, which can lead to side effects like gynecomastia.

ii.   **Eplerenone:** More selective for mineralocorticoid receptors with fewer side effects.

c. Clinical Use:

i.   Aldosterone antagonists are used in advanced CHF to reduce symptoms and improve survival, especially in patients with reduced ejection fraction.

6. Inotropic Agents

a. Mechanism of Action:

i.   Inotropic agents increase the force of cardiac contraction, improving cardiac output.

b. Examples:

i.   **Digoxin:** Increases intracellular calcium, enhancing myocardial contractility. It also has a mild diuretic effect and slows the heart rate.

ii.   **Dobutamine:** Beta-agonist that increases myocardial contractility and cardiac output.

iii. **Milrinone:** Phosphodiesterase inhibitor that increases cyclic AMP, leading to enhanced myocardial contractility and vasodilation.

c. Clinical Use:

i.   Inotropic agents are typically used in acute settings or severe CHF when immediate improvement in cardiac output is needed. They are not usually used for long-term management due to potential side effects and risks.

7. Vasodilators

a. Mechanism of Action:

i.   Vasodilators relax blood vessels, reducing afterload (the resistance the heart must overcome to eject blood) and improving cardiac output.

b. Examples:

i.   **Nitrates:** Such as nitroglycerin, primarily venodilators that reduce preload.

ii. **Hydralazine:** Primarily an arterial vasodilator that reduces afterload.

iii. **Isosorbide dinitrate:** Combined with hydralazine in some cases to manage CHF.

c. Clinical Use:

i. Vasodilators are used to manage symptoms of heart failure by reducing both preload and afterload, improving exercise tolerance, and reducing hospitalization.

8. Sodium-Glucose Cotransporter-2 (SGLT2) Inhibitors

a. Mechanism of Action:

i. SGLT2 inhibitors reduce glucose reabsorption in the kidneys, leading to osmotic diuresis and reduced fluid overload.

b. Examples:

i. Dapagliflozin

ii. Empagliflozin

c. Clinical Use:

i. SGLT2 inhibitors have been shown to improve symptoms, reduce hospitalizations, and prolong survival in CHF, particularly in patients with diabetes.

ANTI-HYPERTENSIVE DRUGS

Hypertension (high blood pressure) is a major risk factor for cardiovascular diseases, including stroke, heart attack, and heart failure. Effective management of hypertension is crucial to reduce these risks and improve overall cardiovascular health. Anti-hypertensive drugs work through various mechanisms to lower blood pressure and can be classified into several categories based on their action and effects.

1. Diuretics

a. Mechanism of Action:

i.   Diuretics reduce blood pressure by decreasing blood volume through increased urine production. This reduces the workload on the heart and decreases peripheral resistance.

b. Types and Examples:

i.   **Thiazide Diuretics:**

1. **Hydrochlorothiazide:** Acts on the distal convoluted tubule to increase sodium and chloride excretion.

2. **Chlorthalidone:** Similar to hydrochlorothiazide but has a longer duration of action.

ii. **Loop Diuretics:**

1. **Furosemide:** Acts on the ascending loop of Henle to inhibit sodium, chloride, and potassium reabsorption.

2. **Bumetanide:** More potent than furosemide.

iii. **Potassium-Sparing Diuretics:**

1. **Spironolactone:** Aldosterone antagonist that reduces sodium reabsorption and potassium excretion.

2. **Eplerenone:** More selective for mineralocorticoid receptors, with fewer hormonal side effects.

c. Clinical Use:

i.   Diuretics are commonly used as first-line therapy for hypertension, especially in patients with fluid retention or heart failure. They are often combined with other antihypertensive agents for better control.

2. Angiotensin-Converting Enzyme (ACE) Inhibitors

a. Mechanism of Action:

i.   ACE inhibitors block the conversion of angiotensin I to angiotensin II, leading to vasodilation and reduced blood pressure. They also decrease aldosterone secretion, which reduces fluid retention.

b. Examples:

i.   Enalapril

ii.   Lisinopril

iii.   Ramipril

iv.   Captopril

c. Clinical Use:

i.   ACE inhibitors are effective in treating hypertension and are beneficial in patients with heart failure, diabetic nephropathy, and chronic kidney disease. They are often used in combination with other antihypertensive drugs.

3. Angiotensin II Receptor Blockers (ARBs)

a. Mechanism of Action:

i.   ARBs block the binding of angiotensin II to its receptors, leading to vasodilation and reduced blood pressure. They also reduce aldosterone release.

b. Examples:

i.   Losartan

ii.   Valsartan

iii.   Candesartan

c. Clinical Use:

i.   ARBs are used as an alternative to ACE inhibitors, particularly in patients who experience cough or angioedema with ACE inhibitors. They are effective for hypertension and offer renal protective effects in diabetic nephropathy.

4. Calcium Channel Blockers (CCBs)

a. Mechanism of Action:

i.   CCBs inhibit calcium entry into vascular smooth muscle and cardiac cells, leading to vasodilation and decreased cardiac contractility. They reduce peripheral resistance and lower blood pressure.

b. Types and Examples:

i.   **Dihydropyridines:** Primarily affect vascular smooth muscle.

1. **Amlodipine**

2. **Nifedipine**

3. **Felodipine**

ii. **Non-Dihydropyridines:** Affect both the heart and blood vessels.

1. **Verapamil:** Reduces heart rate and contractility.

2. **Diltiazem:** Moderate effects on heart rate and vascular resistance.

c. Clinical Use:

i. CCBs are used to treat hypertension, angina, and certain arrhythmias. Dihydropyridines are often preferred for hypertension, while non-dihydropyridines are used for conditions involving the heart.

5. Beta-Blockers

a. Mechanism of Action:

i. Beta-blockers reduce blood pressure by blocking beta-adrenergic receptors in the heart and blood vessels. This decreases heart rate, myocardial contractility, and cardiac output.

b. Examples:

i. **Metoprolol:** Selective beta-1 blocker.

ii. **Atenolol:** Selective beta-1 blocker.

iii. **Carvedilol:** Non-selective beta-blocker with alpha-blocking activity.

iv. **Bisoprolol:** Selective beta-1 blocker with efficacy in heart failure.

c. Clinical Use:

i. Beta-blockers are used to manage hypertension, heart failure, angina, and post-myocardial infarction. They are often combined with other antihypertensive agents for comprehensive control.

6. Alpha-Blockers

a. Mechanism of Action:

i. Alpha-blockers inhibit alpha-adrenergic receptors, leading to vasodilation and reduced blood pressure. They primarily affect the vascular smooth muscle.

b. Examples:

i.   **Prazosin:** Selective alpha-1 blocker.

ii. **Doxazosin:** Selective alpha-1 blocker.

iii. **Terazosin:** Selective alpha-1 blocker.

c. Clinical Use:

i.   Alpha-blockers are used to treat hypertension and benign prostatic hyperplasia. They are often used as adjunctive therapy rather than as first-line treatment.

7. Direct Renin Inhibitors

a. Mechanism of Action:

i.   Direct renin inhibitors block the enzyme renin, which is responsible for the initial step in the renin-angiotensin-aldosterone system, leading to reduced angiotensin I and angiotensin II levels and decreased blood pressure.

b. Example:

i.   **Aliskiren**

c. Clinical Use:

i.   Direct renin inhibitors are used for hypertension and are typically used in combination with other antihypertensive agents.

8. Vasodilators

a. Mechanism of Action:

i.   Vasodilators directly relax vascular smooth muscle, leading to decreased systemic vascular resistance and reduced blood pressure.

b. Examples:

i.   **Hydralazine:** Acts on arterial smooth muscle, reducing afterload.

ii. **Minoxidil:** Potent arterial vasodilator used in severe hypertension.

iii. **Nitroglycerin:** Primarily used for its venodilator effects, reducing preload.

c. Clinical Use:

i. Vasodilators are used for hypertension, especially in combination with other antihypertensive agents. They are also used in specific conditions like heart failure.

CLASSIFICATION:

Drugs used to manage cardiovascular diseases can be classified based on their primary action and therapeutic use. Below is a detailed classification of cardiovascular drugs with examples:

1. Diuretics

a. **Thiazide Diuretics**

i. Hydrochlorothiazide

ii. Chlorthalidone

b. **Loop Diuretics**

i. Furosemide

ii. Bumetanide

iii. Torsemide

c. **Potassium-Sparing Diuretics**

i. Spironolactone

ii. Eplerenone

iii. Amiloride

iv. Triamterene

2. Angiotensin-Converting Enzyme (ACE) Inhibitors

a. Enalapril

b. Lisinopril

c. Ramipril

d. Captopril

e. Quinapril

3. Angiotensin II Receptor Blockers (ARBs)

a. Losartan

b. Valsartan

c. Candesartan

d. Irbesartan

e. Olmesartan

4. Calcium Channel Blockers (CCBs)

a. Dihydropyridines (primarily affect vascular smooth muscle)

i. Amlodipine

ii. Nifedipine

iii. Felodipine

iv. Isradipine

b. Non-Dihydropyridines (affect both heart and blood vessels)

i. Verapamil

ii. Diltiazem

5. Beta-Blockers

a. **Metoprolol** (selective beta-1 blocker)

b. **Atenolol** (selective beta-1 blocker)

c. **Carvedilol** (non-selective beta-blocker with alpha-blocking activity)

d. **Bisoprolol** (selective beta-1 blocker)

e. **Propranolol** (non-selective beta-blocker)

6. Alpha-Blockers

a. **Prazosin** (selective alpha-1 blocker)

b. **Doxazosin** (selective alpha-1 blocker)

c. **Terazosin** (selective alpha-1 blocker)

7. Direct Renin Inhibitors

a. Aliskiren

8. Vasodilators

a. Arterial Vasodilators

i. Hydralazine

ii. Minoxidil

b. Venodilators

i. **Nitroglycerin**

ii. **Isosorbide dinitrate**

iii. **Isosorbide mononitrate**

9. Other Cardiovascular Agents

a. **Nitrates (also considered venodilators)**

i. **Nitroglycerin**

ii. **Isosorbide dinitrate**

b. **Drugs for Heart Failure**

i. **Digoxin** (a cardiac glycoside with inotropic effects)

ii. **Sacubitril/Valsartan** (a combination of neprilysin inhibitor and ARB)

c. **Sodium-Glucose Cotransporter-2 (SGLT2) Inhibitors**

i. **Dapagliflozin**

ii. **Empagliflozin**

A. Hydrochlorothiazide:

a. **Mechanism of Action:**

1. Hydrochlorothiazide acts primarily on the distal convoluted tubule of the nephron in the kidneys.

2. It inhibits the Na+/Cl- symporter, which is responsible for the reabsorption of sodium and chloride ions.

3. This inhibition leads to increased excretion of sodium and chloride, resulting in an osmotic diuresis (increased urine production).

4. The reduction in blood volume leads to decreased cardiac output and decreased blood pressure.

b. **Pharmacokinetics:**

1. **Absorption:** Hydrochlorothiazide is well absorbed from the gastrointestinal tract.

2. **Distribution:** It is distributed throughout the body and has a moderate volume of distribution.

3. **Metabolism:** It is not metabolized by the liver and is excreted unchanged in the urine.

4. **Elimination:** The drug has a relatively short half-life, and its effects last for about 6-12 hours.

c. **Clinical Uses:**

1. **Hypertension:** Hydrochlorothiazide is often used as a first-line treatment for high blood pressure, either alone or in combination with other antihypertensive agents.

2. **Heart Failure:** It helps reduce fluid overload and symptoms such as edema.

3. **Edema:** It is used to manage edema associated with conditions like chronic kidney disease and liver cirrhosis.

d. **Side Effects:**

1. **Electrolyte Imbalances:** Hypokalemia (low potassium), hyponatremia (low sodium), and hypochloremic metabolic alkalosis.

2. **Hyperuricemia:** Can lead to gout exacerbation.

3. **Hyperglycemia:** Potentially increases blood glucose levels.

4. **Dehydration:** Due to excessive diuresis.

5. **Allergic Reactions:** Rash, photosensitivity, or, rarely, severe allergic reactions.

e. **Drug Interactions:**

1. **Digoxin:** Risk of digoxin toxicity due to hypokalemia.

2. **Lithium:** Increased lithium levels and potential toxicity.

3. **NSAIDs:** May reduce the efficacy of hydrochlorothiazide.

B. Chlorthalidone:

a. **Mechanism of Action:**

1. Chlorthalidone is a thiazide-like diuretic with a mechanism similar to hydrochlorothiazide.

2. It inhibits the Na+/Cl- symporter in the distal convoluted tubule, increasing the excretion of sodium and chloride.

3. It also has a mild vasodilatory effect, which contributes to its antihypertensive properties.

b. **Pharmacokinetics:**

1. **Absorption:** Chlorthalidone is well absorbed from the gastrointestinal tract.

2. **Distribution:** It has a large volume of distribution and is highly bound to plasma proteins.

3. **Metabolism:** Chlorthalidone is not metabolized and is excreted unchanged in the urine.

4. **Elimination:** It has a longer half-life than hydrochlorothiazide, with effects lasting up to 24-72 hours, allowing for once-daily dosing.

c. **Clinical Uses:**

1. **Hypertension:** Chlorthalidone is effective for long-term management of high blood pressure and is often used as a first-line treatment.

2. **Heart Failure:** It helps reduce fluid overload and manage symptoms of heart failure.

3. **Edema:** Used to treat edema from various causes, including kidney and liver diseases.

d. **Side Effects:**

1. **Electrolyte Imbalances:** Similar to hydrochlorothiazide, it can cause hypokalemia, hyponatremia, and hypochloremic metabolic alkalosis.

2. **Hyperuricemia:** May exacerbate gout.

3. **Hyperglycemia:** Risk of elevated blood glucose levels.

4. **Dehydration:** Risk of excessive fluid loss.

5. **Photosensitivity:** Increased sensitivity to sunlight.

e. **Drug Interactions:**

1. **Digoxin:** Enhanced risk of toxicity due to hypokalemia.

2. **Lithium:** Potential for increased lithium levels and toxicity.

3. **NSAIDs:** May reduce the diuretic and antihypertensive effects of chlorthalidone.

Comparison Between Hydrochlorothiazide and Chlorthalidone

1. Duration of Action:

a. **Hydrochlorothiazide:** Shorter duration (6-12 hours).

b. **Chlorthalidone:** Longer duration (24-72 hours).

2. Potency:

a. **Hydrochlorothiazide:** Generally less potent.

b. **Chlorthalidone:** More potent and longer-acting.

3. Use in Practice:

a. **Hydrochlorothiazide:** Frequently used due to its well-established efficacy and safety profile.

b. **Chlorthalidone:** Preferred in some guidelines due to its longer duration of action and potentially better blood pressure control over 24 hours.

C. Furosemide:

a. **Mechanism of Action:**

i. **Location of Action:** Furosemide acts on the thick ascending limb of the loop of Henle.

ii. **Action:** It inhibits the $Na+/K+/2Cl-$ cotransporter in the luminal membrane of the epithelial cells in the ascending limb of the loop of Henle.

iii. **Effect:** This inhibition prevents the reabsorption of sodium, potassium, and chloride ions. As a result, there is a significant increase in the excretion of sodium, chloride, and water, leading to a potent diuretic effect.

b. **Pharmacokinetics:**

i. **Absorption:** Furosemide is rapidly absorbed from the gastrointestinal tract with oral administration, but its bioavailability can vary (40-70%).

ii. **Distribution:** It is highly bound to plasma proteins (90-99%) and has a moderate volume of distribution.

iii. **Metabolism:** Furosemide is minimally metabolized by the liver.

iv. **Elimination:** It is excreted mainly in the urine. The half-life is approximately 1-2 hours in individuals with normal renal function, but it can be prolonged in patients with renal impairment.

c. **Clinical Uses:**

i. **Heart Failure:** Used to manage symptoms of heart failure by reducing fluid overload and edema.

ii. **Hypertension:** Effective in the treatment of hypertension, especially when other antihypertensive agents are insufficient.

iii. **Edema:** Useful for edema associated with conditions such as chronic kidney disease, cirrhosis, and nephrotic syndrome.

d. **Side Effects:**

i. **Electrolyte Imbalances:** Hypokalemia, hypomagnesemia, hypocalcemia, and hyponatremia.

ii. **Dehydration:** Risk of excessive fluid loss.

iii. **Ototoxicity:** High doses can lead to hearing loss or tinnitus.

iv. **Hyperuricemia:** May exacerbate gout.

v. **Hypotension:** Due to rapid or excessive fluid loss.

e. **Drug Interactions:**

i. **Digoxin:** Increased risk of digoxin toxicity due to hypokalemia.

ii. **NSAIDs:** May reduce the efficacy of furosemide and increase the risk of renal impairment.

iii. **Aminoglycosides:** Increased risk of ototoxicity when used with furosemide.

D. Bumetanide:

a. **Mechanism of Action:**

i. **Location of Action:** Bumetanide acts on the thick ascending limb of the loop of Henle, similar to furosemide.

ii. **Action:** It inhibits the Na+/K+/2Cl- cotransporter in the luminal membrane of the epithelial cells in the ascending limb of the loop of Henle.

iii. **Effect:** This inhibition results in increased excretion of sodium, chloride, and water, providing a strong diuretic effect.

b. **Pharmacokinetics:**

i. **Absorption:** Bumetanide is rapidly absorbed from the gastrointestinal tract with oral administration, and its bioavailability is high (approximately 80-90%).

ii. **Distribution:** It is highly bound to plasma proteins (95-99%) and has a relatively small volume of distribution.

iii. **Metabolism:** Bumetanide is minimally metabolized by the liver.

iv. **Elimination:** It is excreted primarily in the urine. The half-life is approximately 1-2 hours, similar to furosemide, but the drug can be dosed less frequently due to its potency.

c. **Clinical Uses:**

i. **Heart Failure:** Used to alleviate symptoms of heart failure by reducing fluid overload.

ii. **Hypertension:** Effective in cases where other diuretics are inadequate.

iii. **Edema:** Useful for managing edema from various conditions, including chronic kidney disease and liver cirrhosis.

d. **Side Effects:**

i. **Electrolyte Imbalances:** Hypokalemia, hypomagnesemia, hypocalcemia, and hyponatremia.

ii. **Dehydration:** Risk of excessive fluid loss.

iii. **Ototoxicity:** Rare but possible, especially at high doses.

iv. **Hyperuricemia:** Potentially exacerbates gout.

v. **Hypotension:** Due to rapid or excessive fluid loss.

e. **Drug Interactions:**

i. **Digoxin:** Increased risk of toxicity due to hypokalemia.

ii. **NSAIDs:** May reduce the efficacy of bumetanide and increase the risk of renal impairment.

iii. **Aminoglycosides:** Increased risk of ototoxicity when used with bumetanide.

Comparison Between Furosemide and Bumetanide

1. **Potency:**

   a. **Furosemide:** Generally requires higher doses compared to bumetanide for similar diuretic effects.

   b. **Bumetanide:** More potent than furosemide, allowing for effective diuresis with lower doses.

2. **Bioavailability:**

   a. **Furosemide:** Variable bioavailability (40-70%).

   b. **Bumetanide:** Higher and more consistent bioavailability (80-90%).

3. **Duration of Action:**

   a. **Furosemide:** Shorter duration of action, requiring multiple doses per day.

   b. **Bumetanide:** Similar duration of action but often dosed less frequently due to its potency.

4. **Side Effects:**

   a. Both drugs have similar side effects, but bumetanide's higher potency means that its side effects may be more pronounced at equivalent doses.

E. Torsemide:

a. **Mechanism of Action:**

   i. **Location of Action:** Torsemide acts on the thick ascending limb of the loop of Henle, similar to other loop diuretics like furosemide and bumetanide.

ii. **Action:** It inhibits the Na+/K+/2Cl- cotransporter in the luminal membrane of the epithelial cells in the ascending limb of the loop of Henle.

iii. **Effect:** This inhibition prevents the reabsorption of sodium, potassium, and chloride ions, leading to increased diuresis (increased urine production) and a decrease in blood volume.

b. **Pharmacokinetics:**

i. **Absorption:** Torsemide is well absorbed from the gastrointestinal tract with oral administration, and its bioavailability is about 80-90%.

ii. **Distribution:** It is highly bound to plasma proteins (approximately 99%) and has a moderate volume of distribution.

iii. **Metabolism:** Torsemide is partially metabolized by the liver to inactive metabolites.

iv. **Elimination:** It is excreted primarily in the urine. The half-life is approximately 3-4 hours, but its diuretic effect lasts longer due to its potent action.

c. **Clinical Uses:**

i. **Heart Failure:** Used to manage symptoms of heart failure, including fluid overload and edema.

ii. **Hypertension:** Effective for treating hypertension, often used in combination with other antihypertensive agents.

iii. **Edema:** Utilized for edema associated with conditions such as chronic kidney disease, liver cirrhosis, and nephrotic syndrome.

d. **Side Effects:**

i. **Electrolyte Imbalances:** Hypokalemia, hypomagnesemia, hypocalcemia, and hyponatremia.

ii. **Dehydration:** Risk of excessive fluid loss leading to dehydration.

iii. **Hyperuricemia:** Can exacerbate gout.

iv. **Hypotension:** Due to significant fluid loss.

v.   **Rashes:** Allergic reactions and skin rashes.

e. **Drug Interactions:**

i.   **Digoxin:** Increased risk of digoxin toxicity due to hypokalemia.

ii.   **NSAIDs:** May reduce the efficacy of torsemide and increase the risk of renal impairment.

iii. **Aminoglycosides:** Increased risk of ototoxicity when used concurrently.

F. Spironolactone:

a. **Mechanism of Action:**

i.   **Location of Action:** Spironolactone acts on the distal convoluted tubule and the collecting ducts in the nephron.

ii.   **Action:** It is an aldosterone antagonist, meaning it blocks the action of aldosterone at its receptor site.

iii. **Effect:** By inhibiting aldosterone, spironolactone reduces the reabsorption of sodium and the secretion of potassium. This leads to increased sodium excretion and potassium retention, resulting in a mild diuretic effect.

b. **Pharmacokinetics:**

i.   **Absorption:** Spironolactone is well absorbed from the gastrointestinal tract, though it has a variable bioavailability (around 60-90%).

ii.   **Distribution:** It is highly bound to plasma proteins (about 90%).

iii. **Metabolism:** Spironolactone is metabolized in the liver to active metabolites, including canrenone.

iv.   **Elimination:** It is excreted in the urine. The half-life of spironolactone is approximately 1.4 hours, but its effects last longer due to its active metabolites.

c. **Clinical Uses:**

i.   **Heart Failure:** Used to manage symptoms of heart failure by reducing fluid overload and preventing potassium loss.

ii. **Hypertension:** Effective in treating hypertension, particularly in combination with other antihypertensive agents.

iii. **Edema:** Useful for managing edema due to conditions such as cirrhosis and nephrotic syndrome.

iv. **Hyperaldosteronism:** Used to treat primary hyperaldosteronism (Conn's syndrome).

d. **Side Effects:**

i. **Electrolyte Imbalances:** Hyperkalemia (high potassium levels), hyponatremia, and metabolic acidosis.

ii. **Gynecomastia:** Can cause breast enlargement in males and menstrual irregularities in females.

iii. **Rashes:** Allergic reactions, including rashes and itching.

iv. **Dizziness:** Due to hypotension and electrolyte imbalances.

e. **Drug Interactions:**

i. **ACE Inhibitors and ARBs:** Increased risk of hyperkalemia when used with these drugs.

ii. **Potassium Supplements:** Caution is needed to avoid excessive potassium levels.

iii. **NSAIDs:** May reduce the efficacy of spironolactone and increase the risk of renal impairment.

Comparison Between Torsemide and Spironolactone

1. **Mechanism of Action:**

   a. **Torsemide:** Acts as a loop diuretic by inhibiting Na+/K+/2Cl- cotransporter, leading to potent diuresis.

   b. **Spironolactone:** Acts as an aldosterone antagonist, leading to potassium-sparing diuresis.

2. **Potency and Duration of Action:**

   a. **Torsemide:** More potent and has a longer duration of action compared to furosemide, but less compared to spironolactone.

b. **Spironolactone:** Provides a mild diuretic effect but is more focused on potassium retention and is often used in combination with other diuretics.

3. **Clinical Uses:**

a. **Torsemide:** Used for acute and chronic conditions involving fluid overload, including heart failure and hypertension.

b. **Spironolactone:** Primarily used for conditions requiring potassium retention, such as heart failure, hyperaldosteronism, and hypertension.

4. **Side Effects:**

a. **Torsemide:** Risk of electrolyte imbalances and dehydration, similar to other loop diuretics.

b. **Spironolactone:** Risk of hyperkalemia and hormonal effects, which are less common with loop diuretics.

Multiple Choice Questions (MCQs)

1. Which of the following drugs is classified as a loop diuretic?

   a) Spironolactone

   b) Torsemide

   c) Hydrochlorothiazide

   d) Chlorthalidone

2. What is the primary mechanism of action of ACE inhibitors in managing hypertension?

   a) Blocking sodium reabsorption in the kidneys

   b) Inhibiting calcium channels in the heart

   c) Blocking the conversion of angiotensin I to angiotensin II

   d) Inhibiting beta-adrenergic receptors

3. Which drug is used to manage hyperaldosteronism due to its aldosterone antagonistic properties?

   a) Furosemide

b) Bumetanide

c) Spironolactone

d) Torsemide

4. Which calcium channel blocker primarily affects vascular smooth muscle?

a) Verapamil

b) Diltiazem

c) Amlodipine

d) Atenolol

5. Which of the following is a potassium-sparing diuretic?

a) Furosemide

b) Chlorthalidone

c) Spironolactone

d) Torsemide

6. Which drug class includes Losartan and Valsartan?

a) ACE inhibitors

b) Calcium channel blockers

c) Beta-blockers

d) Angiotensin II receptor blockers (ARBs)

7. What is the primary adverse effect of loop diuretics like Furosemide?

a) Hyperkalemia

b) Hypokalemia

c) Hypernatremia

d) Hypercalcemia

8. Which drug is known for causing gynecomastia as a side effect?

a) Hydrochlorothiazide

b) Furosemide

c) Spironolactone

d) Bumetanide

9. Which drug has the longest duration of action among thiazide diuretics?

a) Hydrochlorothiazide

b) Chlorthalidone

c) Furosemide

d) Bumetanide

10. What is the primary therapeutic use of beta-blockers in cardiovascular medicine?

a) Managing hyperkalemia

b) Reducing heart rate and contractility

c) Increasing sodium reabsorption

d) Blocking calcium channels

11. Which of the following drugs is a direct renin inhibitor?

a) Aliskiren

b) Enalapril

c) Losartan

d) Atenolol

12. Which drug is used to treat edema associated with heart failure by acting on the loop of Henle?

a) Spironolactone

b) Torsemide

c) Aliskiren

d) Chlorthalidone

13. What is the primary mechanism of action of calcium channel blockers like Amlodipine?

a) Inhibiting sodium channels

b) Blocking angiotensin II receptors

c) Inhibiting calcium ion entry into vascular smooth muscle

d) Enhancing sodium reabsorption in the kidneys

14. Which antihypertensive drug is an alpha-blocker?

a) Metoprolol

b) Doxazosin

c) Amlodipine

d) Valsartan

15. Which of the following drugs is a selective beta-1 blocker?

a) Carvedilol

b) Propranolol

c) Atenolol

d) Spironolactone

16. Which drug is a thiazide-like diuretic with a longer duration of action compared to Hydrochlorothiazide?

a) Torsemide

b) Furosemide

c) Chlorthalidone

d) Bumetanide

17. What is the primary clinical use of ARBs in cardiovascular treatment?

a) Managing hyperkalemia

b) Reducing preload and afterload

c) Blocking sodium reabsorption

d) Inhibiting calcium channels

18. Which drug can cause ototoxicity, particularly at high doses?

a) Spironolactone

b) Bumetanide

c) Chlorthalidone

d) Aliskiren

19. Which drug is primarily used in the treatment of hypertension and is often combined with other antihypertensive agents?

a) Digoxin

b) Aliskiren

c) Spironolactone

d) Torsemide

20. Which drug works by inhibiting the Na+/K+/2Cl- cotransporter in the loop of Henle?

    a) Spironolactone

    b) Torsemide

    c) Aliskiren

    d) Chlorthalidone

Short Answer Questions (SAQs)

1. Explain the mechanism of action of loop diuretics like Furosemide.

2. What are the primary clinical uses of ACE inhibitors in managing cardiovascular diseases?

3. Describe the role of ARBs in the treatment of hypertension.

4. How do potassium-sparing diuretics like Spironolactone differ from loop diuretics?

5. Discuss the pharmacokinetics of Hydrochlorothiazide and its clinical implications.

6. What are the side effects associated with the use of calcium channel blockers?

7. How does Chlorthalidone compare to Hydrochlorothiazide in terms of potency and duration of action?

8. Describe the mechanism of action and clinical uses of direct renin inhibitors like Aliskiren.

9. What are the potential adverse effects of beta-blockers in the treatment of cardiovascular diseases?

10. How does Spironolactone act as an aldosterone antagonist in managing heart failure?

11. Discuss the mechanism by which Torsemide exerts its diuretic effect.

12. What are the clinical uses of Bumetanide in the management of cardiovascular conditions?

13. Explain the role of alpha-blockers in the treatment of hypertension.

14. What are the key differences between selective and non-selective beta-blockers?

15. How do vasodilators help manage hypertension, and what are some examples?

16. Describe the adverse effects and contraindications of using loop diuretics.

17. What is the clinical significance of using SGLT2 inhibitors in the treatment of heart failure?

18. Explain the pharmacological effects of nitrates in the management of angina.

19. What are the potential drug interactions associated with the use of Furosemide?

20. How does Spironolactone help in managing conditions like hyperaldosteronism?

Long Answer Questions (LAQs)

1. Discuss the classification, mechanisms of action, and clinical applications of diuretics, focusing on loop diuretics, thiazide diuretics, and potassium-sparing diuretics.

2. Describe the role of ACE inhibitors and ARBs in the management of hypertension and heart failure, including their mechanisms, clinical uses, and potential side effects.

3. Explain the pharmacological management of heart failure, including the use of diuretics, ACE inhibitors, beta-blockers, and inotropic agents.

4. Compare and contrast the uses, mechanisms, and side effects of thiazide diuretics like Hydrochlorothiazide and Chlorthalidone.

5. Discuss the pharmacology, clinical uses, and potential adverse effects of loop diuretics like Furosemide and Bumetanide.

6. Explain the role of calcium channel blockers in the management of cardiovascular diseases, focusing on the differences between dihydropyridines and non-dihydropyridines.

7. Describe the use of beta-blockers in cardiovascular medicine, including their mechanisms, clinical applications, and potential side effects.

8. Discuss the clinical uses and pharmacology of direct renin inhibitors like Aliskiren in the management of hypertension.

9. Explain the role of vasodilators in the management of cardiovascular diseases, including their mechanisms, clinical uses, and potential side effects.

10. Compare the pharmacokinetics, mechanisms of action, and clinical applications of Spironolactone and Torsemide in the treatment of cardiovascular conditions.

Answer Key for MCQs

1. b) Torsemide
2. c) Blocking the conversion of angiotensin I to angiotensin II
3. c) Spironolactone
4. c) Amlodipine
5. c) Spironolactone
6. d) Angiotensin II receptor blockers (ARBs)
7. b) Hypokalemia
8. c) Spironolactone
9. b) Chlorthalidone
10. b) Reducing heart rate and contractility
11. a) Aliskiren
12. b) Torsemide
13. c) Inhibiting calcium ion entry into vascular smooth muscle
14. b) Doxazosin

15.c) Atenolol

16.c) Chlorthalidone

17.b) Reducing preload and afterload

18.b) Bumetanide

19.c) Spironolactone

20.b) Torsemide

CHAPTER – 2

PHARMACOLOGY OF DRUGS ACTING ON CARDIO VASCULAR SYSTEM – II

INTRODUCTION:

Pharmacology of drugs acting on the cardiovascular system encompasses a broad range of medications that influence heart function, blood pressure, and overall cardiovascular health. Here's an overview of key areas covered under this topic:

1. Antiarrhythmic Drugs

  a. **Purpose**: Treat and prevent irregular heart rhythms (arrhythmias).

  b. **Classification**:

    i. **Class I (Sodium Channel Blockers)**: Quinidine, Procainamide, Lidocaine.

    ii. **Class II (Beta Blockers)**: Metoprolol, Propranolol.

    iii. **Class III (Potassium Channel Blockers)**: Sotalol, Dofetilide.

    iv. **Class IV (Calcium Channel Blockers)**: Verapamil, Diltiazem.

2. Antihypertensives

  a. **Purpose**: Lower high blood pressure.

  b. **Classes**:

    i. **Diuretics**: Hydrochlorothiazide, Furosemide.

    ii. **ACE Inhibitors**: Lisinopril, Enalapril.

    iii. **Angiotensin II Receptor Blockers (ARBs)**: Losartan, Valsartan.

    iv. **Calcium Channel Blockers**: Amlodipine, Nifedipine.

    v. **Beta Blockers**: Atenolol, Carvedilol.

3. Vasodilators

  a. **Purpose**: Dilate blood vessels to lower blood pressure and improve blood flow.

b. **Types**:

    i.   **Nitrates**: Nitroglycerin, Isosorbide dinitrate.

    ii.   **Hydralazine**: Often used in combination with other drugs.

    iii. **Sodium Nitroprusside**: Used for acute hypertensive crises.

4. Anticoagulants and Antiplatelets

a. **Purpose**: Prevent blood clot formation.

b. **Anticoagulants**:

    i.   **Warfarin**: Vitamin K antagonist.

    ii.   **Heparin**: Enhances antithrombin III.

    iii. **Direct Oral Anticoagulants (DOACs)**: Dabigatran, Rivaroxaban.

c. **Antiplatelets**:

    i.   **Aspirin**: Inhibits platelet aggregation.

    ii.   **Clopidogrel**: ADP receptor inhibitor.

5. Heart Failure Medications

a. **Purpose**: Manage symptoms and improve heart function in heart failure.

b. **Medications**:

    i.   **ACE Inhibitors**: Help reduce the workload on the heart.

    ii.   **Beta Blockers**: Improve heart function and reduce symptoms.

    iii. **Diuretics**: Reduce fluid buildup.

    iv. **Digoxin**: Increases the force of heart contractions.

6. Lipid-Lowering Agents

a. **Purpose**: Manage dyslipidemia and reduce cardiovascular risk.

b. **Classes**:

    i.   **Statins**: Atorvastatin, Simvastatin.

    ii.   **Fibrates**: Fenofibrate, Gemfibrozil.

    iii. **Ezetimibe**: Reduces cholesterol absorption.

7. Others

a. **Agents for Angina**: Ranolazine, usually used in combination with nitrates and beta-blockers.

b. **Inotropic Agents**: Improve the force of heart muscle contractions (e.g., Dobutamine).

ANTI-ANGINAL DRUGS

Anti-anginal drugs are used to manage angina pectoris, a condition characterized by chest pain due to insufficient blood flow to the heart muscle. The goal of anti-anginal therapy is to reduce the frequency, severity, and duration of angina attacks and improve overall heart function. Here's a detailed look at the main classes of anti-anginal drugs:

1. Nitrates

a. **Mechanism of Action**: Nitrates are converted to nitric oxide in the body, which relaxes vascular smooth muscle, particularly in veins, reducing preload (the amount of blood returning to the heart). This decreases the heart's workload and oxygen demand.

b. **Examples**:

  i. **Nitroglycerin**: Used for acute relief of angina. Available in sublingual tablets, sprays, and patches.

  ii. **Isosorbide Dinitrate**: Often used for chronic management of angina. Available in oral and extended-release forms.

  iii. **Isosorbide Mononitrate**: Similar to isosorbide dinitrate, used for long-term prevention of angina.

c. **Side Effects**: Headache, dizziness, hypotension, and tolerance with prolonged use.

2. Beta-Blockers

a. **Mechanism of Action**: Beta-blockers reduce the heart rate and myocardial contractility by blocking beta-adrenergic receptors. This decreases the heart's oxygen demand and helps prevent angina attacks.

b. **Examples**:

  i. **Atenolol**: A selective beta-1 blocker used for chronic angina.

ii. **Metoprolol**: Another selective beta-1 blocker, effective in controlling angina and improving exercise tolerance.

iii. **Propranolol**: A non-selective beta-blocker used in various types of angina.

c. **Side Effects**: Bradycardia, fatigue, depression, and bronchoconstriction.

3. Calcium Channel Blockers

a. **Mechanism of Action**: Calcium channel blockers inhibit calcium entry into cardiac and smooth muscle cells, leading to reduced myocardial contractility and vasodilation. They primarily reduce afterload (the resistance the heart must overcome to eject blood) and decrease heart rate.

b. **Examples**:

i. **Diltiazem**: A non-dihydropyridine calcium channel blocker that reduces heart rate and vasodilates.

ii. **Verapamil**: Similar to diltiazem, it decreases heart rate and is used for angina and arrhythmias.

iii. **Amlodipine**: A dihydropyridine calcium channel blocker with more significant effects on vascular smooth muscle than the heart.

c. **Side Effects**: Edema, dizziness, headache, and constipation.

4. Ranolazine

a. **Mechanism of Action**: Ranolazine works by modifying cardiac ion currents, reducing sodium overload in cardiac cells, and decreasing myocardial oxygen consumption. It does not significantly affect heart rate or blood pressure.

b. **Uses**: Used for chronic angina, often in combination with other anti-anginal medications.

c. **Side Effects**: Dizziness, headache, constipation, and nausea.

5. Others

a. **Ivabradine**: Reduces heart rate by selectively inhibiting the funny (If) current in the sinoatrial node, which helps reduce angina in patients who cannot tolerate beta-blockers.

b. **Nicorandil**: A nitrate with additional potassium channel-opening effects, providing vasodilation and reducing angina.

Considerations in Therapy

a. **Combination Therapy**: Often, a combination of anti-anginal drugs is used to manage angina more effectively. For example, beta-blockers and nitrates can be combined for better control of symptoms.

b. **Tolerance**: With prolonged use of nitrates, tolerance can develop, necessitating nitrate-free intervals to maintain efficacy.

c. **Patient-Specific Factors**: Individual response to medications, side effects, and contraindications (e.g., in patients with asthma or certain heart conditions) must be considered when choosing anti-anginal therapy.

ANTI-ARRHYTHMIC DRUGS

Anti-arrhythmic drugs are used to manage and prevent irregular heart rhythms (arrhythmias). These drugs work by modifying the electrical activity of the heart to restore normal rhythm. They are classified into several classes based on their mechanisms of action. Here's a detailed overview:

1. Class I: Sodium Channel Blockers

Subclass IA

a. **Mechanism of Action**: These drugs block sodium channels, slowing depolarization during the action potential, which prolongs the refractory period.

b. **Examples**:

i. **Quinidine**: Used for atrial and ventricular arrhythmias. Can cause gastrointestinal disturbances and cinchonism (tinnitus, headache).

ii. **Procainamide**: Used for ventricular arrhythmias and atrial fibrillation. May cause lupus-like symptoms.

iii. **Disopyramide**: Effective in ventricular arrhythmias. Can cause anticholinergic effects (dry mouth, constipation).

Subclass IB

a. **Mechanism of Action**: These drugs block sodium channels during the action potential, but their effect is more prominent during the repolarization phase. They shorten the action potential duration.

b. **Examples**:

i. **Lidocaine**: Commonly used for acute ventricular arrhythmias, especially after myocardial infarction. Side effects include neurological symptoms (tremors, seizures).

ii. **Mexiletine**: Oral analog of lidocaine, used for chronic ventricular arrhythmias. Side effects similar to lidocaine.

iii. **Tocainide**: Less commonly used due to side effects like pulmonary fibrosis.

Subclass IC

a. **Mechanism of Action**: These drugs block sodium channels without significantly affecting the action potential duration, but they markedly slow conduction velocity.

b. **Examples**:

i. **Flecainide**: Used for atrial fibrillation and ventricular arrhythmias. Can cause pro-arrhythmia (new or worsening arrhythmias).

ii. **Propafenone**: Similar to flecainide, used for atrial and ventricular arrhythmias. Has beta-blocking activity.

2. Class II: Beta-Blockers

a. **Mechanism of Action**: These drugs block beta-adrenergic receptors, reducing sympathetic stimulation of the heart. This slows heart rate and decreases automaticity.

b. **Examples**:

i. **Metoprolol**: Selective beta-1 blocker used for various arrhythmias, including atrial fibrillation. Can cause bradycardia and fatigue.

ii. **Propranolol**: Non-selective beta-blocker used for ventricular arrhythmias and atrial fibrillation. Can cause bronchoconstriction and fatigue.

iii. **Esmolol**: Ultra-short-acting beta-blocker used for acute arrhythmias. Side effects include hypotension and bradycardia.

3. Class III: Potassium Channel Blockers

a. **Mechanism of Action**: These drugs block potassium channels, prolonging repolarization and the refractory period, which helps stabilize the heart rhythm.

b. **Examples**:

i. **Sotalol**: Used for ventricular and atrial arrhythmias. Can cause torsades de pointes (a type of ventricular tachycardia) and renal function abnormalities.

ii. **Dofetilide**: Used for atrial fibrillation and atrial flutter. Requires close monitoring due to risk of pro-arrhythmia and renal dose adjustment.

4. Class IV: Calcium Channel Blockers

a. **Mechanism of Action**: These drugs block calcium channels, particularly in the heart, reducing conduction through the AV node and decreasing heart rate.

b. **Examples**:

i. **Verapamil**: Used for atrial fibrillation, atrial flutter, and some ventricular arrhythmias. Can cause hypotension, constipation, and bradycardia.

ii. **Diltiazem**: Similar to verapamil but with a slightly different profile. Used for similar indications and side effects.

5. Other Anti-arrhythmic Drugs

a. **Adenosine**

   i. **Mechanism of Action**: Activates adenosine receptors, leading to hyperpolarization of the AV node and rapid termination of certain types of supraventricular tachycardia.

   ii. **Uses**: Acute treatment of paroxysmal supraventricular tachycardia (PSVT).

   iii. **Side Effects**: Flushing, chest discomfort, and short-term asystole.

b. **Digoxin**

   i. **Mechanism of Action**: Increases vagal tone and decreases conduction through the AV node, which helps control ventricular rate in atrial fibrillation and atrial flutter.

   ii. **Uses**: Atrial fibrillation, atrial flutter, and heart failure.

   iii. **Side Effects**: Nausea, visual disturbances (yellow-green halos), and toxicity, especially in patients with renal impairment.

Considerations in Therapy

a. **Selection of Therapy**: Choice of anti-arrhythmic drug depends on the type of arrhythmia, patient comorbidities, and potential side effects.

b. **Monitoring**: Many anti-arrhythmic drugs require close monitoring for efficacy and adverse effects, including ECG changes and serum drug levels.

c. **Drug Interactions**: Anti-arrhythmic drugs can interact with other medications, affecting their effectiveness and increasing the risk of side effects.

ANTI-HYPERLIPIDEMIC DRUGS

Anti-hyperlipidemic drugs are used to manage dyslipidemia, a condition characterized by abnormal levels of lipids (cholesterol and triglycerides) in the blood. These drugs help reduce the risk of cardiovascular diseases by lowering elevated lipid levels. Here's a detailed overview of the main classes of anti-hyperlipidemic drugs:

1. Statins

    a. **Mechanism of Action**: Statins inhibit HMG-CoA reductase, an enzyme crucial for the synthesis of cholesterol in the liver. This leads to reduced cholesterol levels and increased uptake of low-density lipoprotein (LDL) from the blood.

    b. **Examples**:

        i. **Atorvastatin**: One of the most potent statins, used to lower LDL cholesterol and reduce cardiovascular events.

        ii. **Simvastatin**: Effective in reducing LDL cholesterol and triglycerides.

        iii. **Rosuvastatin**: Known for its strong LDL-lowering effects and potential to raise high-density lipoprotein (HDL) cholesterol.

    c. **Side Effects**: Muscle pain, liver enzyme elevation, and in rare cases, rhabdomyolysis.

2. Bile Acid Sequestrants

    a. **Mechanism of Action**: These drugs bind bile acids in the intestine, preventing their reabsorption. This leads to increased conversion of cholesterol to bile acids and lower blood cholesterol levels.

    b. **Examples**:

        i. **Cholestyramine**: Used to lower LDL cholesterol. Can cause gastrointestinal issues like constipation and bloating.

        ii. **Colestipol**: Similar to cholestyramine, used to manage LDL levels.

        iii. **Colesevelam**: Less likely to cause gastrointestinal side effects and can also help with glycemic control in diabetes.

    c. **Side Effects**: Constipation, bloating, and potential interference with the absorption of other medications.

3. Niacin (Vitamin B3)

a. **Mechanism of Action**: Niacin lowers LDL cholesterol and triglycerides and raises HDL cholesterol. It works by inhibiting the release of free fatty acids from adipose tissue, reducing hepatic production of VLDL (very-low-density lipoprotein) and LDL.

b. **Examples**:
   i. **Immediate-release Niacin**: Effective but often causes flushing.
   ii. **Extended-release Niacin**: Less flushing but can be associated with liver toxicity.

c. **Side Effects**: Flushing, itching, liver toxicity, and gastrointestinal disturbances.

4. Fibric Acid Derivatives (Fibrates)

a. **Mechanism of Action**: Fibrates activate peroxisome proliferator-activated receptors (PPARs), which increase the oxidation of fatty acids and decrease the synthesis of triglycerides.

b. **Examples**:
   i. **Fenofibrate**: Effective in lowering triglycerides and can also modestly increase HDL cholesterol.
   ii. **Gemfibrozil**: Used to reduce triglycerides but can interact with statins, increasing the risk of myopathy.

c. **Side Effects**: Gastrointestinal symptoms, muscle pain, and liver enzyme changes.

5. Cholesterol Absorption Inhibitors

a. **Mechanism of Action**: These drugs inhibit the absorption of cholesterol from the intestines, leading to decreased levels of cholesterol in the blood.

b. **Examples**:
   i. **Ezetimibe**: Used alone or in combination with statins to lower LDL cholesterol. Well-tolerated with few side effects.

c. **Side Effects**: Gastrointestinal issues and, rarely, liver enzyme elevation.

6. PCSK9 Inhibitors

a. **Mechanism of Action**: PCSK9 inhibitors prevent the degradation of LDL receptors in the liver, increasing the uptake of LDL from the blood.

b. **Examples**:

    i. **Alirocumab**: Used for patients with familial hypercholesterolemia or those who cannot achieve target LDL levels with statins alone.

    ii. **Evolocumab**: Similar to alirocumab, effective in significantly lowering LDL levels.

c. **Side Effects**: Injection site reactions, flu-like symptoms, and in rare cases, neurocognitive effects.

7. Omega-3 Fatty Acids

a. **Mechanism of Action**: Omega-3 fatty acids reduce triglyceride levels through various mechanisms, including decreasing hepatic production of triglycerides and increasing their clearance.

b. **Examples**:

    i. **Eicosapentaenoic Acid (EPA)**: Found in fish oil supplements, used to lower triglycerides.

    ii. **Docosahexaenoic Acid (DHA)**: Often combined with EPA in supplements.

c. **Side Effects**: Gastrointestinal upset, fishy aftertaste, and increased bleeding risk at high doses.

Considerations in Therapy

a. **Individualization**: Therapy should be tailored based on the patient's lipid profile, comorbid conditions, and risk of cardiovascular events.

b. **Monitoring**: Regular monitoring of lipid levels, liver function tests (especially for statins), and potential side effects is important for optimizing therapy.

c. **Combination Therapy**: Often, a combination of different classes of lipid-lowering drugs is used to achieve target lipid levels and reduce cardiovascular risk.

DRUG USED IN THE THERAPY OF SHOCK

Shock is a critical condition characterized by inadequate blood flow to the tissues, leading to cellular and organ dysfunction. The treatment of shock involves stabilizing blood pressure, improving tissue perfusion, and addressing the underlying cause. Here's a detailed overview of the drugs used in the therapy of shock:

1. Vasopressors

Vasopressors are used to increase blood pressure by causing vasoconstriction, thereby improving blood flow and perfusion to vital organs.

a. **Norepinephrine**

    i. **Mechanism of Action**: Acts on alpha-1 adrenergic receptors to cause vasoconstriction and increase systemic vascular resistance. It also has some beta-1 adrenergic activity, which can increase heart rate and cardiac output.

    ii. **Uses**: Commonly used in septic shock and other forms of shock with low blood pressure.

    iii. **Side Effects**: Hypertension, arrhythmias, and tissue necrosis if extravasated.

b. **Epinephrine**

    i. **Mechanism of Action**: Acts on both alpha-1 and beta-adrenergic receptors. Increases blood pressure through vasoconstriction (alpha-1) and improves cardiac output through increased heart rate and contractility (beta-1).

    ii. **Uses**: Used in anaphylactic shock and sometimes in cardiogenic shock.

    iii. **Side Effects**: Tachycardia, hypertension, and anxiety.

c. **Dopamine**

   i. **Mechanism of Action**: Acts on dopamine receptors, beta-1 receptors, and alpha-1 receptors depending on the dose. At low doses, it increases renal blood flow; at moderate doses, it increases cardiac output; at high doses, it causes vasoconstriction.

   ii. **Uses**: Used in cardiogenic shock and sometimes in septic shock.

   iii. **Side Effects**: Tachycardia, arrhythmias, and vasoconstriction.

d. **Phenylephrine**

   i. **Mechanism of Action**: Selective alpha-1 adrenergic receptor agonist, causing vasoconstriction and increasing systemic vascular resistance.

   ii. **Uses**: Used for hypotension, particularly in neurogenic shock.

   iii. **Side Effects**: Hypertension, reflex bradycardia, and reduced cardiac output.

2. Inotropes

Inotropes improve cardiac contractility and output, which is crucial in conditions like cardiogenic shock.

a. **Dobutamine**

   i. **Mechanism of Action**: Primarily acts on beta-1 adrenergic receptors, increasing cardiac contractility and output with less effect on heart rate compared to other inotropes.

   ii. **Uses**: Used in cardiogenic shock and heart failure.

   iii. **Side Effects**: Tachycardia, arrhythmias, and hypotension.

b. **Milrinone**

   i. **Mechanism of Action**: Phosphodiesterase-3 inhibitor, leading to increased intracellular cyclic AMP, which enhances cardiac contractility and causes vasodilation.

   ii. **Uses**: Used in cardiogenic shock and severe heart failure.

iii. **Side Effects**: Hypotension, arrhythmias, and potentially elevated liver enzymes.

3. Fluid Resuscitation

Fluid resuscitation is a key component in the management of shock, especially hypovolemic shock.

a. **Crystalloids**

    i. **Examples**: Normal saline (0.9% NaCl), Ringer's lactate.

    ii. **Mechanism of Action**: Increase intravascular volume and improve tissue perfusion.

    iii. **Uses**: Initial fluid resuscitation in most types of shock.

    iv. **Side Effects**: Fluid overload, electrolyte imbalances.

b. **Colloids**

    i. **Examples**: Hydroxyethyl starch (HES), Dextran, Albumin.

    ii. **Mechanism of Action**: Increase oncotic pressure in the blood, drawing fluid into the intravascular space.

    iii. **Uses**: Used in cases where crystalloids are insufficient, though their use has declined due to potential side effects.

    iv. **Side Effects**: Allergic reactions, coagulopathy, and renal impairment.

4. Adjuvant Medications

These drugs are used to support overall management of shock and its complications.

a. **Antibiotics**

    i. **Uses**: Essential in septic shock to treat underlying infections.

    ii. **Example**: Broad-spectrum antibiotics like Piperacillin-tazobactam or Ceftriaxone.

    iii. **Side Effects**: Allergic reactions, gastrointestinal disturbances.

b. **Steroids**

i. **Uses**: May be used in septic shock to reduce inflammation and support adrenal function.

ii. **Example**: Hydrocortisone.

iii. **Side Effects**: Hyperglycemia, infection risk, and gastrointestinal upset.

c. **Vasodilators**

i. **Examples**: Sodium nitroprusside, Nitroglycerin.

ii. **Uses**: Used in cases of shock with severe hypertension or heart failure.

iii. **Side Effects**: Hypotension, cyanide toxicity (with nitroprusside).

Considerations in Therapy

a. **Monitoring**: Continuous monitoring of vital signs, including blood pressure, heart rate, and oxygen saturation, is essential. Also, monitoring of fluid balance, electrolytes, and renal function is crucial.

b. **Underlying Cause**: Addressing the underlying cause of shock (e.g., infection, blood loss, cardiac dysfunction) is critical in conjunction with supportive therapy.

c. **Individualization**: Treatment should be tailored based on the type of shock (e.g., hypovolemic, cardiogenic, septic) and the patient's clinical condition.

HEMATINIC

Hematinics are medications that enhance the production and function of red blood cells and hemoglobin, which is crucial for oxygen transport in the blood. They are particularly important in treating various forms of anemia, which can affect cardiovascular health by reducing oxygen delivery to tissues. Here's a detailed overview of the drugs used as hematinics:

Iron Supplements:

Iron supplements are essential for treating iron deficiency anemia, which is a common type of anemia characterized by insufficient iron levels in the body.

Iron is crucial for the production of hemoglobin, which is necessary for oxygen transport in the blood. Here's a detailed overview of iron supplements, their mechanisms, uses, and side effects:

1. Oral Iron Supplements

Oral iron supplements are commonly used to treat mild to moderate iron deficiency anemia. They are typically well-tolerated and effective in increasing iron levels in the body.

a. **Ferrous Sulfate**

   i. **Mechanism of Action**: Provides elemental iron, which is absorbed in the small intestine and used to produce hemoglobin in red blood cells.

   ii. **Uses**: First-line treatment for iron deficiency anemia; also used for prevention in high-risk populations (e.g., pregnant women).

   iii. **Dosage**: Typically 325 mg of ferrous sulfate, providing 65 mg of elemental iron, taken once or twice daily.

   iv. **Side Effects**: Gastrointestinal issues such as constipation, nausea, abdominal pain, and black stools. Tolerance can be improved by taking the supplement with food or using slow-release formulations.

b. **Ferrous Gluconate**

   i. **Mechanism of Action**: Similar to ferrous sulfate, provides elemental iron for hemoglobin synthesis.

   ii. **Uses**: Used as an alternative to ferrous sulfate, especially for patients who experience gastrointestinal side effects with other iron supplements.

   iii. **Dosage**: Typically 325 mg of ferrous gluconate, providing 36 mg of elemental iron, taken two to three times daily.

   iv. **Side Effects**: Similar to ferrous sulfate but may be better tolerated by some patients.

c. **Ferrous Fumarate**

   i. **Mechanism of Action**: Provides elemental iron for incorporation into hemoglobin.

   ii. **Uses**: Another alternative to ferrous sulfate, often used when higher doses of iron are required.

   iii. **Dosage**: Typically 324 mg of ferrous fumarate, providing 106 mg of elemental iron, taken once or twice daily.

   iv. **Side Effects**: Gastrointestinal issues such as constipation and nausea.

2. Intravenous Iron Supplements

Intravenous (IV) iron supplements are used for patients who cannot tolerate oral iron, have severe iron deficiency anemia, or have conditions that impair iron absorption.

a. **Iron Dextran**

   i. **Mechanism of Action**: Provides iron directly into the bloodstream, bypassing the gastrointestinal tract.

   ii. **Uses**: Used for severe iron deficiency anemia, particularly in patients who cannot take oral iron or have chronic kidney disease.

   iii. **Dosage**: Dosage varies based on individual needs and iron deficit. Administered via IV infusion or injection.

   iv. **Side Effects**: Risk of allergic reactions, hypotension, and local reactions at the injection site.

b. **Iron Sucrose**

   i. **Mechanism of Action**: Provides iron directly into the bloodstream.

   ii. **Uses**: Commonly used for iron deficiency anemia in chronic kidney disease patients.

   iii. **Dosage**: Administered via IV infusion, with doses tailored to the patient's iron requirements.

iv. **Side Effects**: Generally well-tolerated, but may cause allergic reactions, hypotension, and gastrointestinal symptoms.

c. **Ferric Gluconate**

   i. **Mechanism of Action**: Provides iron for direct absorption into the bloodstream.

   ii. **Uses**: Used for iron deficiency anemia, especially in patients undergoing dialysis.

   iii. **Dosage**: Administered via IV infusion, with dosing based on the patient's iron needs.

   iv. **Side Effects**: Similar to other IV iron preparations, with potential for allergic reactions and local reactions at the infusion site.

d. **Ferumoxytol**

   i. **Mechanism of Action**: Provides iron in a nanoparticle form, allowing for rapid absorption.

   ii. **Uses**: Used for iron deficiency anemia in patients with chronic kidney disease.

   iii. **Dosage**: Administered via IV injection, usually in two doses.

   iv. **Side Effects**: May cause dizziness, hypotension, and nausea. Risk of allergic reactions.

Considerations in Therapy

a. **Iron Absorption**: Iron is best absorbed on an empty stomach, but if gastrointestinal side effects occur, taking it with food may improve tolerance. Vitamin C can enhance iron absorption, so some supplements include vitamin C.

b. **Monitoring**: Regular monitoring of hemoglobin levels, serum ferritin, and transferrin saturation is important to assess the effectiveness of therapy and adjust dosages as needed.

c. **Duration of Therapy**: Treatment typically continues until iron stores are replenished and anemia is resolved, which may take several months.

d. **Side Effects Management**: Managing side effects, such as gastrointestinal discomfort, by adjusting the dose or form of iron (e.g., using slow-release formulations) can improve patient adherence.

Vitamin B12 Supplements:

Vitamin B12, also known as cobalamin, is essential for the production of red blood cells and the proper functioning of the nervous system. It plays a critical role in DNA synthesis and the formation of hemoglobin, making it important in the treatment of anemia, particularly megaloblastic anemia caused by Vitamin B12 deficiency. Here's a detailed overview of Vitamin B12 supplements:

1. Forms of Vitamin B12 Supplements

   a. **Cyanocobalamin**

      i. **Mechanism of Action**: A synthetic form of Vitamin B12 that is converted to the active forms (methylcobalamin and adenosylcobalamin) in the body. It is crucial for DNA synthesis and red blood cell production.

      ii. **Uses**: Used to treat and prevent Vitamin B12 deficiency, which can lead to megaloblastic anemia and neurological issues.

      iii. **Dosage**: Oral dosage typically ranges from 500 to 1000 mcg daily for deficiency treatment. Intramuscular injections are often given in doses of 1000 mcg once a month or as needed for severe deficiencies.

      iv. **Side Effects**: Generally well-tolerated. Rare side effects include mild gastrointestinal upset and allergic reactions.

   b. **Hydroxocobalamin**

      i. **Mechanism of Action**: A naturally occurring form of Vitamin B12 that is also converted to the active forms in the body. It has a longer half-life than cyanocobalamin.

      ii. **Uses**: Used in Vitamin B12 deficiency, particularly in cases of malabsorption, and for treating cyanide poisoning (in high doses).

iii. **Dosage**: For deficiency treatment, doses are similar to cyanocobalamin, typically 1000 mcg administered intramuscularly or orally as needed.

iv. **Side Effects**: Similar to cyanocobalamin, including rare allergic reactions and gastrointestinal issues.

c. **Methylcobalamin**

i. **Mechanism of Action**: An active form of Vitamin B12 that is directly involved in methylation reactions and neurological function.

ii. **Uses**: Used in treating Vitamin B12 deficiency, especially when neurological symptoms are present.

iii. **Dosage**: Oral doses typically range from 1000 to 5000 mcg daily. Intramuscular or sublingual forms may also be used.

iv. **Side Effects**: Generally well-tolerated with minimal side effects; occasional mild gastrointestinal symptoms.

d. **Adenosylcobalamin**

i. **Mechanism of Action**: Another active form of Vitamin B12 that is involved in energy metabolism and red blood cell production.

ii. **Uses**: Used in Vitamin B12 deficiency, particularly in cases with neurological involvement.

iii. **Dosage**: Oral or sublingual doses typically range from 1000 to 5000 mcg daily.

iv. **Side Effects**: Generally well-tolerated, with minimal side effects similar to other forms of Vitamin B12.

2. Mechanism of Action

Vitamin B12 is vital for:

a. **DNA Synthesis**: Essential for the synthesis of DNA and RNA, crucial for cell division and the production of red blood cells.

b. **Red Blood Cell Production**: Plays a key role in producing and maintaining healthy red blood cells, preventing megaloblastic anemia.

c. **Neurological Function**: Important for the maintenance of myelin, the protective sheath surrounding nerves, and for proper neurological function.

3. Clinical Uses

a. **Vitamin B12 Deficiency**: Treatment of anemia caused by Vitamin B12 deficiency, often seen in conditions like pernicious anemia, gastrointestinal disorders, or in individuals with poor dietary intake.

b. **Megaloblastic Anemia**: A type of anemia characterized by large, immature, and dysfunctional red blood cells due to Vitamin B12 deficiency.

c. **Neurological Symptoms**: Management of neurological symptoms associated with Vitamin B12 deficiency, such as peripheral neuropathy, cognitive dysfunction, and mood disturbances.

4. Side Effects

Vitamin B12 supplements are generally well-tolerated. However, potential side effects include:

a. **Gastrointestinal Issues**: Mild nausea, diarrhea, or abdominal discomfort.

b. **Allergic Reactions**: Rare, but can include rash, itching, or anaphylaxis in sensitive individuals.

c. **Injection Site Reactions**: For intramuscular forms, possible pain or irritation at the injection site.

5. Considerations in Therapy

a. **Diagnosis and Monitoring**: Accurate diagnosis of Vitamin B12 deficiency is crucial, often involving blood tests such as serum Vitamin B12 levels, methylmalonic acid (MMA), and homocysteine levels. Monitoring of response to therapy is important, with follow-up blood tests to ensure adequate replenishment and resolution of anemia.

b. **Dietary Intake**: Vegetarians and vegans are at higher risk for Vitamin B12 deficiency due to its limited dietary sources. Supplementation is often recommended for these populations.

c. **Absorption Issues**: Patients with conditions affecting Vitamin B12 absorption (e.g., pernicious anemia, gastrointestinal surgeries) may require higher doses or alternative forms (e.g., injections).

Folate Supplements:

Folate, also known as Vitamin B9, is crucial for DNA synthesis, cell division, and the production of red blood cells. Folate deficiency can lead to megaloblastic anemia, characterized by the production of abnormally large and dysfunctional red blood cells. Here's a detailed overview of folate supplements, their mechanisms, uses, and side effects:

1. Forms of Folate Supplements

a. **Folic Acid**

   i. **Mechanism of Action**: A synthetic form of folate that is converted to the active forms (tetrahydrofolate) in the body. It is essential for DNA synthesis and red blood cell production.

   ii. **Uses**: Used to treat and prevent folate deficiency, which can cause megaloblastic anemia and other health issues. Also used in prenatal vitamins to prevent neural tube defects in pregnancy.

   iii. **Dosage**: Commonly 400 to 800 mcg daily for adults; higher doses may be required for deficiency treatment or in specific conditions (e.g., pregnancy, certain medications).

   iv. **Side Effects**: Generally well-tolerated. Rare side effects include gastrointestinal disturbances and allergic reactions.

b. **L-Methylfolate**

   i. **Mechanism of Action**: The active form of folate that is readily utilized by the body. It bypasses the need for conversion from folic acid and directly participates in metabolic processes.

ii.   **Uses**: Used for treating folate deficiency, particularly in individuals with metabolic disorders affecting folate metabolism (e.g., MTHFR gene mutations).

iii.   **Dosage**: Typically 400 to 1000 mcg daily, based on individual needs and response to therapy.

iv.   **Side Effects**: Generally well-tolerated with minimal side effects. Occasionally mild gastrointestinal symptoms.

c. **Folate (5-MTHF)**

i.   **Mechanism of Action**: Another form of the active folate, which is directly involved in the body's methylation processes and red blood cell production.

ii.   **Uses**: Similar to L-methylfolate, used in conditions where the active form of folate is required or when there are absorption issues with synthetic folic acid.

iii.   **Dosage**: Typically 400 to 800 mcg daily, but dosages can vary based on specific needs.

iv.   **Side Effects**: Generally well-tolerated; similar side effects to other forms of folate supplements.

2. Mechanism of Action

Folate is essential for:

a. **DNA and RNA Synthesis**: Necessary for the synthesis of nucleic acids, which are vital for cell division and growth.

b. **Red Blood Cell Production**: Helps in the formation and maturation of red blood cells, preventing megaloblastic anemia.

c. **Homocysteine Metabolism**: Involved in the metabolism of homocysteine, an amino acid that, at elevated levels, is associated with cardiovascular disease.

3. Clinical Uses

a. **Folate Deficiency**: Treatment of anemia caused by folate deficiency, commonly seen in individuals with poor dietary intake, malabsorption issues, or increased requirements (e.g., pregnancy).

b. **Megaloblastic Anemia**: A type of anemia caused by folate deficiency, characterized by large, immature red blood cells.

c. **Pregnancy**: Prevention of neural tube defects (e.g., spina bifida) in the developing fetus by ensuring adequate folate levels.

d. **Homocysteine Reduction**: Lowering elevated homocysteine levels, which is beneficial for cardiovascular health.

4. Side Effects

Folate supplements are typically well-tolerated, but potential side effects can include:

a. **Gastrointestinal Issues**: Nausea, abdominal discomfort, and flatulence.

b. **Allergic Reactions**: Rare but can include rash, itching, and swelling.

c. **Potential Masking of Vitamin B12 Deficiency**: High doses of folate can mask Vitamin B12 deficiency, leading to potential neurological complications.

5. Considerations in Therapy

a. **Diagnosis and Monitoring**: Proper diagnosis of folate deficiency often involves blood tests such as serum folate levels and red blood cell indices. Monitoring is essential to assess the effectiveness of therapy and prevent complications.

b. **Dietary Sources**: Folate is found in various foods such as leafy greens, legumes, and fortified cereals. Supplementation is often used when dietary intake is insufficient or in specific clinical situations.

c. **Interaction with Medications**: Some medications can affect folate metabolism or absorption, including anticonvulsants and certain chemotherapeutic agents. Dose adjustments may be necessary in these cases.

Erythropoiesis-Stimulating Agents (ESAs):

Erythropoiesis-stimulating agents (ESAs) are medications designed to stimulate the production of red blood cells (RBCs) by acting on the bone marrow. They are primarily used in the treatment of anemia, especially in patients with chronic kidney disease (CKD) or those undergoing chemotherapy. Here's a detailed overview of ESAs, including their mechanisms of action, uses, and potential side effects:

1. Mechanism of Action

ESAs mimic the action of erythropoietin, a hormone naturally produced by the kidneys that stimulates erythropoiesis (the production of red blood cells) in the bone marrow. They work by binding to the erythropoietin receptors on erythroid progenitor cells in the bone marrow, leading to:

a. **Increased RBC Production**: Enhances the proliferation and differentiation of erythroid progenitor cells into mature red blood cells.

b. **Improved Hemoglobin Levels**: Results in increased hemoglobin levels and improved oxygen-carrying capacity of the blood.

2. Types of Erythropoiesis-Stimulating Agents

a. **Erythropoietin (Epoetin alfa)**

    i. **Mechanism of Action**: A synthetic form of erythropoietin. It stimulates erythropoiesis by binding to erythropoietin receptors on erythroid progenitor cells in the bone marrow.

    ii. **Uses**: Used to treat anemia associated with chronic kidney disease, cancer chemotherapy, and certain other conditions.

    iii. **Dosage**: Administered subcutaneously or intravenously. Dosage varies based on the condition being treated and the patient's response. Common dosing ranges from 50 to 300 units/kg 1-3 times a week.

    iv. **Side Effects**: May include hypertension, headache, nausea, and risk of thromboembolic events (e.g., stroke, heart attack).

b. **Darbepoetin alfa**

    i. **Mechanism of Action**: A modified form of erythropoietin with a longer half-life, allowing for less frequent dosing. It stimulates erythropoiesis in a similar manner to erythropoietin.

    ii. **Uses**: Similar to epoetin alfa, used for anemia due to chronic kidney disease and chemotherapy.

    iii. **Dosage**: Administered subcutaneously or intravenously. Dosage typically ranges from 0.45 to 0.75 mcg/kg every 1-4 weeks, depending on the patient's needs and response.

    iv. **Side Effects**: Similar to epoetin alfa, including hypertension, headache, and thromboembolic events.

c. **Methoxy Polyethylene Glycol-Epoetin Beta (Mircera)**

    i. **Mechanism of Action**: An extended-release form of erythropoietin that combines epoetin beta with a polyethylene glycol (PEG) moiety to extend its duration of action.

    ii. **Uses**: Used for the treatment of anemia associated with chronic kidney disease, with dosing less frequent compared to other ESAs.

    iii. **Dosage**: Administered subcutaneously or intravenously. Typical dosing ranges from 0.6 to 1.2 mcg/kg every 2-4 weeks.

    iv. **Side Effects**: Similar to other ESAs, including hypertension, headache, and increased risk of cardiovascular events.

3. Clinical Uses

a. **Chronic Kidney Disease (CKD)**: Anemia is common in CKD due to reduced erythropoietin production. ESAs help manage anemia and improve quality of life in these patients.

b. **Cancer Chemotherapy**: Anemia can occur as a side effect of chemotherapy. ESAs are used to reduce the need for blood transfusions and improve anemia-related symptoms.

c. **Preoperative Anemia**: ESAs may be used to correct anemia before surgery, especially in patients at high risk of blood loss.

4. Side Effects and Risks

a. **Hypertension**: ESAs can cause or exacerbate high blood pressure, which needs to be monitored and managed.

b. **Thromboembolic Events**: Increased risk of serious cardiovascular events, such as stroke, heart attack, and deep vein thrombosis, especially when hemoglobin levels are increased too rapidly.

c. **Headache and Fatigue**: Common side effects that can affect the patient's quality of life.

d. **Allergic Reactions**: Rare but possible, including rash, itching, or more severe reactions.

5. Monitoring and Considerations

a. **Hemoglobin Levels**: Regular monitoring of hemoglobin and hematocrit levels is essential to avoid excessive increases in hemoglobin, which can increase the risk of thromboembolic events.

b. **Dosage Adjustment**: Dosages should be adjusted based on the patient's response and hemoglobin levels to ensure efficacy while minimizing risks.

c. **Blood Pressure Management**: Monitoring and managing blood pressure is crucial to reduce the risk of hypertension associated with ESA therapy.

d. **Iron Levels**: Adequate iron levels are necessary for effective erythropoiesis. Patients on ESAs may require iron supplementation if their iron stores are insufficient.

Hematinics for Specific Conditions:

Hematinics are agents used to treat or prevent anemia by promoting the production of red blood cells (RBCs) or correcting deficiencies in essential components of blood formation. In the context of specific conditions, hematinics are tailored to address the underlying causes of anemia. Here's a detailed overview of hematinics used for specific conditions:

1. Anemia Due to Iron Deficiency

Iron Supplements

   a. **Forms**: Oral (ferrous sulfate, ferrous gluconate, ferrous fumarate) and intravenous (iron dextran, iron sucrose, ferric carboxymaltose).

   b. **Mechanism of Action**: Provide elemental iron, which is necessary for the synthesis of hemoglobin and erythropoiesis.

   c. **Uses**: Treats anemia caused by iron deficiency due to inadequate dietary intake, absorption issues, or blood loss.

   d. **Dosage**: Oral doses typically range from 50 to 200 mg of elemental iron daily. Intravenous doses vary depending on the product and clinical scenario.

   e. **Side Effects**: Gastrointestinal disturbances (nausea, constipation, black stools), allergic reactions (for intravenous forms).

2. Anemia Due to Vitamin B12 Deficiency

Vitamin B12 Supplements

   a. **Forms**: Oral (cyanocobalamin, methylcobalamin), sublingual, intramuscular injections (cyanocobalamin).

   b. **Mechanism of Action**: Essential for DNA synthesis and RBC formation. Supplements correct the deficiency and improve red blood cell production.

   c. **Uses**: Treats megaloblastic anemia caused by Vitamin B12 deficiency due to poor dietary intake, absorption issues, or specific conditions (e.g., pernicious anemia).

   d. **Dosage**: Oral doses typically 500 to 1000 mcg daily; intramuscular injections often 1000 mcg monthly.

   e. **Side Effects**: Generally well-tolerated; rare allergic reactions, mild gastrointestinal symptoms.

3. Anemia Due to Folate Deficiency

Folate Supplements

    a. **Forms**: Oral (folic acid, L-methylfolate).

    b. **Mechanism of Action**: Provides folate, necessary for DNA synthesis and RBC production. Corrects folate deficiency and resolves megaloblastic anemia.

    c. **Uses**: Treats anemia caused by folate deficiency due to poor dietary intake, malabsorption, or specific conditions (e.g., pregnancy).

    d. **Dosage**: Typically 400 to 800 mcg daily.

    e. **Side Effects**: Mild gastrointestinal symptoms; potential for masking Vitamin B12 deficiency.

4. Anemia Due to Chronic Kidney Disease (CKD)

Erythropoiesis-Stimulating Agents (ESAs)

    a. **Forms**: Epoetin alfa, darbepoetin alfa, methoxy polyethylene glycol-epoetin beta.

    b. **Mechanism of Action**: Stimulate erythropoiesis in the bone marrow, increasing red blood cell production.

    c. **Uses**: Treats anemia associated with CKD or other conditions where endogenous erythropoietin is insufficient.

    d. **Dosage**: Varies based on specific ESA, typically administered subcutaneously or intravenously.

    e. **Side Effects**: Hypertension, headache, risk of thromboembolic events, allergic reactions.

5. Anemia Due to Chemotherapy

Erythropoiesis-Stimulating Agents (ESAs)

    a. **Forms**: Epoetin alfa, darbepoetin alfa.

    b. **Mechanism of Action**: Stimulate RBC production to counteract anemia induced by chemotherapy.

c. **Uses**: Used to reduce the need for blood transfusions and improve anemia-related symptoms in cancer patients undergoing chemotherapy.

d. **Dosage**: Administered based on patient needs, typically subcutaneously or intravenously.

e. **Side Effects**: Similar to those for CKD, including risk of cardiovascular events.

6. Anemia Due to Bone Marrow Disorders

Hematopoietic Growth Factors

a. **Forms**: Granulocyte colony-stimulating factor (G-CSF), granulocyte-macrophage colony-stimulating factor (GM-CSF).

b. **Mechanism of Action**: Stimulate the production of hematopoietic cells in the bone marrow, including red blood cells.

c. **Uses**: Used for anemia due to conditions like aplastic anemia or myelodysplastic syndromes.

d. **Dosage**: Doses vary depending on the specific growth factor and condition.

e. **Side Effects**: Possible bone pain, flu-like symptoms, risk of splenomegaly.

7. Anemia Due to Chronic Inflammatory Diseases

Disease-Modifying Anti-Rheumatic Drugs (DMARDs)

a. **Forms**: Methotrexate, hydroxychloroquine.

b. **Mechanism of Action**: Address underlying inflammatory conditions that contribute to anemia.

c. **Uses**: Treat anemia associated with chronic inflammatory diseases such as rheumatoid arthritis or systemic lupus erythematosus.

d. **Dosage**: Varies based on specific drug and condition.

e. **Side Effects**: Depend on the DMARD used; can include gastrointestinal symptoms, liver toxicity, and bone marrow suppression.

8. Anemia Due to Blood Loss

Iron Supplements and **Blood Transfusions**

a. **Forms**: Oral or intravenous iron; whole blood or red blood cell concentrates.

b. **Mechanism of Action**: Iron supplements replenish iron stores; blood transfusions provide immediate red blood cells to correct anemia.

c. **Uses**: Treats anemia resulting from acute or chronic blood loss (e.g., gastrointestinal bleeding, surgery).

d. **Dosage**: Iron doses as mentioned above; transfusion volumes based on clinical need.

e. **Side Effects**: Iron supplements may cause gastrointestinal disturbances; blood transfusions carry risks of allergic reactions, transfusion reactions, and iron overload.

Multiple Choice Questions (MCQs)

1. Which class of antiarrhythmic drugs blocks sodium channels and slows depolarization during the action potential?

    a) Class II

    b) Class I

    c) Class III

    d) Class IV

2. Which of the following is a beta-blocker used for the management of angina?

    a) Verapamil

    b) Amlodipine

    c) Metoprolol

    d) Ranolazine

3. Which drug is a nitrate used for the acute relief of angina?

a) Atenolol

b) Nitroglycerin

c) Diltiazem

d) Digoxin

4. What is the primary action of calcium channel blockers in the management of angina?

a) Increase heart rate

b) Reduce myocardial oxygen consumption

c) Block sodium channels

d) Increase blood pressure

5. Which anti-arrhythmic drug is known to cause torsades de pointes?

a) Lidocaine

b) Quinidine

c) Sotalol

d) Digoxin

6. Which of the following is a statin used to lower LDL cholesterol?

a) Fenofibrate

b) Atorvastatin

c) Ezetimibe

d) Colestipol

7. Which drug is a potassium channel blocker used in the treatment of ventricular and atrial arrhythmias?

a) Sotalol

b) Propranolol

c) Lidocaine

d) Verapamil

8. Which vasopressor is commonly used in septic shock to increase blood pressure?

a) Dopamine

b) Norepinephrine

c) Epinephrine

d) Phenylephrine

9. Which medication is used as a first-line treatment for iron deficiency anemia?

a) Vitamin B12

b) Folate

c) Ferrous sulfate

d) Epoetin alfa

10. Which anticoagulant enhances antithrombin III activity?

a) Warfarin

b) Heparin

c) Aspirin

d) Clopidogrel

11. Which drug is used in the treatment of angina by reducing the funny (If) current in the sinoatrial node?

a) Ivabradine

b) Nicorandil

c) Ranolazine

d) Amlodipine

12. Which of the following drugs is a PCSK9 inhibitor used to lower LDL cholesterol?

a) Atorvastatin

b) Ezetimibe

c) Alirocumab

d) Niacin

13. Which of the following is a hematinic used to stimulate red blood cell production in chronic kidney disease?

a) Folic acid

b) Ferrous fumarate

c) Epoetin alfa

d) Vitamin B12

14. Which inotrope is primarily used to increase cardiac contractility in cardiogenic shock?

   a) Dobutamine

   b) Milrinone

   c) Norepinephrine

   d) Phenylephrine

15. Which of the following is a bile acid sequestrant used to lower LDL cholesterol?

   a) Ezetimibe

   b) Fenofibrate

   c) Cholestyramine

   d) Simvastatin

16. Which of the following is an extended-release form of erythropoietin used to treat anemia in chronic kidney disease?

   a) Epoetin alfa

   b) Darbepoetin alfa

   c) Methoxy polyethylene glycol-epoetin beta

   d) Ferumoxytol

17. Which drug is used for the treatment of cyanide poisoning in high doses?

   a) Folic acid

   b) Hydroxocobalamin

   c) Methotrexate

   d) Iron dextran

18. Which anti-arrhythmic drug is used for acute termination of paroxysmal supraventricular tachycardia (PSVT)?

   a) Adenosine

b) Dofetilide

c) Flecainide

d) Quinidine

19. Which drug acts by inhibiting HMG-CoA reductase, leading to reduced cholesterol synthesis?

a) Fenofibrate

b) Niacin

c) Atorvastatin

d) Ezetimibe

20. Which of the following is a non-dihydropyridine calcium channel blocker used to manage angina and arrhythmias?

a) Amlodipine

b) Verapamil

c) Nifedipine

d) Ranolazine

Short Answer Questions (SAQs)

1. Describe the mechanism of action of beta-blockers in the management of angina.

2. What are the clinical uses of nitrates in cardiovascular therapy?

3. Explain the role of statins in managing hyperlipidemia.

4. How do calcium channel blockers help in the treatment of arrhythmias?

5. What are the potential side effects of ACE inhibitors?

6. Describe the mechanism of action of antiplatelet drugs like aspirin.

7. What is the clinical significance of using digoxin in heart failure?

8. Explain how diuretics contribute to the management of hypertension.

9. What are the key differences between fibrates and statins in lipid management?

10. How does dobutamine work in managing cardiogenic shock?

11.Discuss the therapeutic uses of warfarin and its monitoring requirements.

12.What is the role of erythropoiesis-stimulating agents in treating anemia?

13.Explain the pharmacological management of anaphylactic shock.

14.How do PCSK9 inhibitors help in lowering LDL cholesterol levels?

15.Describe the mechanism of action of vasopressors in shock management.

16.What are the indications and contraindications for the use of beta-blockers?

17.Explain the importance of folate in preventing neural tube defects.

18.How does ranolazine help in the management of chronic angina?

19.Discuss the clinical applications of omega-3 fatty acids in cardiovascular therapy.

20.What are the side effects and risks associated with the use of inotropes in shock?

Long Answer Questions (LAQs)

1. Discuss the classification, mechanisms of action, and clinical applications of antiarrhythmic drugs.

2. Explain the role of antihypertensive drugs in managing blood pressure, including the mechanisms, clinical uses, and side effects of major classes.

3. Describe the pharmacological management of heart failure, focusing on the roles of ACE inhibitors, beta-blockers, diuretics, and digoxin.

4. Discuss the use of lipid-lowering agents in the prevention of cardiovascular diseases, including the different classes, their mechanisms, and side effects.

5. Explain the pharmacology of anti-anginal drugs, including their mechanisms of action, clinical uses, and potential side effects.

6. Discuss the use of anticoagulants and antiplatelets in preventing thromboembolic events, including their mechanisms, clinical applications, and monitoring.

7. Explain the management of shock, including the roles of vasopressors, inotropes, and fluid resuscitation in different types of shock.

8. Describe the role of hematinics in the treatment of anemia, including the different types of anemia and the corresponding treatment options.

9. Discuss the pharmacological management of arrhythmias, focusing on the choice of drugs based on the type of arrhythmia and patient-specific factors.

10. Explain the role of erythropoiesis-stimulating agents in chronic kidney disease and chemotherapy-induced anemia, including their mechanisms, clinical uses, and monitoring.

Answer Key for MCQs

1. b) Class I
2. c) Metoprolol
3. b) Nitroglycerin
4. b) Reduce myocardial oxygen consumption
5. c) Sotalol
6. b) Atorvastatin
7. a) Sotalol
8. b) Norepinephrine
9. c) Ferrous sulfate
10. b) Heparin
11. a) Ivabradine
12. c) Alirocumab
13. c) Epoetin alfa
14. a) Dobutamine
15. c) Cholestyramine
16. c) Methoxy polyethylene glycol-epoetin beta
17. b) Hydroxocobalamin
18. a) Adenosine
19. c) Atorvastatin
20. b) Verapamil

CHAPTER – 3

PHARMACOLOGY OF DRUGS ACTING ON CARDIO VASCULAR SYSTEM – III

INTRODUCTION:

The study of the pharmacology of drugs acting on the cardiovascular system is divided into various segments, each focusing on different classes of drugs and their effects on the heart and blood vessels. The third part of this series, "Pharmacology of Drugs Acting on the Cardiovascular System-III," typically delves into more specific and advanced categories of cardiovascular drugs.

Key Areas Covered:

1. **Anti-hypertensive Agents:**
   a. These drugs are used to manage high blood pressure, a major risk factor for cardiovascular diseases. Classes of anti-hypertensive agents include diuretics, beta-blockers, calcium channel blockers, ACE inhibitors, angiotensin II receptor blockers (ARBs), and others. Each class has a unique mechanism of action, pharmacokinetics, and side effect profile.

2. **Anti-arrhythmic Drugs:**
   a. This section focuses on drugs used to treat arrhythmias, which are disorders of the heart rate or rhythm. The classification of anti-arrhythmic drugs includes Class I (sodium channel blockers), Class II (beta-blockers), Class III (potassium channel blockers), Class IV (calcium channel blockers), and miscellaneous drugs. The specific mechanism of action and clinical uses of each class are discussed.

3. **Drugs Affecting Lipid Metabolism:**

a. These drugs are crucial in the management of dyslipidemias, conditions characterized by abnormal lipid levels in the blood, which are significant risk factors for cardiovascular diseases. This includes statins, fibrates, bile acid sequestrants, and newer agents like PCSK9 inhibitors. The pharmacology, mechanism of action, and therapeutic uses of these agents are covered in detail.

4. **Drugs Used in Heart Failure:**

a. Heart failure is a complex clinical syndrome that requires a multifaceted approach in its pharmacological management. This segment covers drugs like ACE inhibitors, ARBs, beta-blockers, diuretics, aldosterone antagonists, and newer agents like angiotensin receptor-neprilysin inhibitors (ARNIs). The focus is on their role in improving survival, reducing symptoms, and preventing disease progression.

5. **Vasodilators and Drugs Used in Angina:**

a. This part examines drugs that alleviate angina pectoris (chest pain due to reduced blood flow to the heart). Nitrates, calcium channel blockers, and beta-blockers are the primary drugs discussed here. Their mechanism of action, impact on myocardial oxygen demand and supply, and clinical applications are explored.

COAGULANTS AND ANTICOAGULANTS

Coagulants and anticoagulants are critical components in the pharmacology of drugs acting on the cardiovascular system, particularly in the management of blood clotting disorders. Understanding these agents is essential for preventing and treating thromboembolic events, which can lead to conditions like stroke, myocardial infarction, deep vein thrombosis (DVT), and pulmonary embolism. Below is a detailed explanation of both coagulants and anticoagulants.

1. Coagulants

Coagulants, also known as procoagulants or hemostatic agents, promote blood clot formation and are used to manage bleeding disorders, such as hemophilia, vitamin K deficiency, or during surgery to control excessive bleeding.

Types of Coagulants:

a) **Vitamin K and Vitamin K Analogues:**

   i.   **Mechanism of Action:** Vitamin K is essential for the synthesis of clotting factors II, VII, IX, and X in the liver. It acts as a cofactor for the enzyme gamma-glutamyl carboxylase, which is responsible for activating these clotting factors.

   ii. **Uses:** Used in conditions like vitamin K deficiency, warfarin overdose, and to prevent hemorrhagic disease of the newborn.

   iii. **Examples:** Phytomenadione (Vitamin K1), Menadione (Vitamin K3).

b) **Clotting Factors:**

   i.   **Mechanism of Action:** These are specific proteins that are essential for the coagulation cascade. They are administered directly to replenish deficient clotting factors in patients with hemophilia or other coagulation disorders.

   ii. **Uses:** Used in treating hemophilia (Factor VIII for Hemophilia A, Factor IX for Hemophilia B) and other clotting factor deficiencies.

   iii. **Examples:** Factor VIII, Factor IX concentrates, Prothrombin complex concentrates.

c) **Fibrinogen and Fibrin Sealants:**

   i.   **Mechanism of Action:** Fibrinogen is converted to fibrin by thrombin, which then forms a stable clot. Fibrin sealants are used topically during surgery to promote hemostasis.

   ii. **Uses:** Used during surgical procedures to control bleeding and in managing congenital or acquired fibrinogen deficiency.

   iii. **Examples:** Cryoprecipitate, Fibrinogen concentrate, Fibrin sealant.

d) **Antifibrinolytics:**

   i.   **Mechanism of Action:** These agents inhibit the breakdown of fibrin clots by blocking the conversion of plasminogen to plasmin.

   ii.   **Uses:** Used in situations where there is excessive bleeding, such as during surgery or in conditions like fibrinolytic bleeding.

   iii. **Examples:** Tranexamic acid, Aminocaproic acid.

2. Anticoagulants

Anticoagulants are drugs that prevent the formation of new clots and the expansion of existing clots. They are primarily used in the prevention and treatment of thromboembolic disorders.

Types of Anticoagulants:

a) **Heparins:**

   i.   **Mechanism of Action:** Heparins enhance the activity of antithrombin III, which inhibits thrombin (Factor IIa) and Factor Xa, leading to reduced clot formation.

   ii.   **Uses:** Used in the prophylaxis and treatment of DVT, pulmonary embolism, and in acute coronary syndromes. They are also used during surgery to prevent clot formation.

   iii. **Examples:** Unfractionated heparin, Low Molecular Weight Heparins (LMWHs) like Enoxaparin, Dalteparin.

b) **Vitamin K Antagonists:**

   i.   **Mechanism of Action:** These drugs inhibit the synthesis of Vitamin K-dependent clotting factors (II, VII, IX, and X) by blocking the action of Vitamin K epoxide reductase.

   ii.   **Uses:** Long-term anticoagulation in conditions like atrial fibrillation, mechanical heart valves, and prevention of thromboembolic events.

   iii. **Examples:** Warfarin, Acenocoumarol.

c) **Direct Oral Anticoagulants (DOACs):**

i. **Mechanism of Action:** These include direct thrombin inhibitors and direct Factor Xa inhibitors, which prevent clot formation by specifically targeting these clotting factors.

ii. **Uses:** Used for the prevention of stroke in non-valvular atrial fibrillation, treatment and prevention of DVT and pulmonary embolism.

iii. **Examples:**

    1. **Direct Thrombin Inhibitors:** Dabigatran.

    2. **Direct Factor Xa Inhibitors:** Rivaroxaban, Apixaban, Edoxaban.

d) Thrombin Inhibitors:

i. **Mechanism of Action:** These inhibit thrombin directly, preventing the conversion of fibrinogen to fibrin.

ii. **Uses:** Used in situations where heparins are contraindicated, such as in patients with heparin-induced thrombocytopenia (HIT).

iii. **Examples:** Bivalirudin, Argatroban.

e) Factor Xa Inhibitors:

i. **Mechanism of Action:** These directly inhibit Factor Xa, reducing thrombin generation and clot formation.

ii. **Uses:** Similar to DOACs, these are used for stroke prevention in atrial fibrillation, and treatment and prevention of DVT and pulmonary embolism.

iii. **Examples:** Fondaparinux.

f) Fibrinolytics/Thrombolytics:

i. **Mechanism of Action:** These drugs promote the conversion of plasminogen to plasmin, which breaks down fibrin clots. They are used to dissolve clots in acute thromboembolic events.

ii. **Uses:** Acute myocardial infarction, ischemic stroke, and massive pulmonary embolism.

iii. **Examples:** Alteplase, Streptokinase, Tenecteplase.

FIBRINOLYTICS

Fibrinolytics, also known as thrombolytics, are a class of drugs that dissolve blood clots (thrombi) that have already formed within blood vessels. These drugs are critical in the treatment of acute thromboembolic events, such as myocardial infarction (heart attack), ischemic stroke, and massive pulmonary embolism, where rapid restoration of blood flow is necessary to prevent tissue damage and death.

1. Mechanism of Action

Fibrinolytics work by activating the fibrinolytic system, which is the body's natural mechanism for breaking down clots. The key enzyme in this process is plasmin, which digests fibrin, the structural component of blood clots.

a. **Activation of Plasminogen:** Fibrinolytics convert plasminogen, an inactive precursor, into plasmin. Plasmin then breaks down fibrin into fibrin degradation products, effectively dissolving the clot. The main fibrinolytic drugs work by different mechanisms to activate plasminogen:

  i. **Tissue Plasminogen Activator (t-PA):** This is a naturally occurring enzyme that binds to fibrin in a thrombus and converts plasminogen to plasmin. Synthetic or recombinant forms of t-PA are used as fibrinolytic drugs.

  ii. **Streptokinase:** This bacterial protein forms a complex with plasminogen, leading to a conformational change that activates plasminogen to plasmin.

  iii. **Urokinase:** A naturally occurring enzyme in the human body, urokinase directly converts plasminogen to plasmin without the need for fibrin binding.

2. Types of Fibrinolytics

a) **Alteplase (t-PA):**

i. **Mechanism of Action:** Alteplase is a recombinant form of human tissue plasminogen activator (t-PA). It preferentially binds to fibrin in clots, leading to localized clot lysis.

ii. **Uses:** Alteplase is used in the treatment of acute ischemic stroke (within 3-4.5 hours of symptom onset), acute myocardial infarction (particularly when percutaneous coronary intervention is not available), and acute massive pulmonary embolism.

iii. **Administration:** Given intravenously, usually as a bolus followed by an infusion.

iv. **Adverse Effects:** The major risk is bleeding, including intracranial hemorrhage.

b) **Tenecteplase:**

i. **Mechanism of Action:** Tenecteplase is a genetically engineered variant of alteplase with a longer half-life and greater fibrin specificity. It is more resistant to inactivation by its natural inhibitor, plasminogen activator inhibitor-1 (PAI-1).

ii. **Uses:** Used in the management of acute myocardial infarction.

iii. **Administration:** Administered as a single intravenous bolus, making it easier to use in emergency situations compared to alteplase.

iv. **Adverse Effects:** Similar to alteplase, with a risk of bleeding.

c) **Streptokinase:**

i. **Mechanism of Action:** Streptokinase forms a complex with plasminogen, leading to its activation and the subsequent breakdown of fibrin clots. Unlike t-PA, streptokinase does not specifically target fibrin-bound plasminogen, which can lead to a more generalized activation of plasminogen throughout the body.

ii. **Uses:** It is used for acute myocardial infarction, DVT, and pulmonary embolism but less frequently now due to the development of more fibrin-specific agents.

iii. **Administration:** Administered intravenously, often as a loading dose followed by an infusion.

iv. **Adverse Effects:** Risk of systemic bleeding and allergic reactions, particularly since it is derived from streptococcal bacteria.

d) **Urokinase:**

   i. **Mechanism of Action:** Urokinase directly converts plasminogen to plasmin, leading to fibrinolysis. It does not require the presence of fibrin for its action.

   ii. **Uses:** Used for lysis of pulmonary emboli and in cases of catheter occlusion.

   iii. **Administration:** Given intravenously.

   iv. **Adverse Effects:** Systemic bleeding is a significant risk, similar to other fibrinolytics.

e) **Reteplase:**

   i. **Mechanism of Action:** Reteplase is a modified form of t-PA with a longer half-life, allowing it to be administered as a bolus injection. It has reduced fibrin specificity compared to alteplase but is still used for its convenience.

   ii. **Uses:** Primarily used in acute myocardial infarction.

   iii. **Administration:** Administered as two bolus injections, 30 minutes apart.

   iv. **Adverse Effects:** Bleeding, including intracranial hemorrhage.

3. Clinical Applications

Fibrinolytics are primarily used in emergency settings where rapid clot dissolution is required to restore blood flow and prevent irreversible tissue damage. Key clinical indications include:

   a. **Acute Myocardial Infarction (AMI):** Fibrinolytics are used when percutaneous coronary intervention (PCI) is not available or cannot be performed in a timely manner. They are most effective when administered within 12 hours of symptom onset.

b. **Acute Ischemic Stroke:** Fibrinolytics like alteplase are the only FDA-approved treatment for acute ischemic stroke and must be administered within 3 to 4.5 hours of symptom onset for optimal benefit.

c. **Pulmonary Embolism (PE):** For massive pulmonary embolism with hemodynamic instability, fibrinolytics can rapidly reduce clot burden and improve outcomes.

d. **Deep Vein Thrombosis (DVT) and Peripheral Arterial Occlusion:** While less commonly used, fibrinolytics can be considered in cases of extensive thrombosis where the risk of limb loss is high.

4. Adverse Effects

The most significant adverse effect of fibrinolytic therapy is bleeding, which can be life-threatening, especially intracranial hemorrhage. Other potential adverse effects include:

a. **Hypotension:** Particularly with streptokinase due to systemic plasminogen activation.

b. **Allergic Reactions:** Common with streptokinase due to its bacterial origin, but rare with other fibrinolytics.

c. **Reperfusion Arrhythmias:** Sudden restoration of blood flow, especially in myocardial infarction, can lead to arrhythmias.

5. Contraindications

Fibrinolytic therapy is contraindicated in situations where the risk of bleeding outweighs the benefits. Absolute contraindications include:

a. Recent hemorrhagic stroke

b. Active internal bleeding

c. Known intracranial neoplasm

d. Recent major surgery or trauma (within 3 weeks)

e. Known bleeding diathesis

ANTI-PLATELET DRUGS

Antiplatelet drugs are a crucial class of medications used to prevent blood clot formation by inhibiting platelet aggregation. These drugs are widely used in the prevention and treatment of cardiovascular diseases such as myocardial infarction, stroke, and peripheral arterial disease. Understanding their pharmacology is essential for optimizing patient care in these conditions.

1. Mechanism of Action

Antiplatelet drugs work by interfering with various pathways involved in platelet activation and aggregation. Platelets play a critical role in hemostasis, the process by which the body stops bleeding, but their excessive activation can lead to the formation of unwanted clots (thrombi) in arteries, leading to cardiovascular events.

The main mechanisms of action include:

a. **Inhibition of Cyclooxygenase-1 (COX-1):** This reduces the synthesis of thromboxane A2 (TXA2), a potent promoter of platelet aggregation.

b. **Inhibition of the P2Y12 ADP Receptor:** This prevents the activation of the glycoprotein IIb/IIIa receptor, which is necessary for platelets to bind fibrinogen and aggregate.

c. **Inhibition of Phosphodiesterase (PDE):** This increases cyclic AMP (cAMP) levels within platelets, which inhibits platelet activation.

d. **Inhibition of Glycoprotein IIb/IIIa Receptor:** This directly blocks the final common pathway for platelet aggregation by preventing fibrinogen binding.

2. Types of Antiplatelet Drugs

a) Aspirin (Acetylsalicylic Acid):

i. **Mechanism of Action:** Aspirin irreversibly inhibits the enzyme cyclooxygenase-1 (COX-1) in platelets, leading to a decrease in the production of thromboxane A2 (TXA2). TXA2 is a potent promoter of platelet aggregation and vasoconstriction. By inhibiting its synthesis, aspirin effectively reduces platelet aggregation.

ii. **Uses:** Aspirin is widely used for the primary and secondary prevention of cardiovascular events such as myocardial infarction, stroke, and transient ischemic attacks (TIAs). It is also used in the prevention of thromboembolic complications in patients with atrial fibrillation and following coronary artery bypass grafting (CABG).

iii. **Dosage:** Low-dose aspirin (75-325 mg/day) is typically used for its antiplatelet effects.

iv. **Adverse Effects:** Gastrointestinal irritation, peptic ulcers, and bleeding are common side effects. Long-term use may increase the risk of gastrointestinal bleeding.

b) P2Y12 ADP Receptor Inhibitors:

These drugs block the P2Y12 receptor on platelets, which is a key receptor in the ADP-mediated pathway of platelet activation.

i. **Clopidogrel:**

1. **Mechanism of Action:** Clopidogrel is a prodrug that requires hepatic conversion to its active metabolite, which irreversibly inhibits the P2Y12 ADP receptor on platelets. This prevents ADP-mediated activation of the glycoprotein IIb/IIIa complex, thereby reducing platelet aggregation.

2. **Uses:** Clopidogrel is used in the prevention of atherosclerotic events in patients with recent myocardial infarction, stroke, or established peripheral arterial disease. It is also used in patients undergoing percutaneous coronary intervention (PCI) and those who are intolerant to aspirin.

3. **Adverse Effects:** Bleeding is the most significant adverse effect. Other side effects include gastrointestinal disturbances, rash, and, rarely, thrombotic thrombocytopenic purpura (TTP).

ii. **Prasugrel:**

1. **Mechanism of Action:** Like clopidogrel, prasugrel is a prodrug that irreversibly inhibits the P2Y12 receptor. It has a faster onset of action and is more potent than clopidogrel.

2. **Uses:** Primarily used in patients with acute coronary syndrome (ACS) undergoing PCI.

3. **Adverse Effects:** Higher risk of bleeding compared to clopidogrel. It is contraindicated in patients with a history of stroke or transient ischemic attack due to the increased risk of bleeding.

iii. **Ticagrelor:**

1. **Mechanism of Action:** Ticagrelor is a direct, reversible inhibitor of the P2Y12 receptor. Unlike clopidogrel and prasugrel, it does not require metabolic activation and has a more rapid onset and offset of action.

2. **Uses:** Used in combination with aspirin for the prevention of thrombotic events in patients with ACS, including those undergoing PCI.

3. **Adverse Effects:** Bleeding is a common side effect. Other side effects include dyspnea (shortness of breath) and an increase in serum uric acid and creatinine levels.

iv. **Cangrelor:**

1. **Mechanism of Action:** Cangrelor is an intravenous P2Y12 inhibitor with a rapid onset and offset of action, used in situations requiring immediate and potent platelet inhibition.

2. **Uses:** Used during PCI in patients who have not been pre-treated with an oral P2Y12 inhibitor and in whom glycoprotein IIb/IIIa inhibitors are not planned.

3. **Adverse Effects:** Bleeding is the primary concern.

c) Glycoprotein IIb/IIIa Inhibitors:

These drugs block the glycoprotein IIb/IIIa receptor on platelets, which is the final common pathway for platelet aggregation.

i. **Abciximab:**
1. **Mechanism of Action:** Abciximab is a monoclonal antibody that binds to the glycoprotein IIb/IIIa receptor on platelets, preventing fibrinogen from binding and thus inhibiting platelet aggregation.
2. **Uses:** Used as an adjunct to PCI to prevent ischemic complications, particularly in patients with unstable angina or non-ST elevation myocardial infarction (NSTEMI).
3. **Adverse Effects:** Bleeding, particularly at the site of arterial puncture for catheterization, is a common side effect. Thrombocytopenia (low platelet count) can also occur.

ii. **Eptifibatide and Tirofiban:**
1. **Mechanism of Action:** These are small molecule inhibitors that reversibly bind to the glycoprotein IIb/IIIa receptor, preventing platelet aggregation.
2. **Uses:** Used in the treatment of ACS and as an adjunct in PCI.
3. **Adverse Effects:** Similar to abciximab, the primary side effect is bleeding.

d) Phosphodiesterase (PDE) Inhibitors:

These drugs inhibit the enzyme phosphodiesterase, leading to an increase in cAMP within platelets, which inhibits platelet activation.

i. **Dipyridamole:**
1. **Mechanism of Action:** Dipyridamole inhibits phosphodiesterase and blocks the reuptake of adenosine, leading to increased cAMP levels and inhibition of platelet aggregation.
2. **Uses:** Used in combination with aspirin for secondary prevention of stroke and transient ischemic attacks. It is also used in

combination with warfarin for the prevention of thromboembolic complications in patients with prosthetic heart valves.

   3. **Adverse Effects:** Headache, dizziness, and gastrointestinal disturbances are common side effects. It may also cause hypotension.

ii. **Cilostazol:**

   1. **Mechanism of Action:** Cilostazol is a selective PDE3 inhibitor that increases cAMP in platelets and blood vessels, inhibiting platelet aggregation and causing vasodilation.

   2. **Uses:** Used primarily for the treatment of intermittent claudication in peripheral arterial disease.

   3. **Adverse Effects:** Headache, palpitations, and diarrhea are common side effects. Cilostazol is contraindicated in patients with heart failure due to the risk of arrhythmias.

3. Clinical Applications

Antiplatelet drugs are used in a variety of clinical settings, particularly in the prevention and treatment of cardiovascular diseases:

a. **Acute Coronary Syndromes (ACS):** Antiplatelet therapy is a cornerstone in the management of ACS, including unstable angina, NSTEMI, and ST-elevation myocardial infarction (STEMI). Dual antiplatelet therapy (DAPT), typically with aspirin and a P2Y12 inhibitor, is often used.

b. **Percutaneous Coronary Intervention (PCI):** Antiplatelet drugs are used before, during, and after PCI to prevent stent thrombosis and other thrombotic complications.

c. **Stroke Prevention:** In patients with a history of ischemic stroke or TIA, antiplatelet therapy, typically with aspirin or a combination of aspirin and dipyridamole, is used to reduce the risk of recurrent stroke.

d. **Atrial Fibrillation:** In patients who cannot tolerate anticoagulation, antiplatelet therapy may be used to reduce the risk of stroke, although anticoagulants are generally preferred.

e. **Peripheral Arterial Disease (PAD):** Antiplatelet drugs, especially aspirin and cilostazol, are used to reduce the risk of cardiovascular events and improve symptoms of intermittent claudication.

4. Adverse Effects and Contraindications

a. **Bleeding:** The most significant adverse effect of antiplatelet therapy is bleeding, including gastrointestinal bleeding and intracranial hemorrhage. The risk increases with the use of multiple antiplatelet agents (e.g., DAPT).

b. **Gastrointestinal Disturbances:** Common with aspirin and other antiplatelet drugs, particularly with prolonged use.

c. **Hypersensitivity Reactions:** Rare, but possible, especially with aspirin.

d. **Contraindications:** These include active bleeding, peptic ulcer disease, hypersensitivity to the drug, and in some cases, conditions like severe hepatic or renal impairment.

PLASMA VOLUME EXPANDERS

Plasma volume expanders are intravenous fluids used to increase the volume of plasma in the circulatory system. They are primarily employed in the treatment of hypovolemia, a condition where there is a reduced volume of blood plasma, often due to severe blood loss, dehydration, or burns. By expanding the plasma volume, these agents help restore hemodynamic stability, improve tissue perfusion, and prevent shock.

1. Mechanism of Action

Plasma volume expanders work by increasing the volume of plasma in the blood, thereby improving circulatory function. They do this by two main mechanisms:

a. **Osmotic Effect:** Some plasma volume expanders, like colloids, exert an osmotic pressure that draws water from the interstitial and intracellular spaces into the intravascular space, thereby increasing plasma volume.

b. **Volume Expansion:** Crystalloids and colloids physically add to the volume of plasma, increasing the overall intravascular fluid volume, which helps maintain blood pressure and improves cardiac output.

2. Types of Plasma Volume Expanders

Plasma volume expanders can be broadly categorized into crystalloids and colloids.

a) Crystalloids

Crystalloids are solutions of electrolytes in water that freely cross capillary walls, distributing throughout the extracellular space. They are the most commonly used plasma expanders.

i. **Normal Saline (0.9% Sodium Chloride):**

   1. **Composition:** Isotonic solution containing 154 mEq/L of sodium and chloride.

   2. **Mechanism of Action:** Expands the extracellular fluid (ECF) compartment by adding volume directly to the intravascular space. However, because it freely distributes across capillary membranes, a significant portion of the administered volume quickly moves into the interstitial space.

   3. **Uses:** Used in hypovolemia, dehydration, and as a vehicle for drug administration.

   4. **Adverse Effects:** Large volumes can lead to hyperchloremic metabolic acidosis, fluid overload, and edema.

ii. **Ringer's Lactate (Lactated Ringer's Solution):**

   1. **Composition:** Isotonic solution containing sodium, potassium, calcium, chloride, and lactate (which acts as a buffer).

2. **Mechanism of Action:** Similar to normal saline but with the added benefit of lactate, which is metabolized to bicarbonate, helping to buffer metabolic acidosis.

3. **Uses:** Preferred in cases of hypovolemia, especially in patients with acidosis, burns, or surgical patients.

4. **Adverse Effects:** Electrolyte imbalances (hyperkalemia in renal failure patients), fluid overload.

iii. **Dextrose 5% in Water (D5W):**

1. **Composition:** Hypotonic solution that contains 5% dextrose (glucose) in water.

2. **Mechanism of Action:** Initially increases intravascular volume, but as dextrose is metabolized, free water is left behind, which rapidly moves into the intracellular space.

3. **Uses:** Used for fluid replacement in cases where both hydration and calorie supply are needed.

4. **Adverse Effects:** Can cause hyponatremia, especially in large volumes, and should not be used for volume replacement in hypovolemic patients.

b) Colloids

Colloids are solutions that contain large molecules, such as proteins or polysaccharides, that do not easily cross capillary walls, thus staying within the intravascular space longer than crystalloids. They exert a colloid osmotic pressure that draws fluid into the intravascular space from the interstitial space.

i. **Albumin:**

1. **Composition:** A natural colloid made from human plasma, available in concentrations of 5% (isotonic) and 25% (hypertonic).

2. **Mechanism of Action:** Increases plasma oncotic pressure, drawing fluid into the intravascular space from the interstitial and intracellular compartments.

3. **Uses:** Used in hypovolemic shock, burns, and hypoalbuminemia. The 25% solution is often used in patients with significant edema, such as those with liver cirrhosis or nephrotic syndrome.

4. **Adverse Effects:** Risk of anaphylaxis, fluid overload, and it is expensive.

ii. **Hydroxyethyl Starch (HES):**

1. **Composition:** Synthetic colloid made from modified starches, available in varying molecular weights (e.g., HES 130/0.4).

2. **Mechanism of Action:** Increases plasma volume by staying within the intravascular compartment longer, with varying effects depending on the molecular weight and degree of substitution of the starch.

3. **Uses:** Used in hypovolemia and shock, particularly in the perioperative and critical care settings.

4. **Adverse Effects:** Can cause coagulopathy, acute kidney injury, and pruritus. The use of HES has declined due to safety concerns.

iii. **Dextrans:**

1. **Composition:** Synthetic colloids made from polysaccharides with varying molecular weights (e.g., Dextran 40, Dextran 70).

2. **Mechanism of Action:** Expand plasma volume by drawing water into the intravascular space, with a longer duration of action compared to crystalloids.

3. **Uses:** Used in hypovolemia, although their use has declined due to potential side effects.

4. **Adverse Effects:** Can cause anaphylaxis, acute kidney injury, and interfere with blood typing and crossmatching.

iv. **Gelatins:**

1. **Composition:** Synthetic colloid made from hydrolyzed bovine collagen, with low molecular weight.

   2. **Mechanism of Action:** Acts similarly to other colloids, expanding plasma volume and staying intravascular longer than crystalloids.

   3. **Uses:** Used in hypovolemia and shock, although less commonly due to concerns about efficacy and safety.

   4. **Adverse Effects:** Risk of anaphylaxis, renal impairment, and coagulopathy.

3. Clinical Applications

Plasma volume expanders are used in various clinical scenarios where rapid restoration of intravascular volume is necessary:

   a. **Hypovolemic Shock:** Rapid administration of volume expanders is crucial in treating shock due to blood loss, severe dehydration, or burns. Colloids and crystalloids are chosen based on the severity of the shock and the underlying condition.

   b. **Perioperative Fluid Management:** Plasma expanders are used during surgery to maintain hemodynamic stability, especially in major surgeries with significant blood loss.

   c. **Burns:** Patients with extensive burns require large volumes of fluid replacement to compensate for fluid loss and to maintain tissue perfusion.

   d. **Septic Shock:** In septic shock, plasma volume expanders are used as part of the initial resuscitation to improve tissue perfusion and oxygenation.

4. Adverse Effects and Contraindications

   a. **Fluid Overload:** Excessive administration of plasma volume expanders can lead to fluid overload, resulting in pulmonary edema, heart failure, and increased intra-abdominal pressure.

   b. **Electrolyte Imbalance:** Crystalloids can cause electrolyte disturbances, such as hyperchloremic acidosis with normal saline or hyperkalemia with Ringer's lactate.

c. **Coagulopathy:** Some colloids, particularly synthetic ones like HES and dextrans, can interfere with blood coagulation, increasing the risk of bleeding.

d. **Kidney Injury:** Certain colloids, especially HES, have been associated with an increased risk of acute kidney injury.

e. **Allergic Reactions:** Anaphylaxis is a rare but serious adverse effect of colloids like albumin, dextrans, and gelatins.

f. **Contraindications:** Plasma expanders are contraindicated in patients with fluid overload, severe heart failure, or conditions where increased intravascular volume could be detrimental.

CLASSIFICATION:

The classification of drugs acting on the cardiovascular system can be quite broad, especially in the context of Pharmacology of drugs acting on the cardiovascular system-III. Here's a breakdown of the main categories within this section, along with examples:

1. Coagulants

a. **Definition:** Coagulants are agents that promote blood coagulation, helping to prevent excessive bleeding.

b. **Examples:**

   i. **Vitamin K:** Essential for the synthesis of clotting factors.

   ii. **Fibrinogen:** A plasma protein that is converted into fibrin in the blood clotting process.

   iii. **Protamine Sulfate:** Used to reverse the effects of heparin.

2. Anticoagulants

a. **Definition:** Anticoagulants prevent the formation of new blood clots or the extension of existing clots.

b. **Examples:**

   i. **Heparin:** An intravenous anticoagulant that activates antithrombin III, inhibiting thrombin and factor Xa.

ii. **Warfarin:** An oral anticoagulant that inhibits vitamin K-dependent clotting factors.

iii. **Dabigatran:** A direct thrombin inhibitor used as an oral anticoagulant.

3. Fibrinolytics (Thrombolytics)

a. **Definition:** Fibrinolytics dissolve existing clots by converting plasminogen to plasmin, which breaks down fibrin.

b. **Examples:**

i. **Alteplase (tPA):** A recombinant tissue plasminogen activator used in acute ischemic stroke, myocardial infarction, and pulmonary embolism.

ii. **Streptokinase:** A bacterial-derived fibrinolytic agent.

iii. **Reteplase:** A genetically engineered variant of tPA with a longer half-life.

4. Antiplatelet Drugs

a. **Definition:** Antiplatelet drugs inhibit platelet aggregation, reducing the risk of arterial thrombosis.

b. **Examples:**

i. **Aspirin:** Inhibits cyclooxygenase (COX) enzyme, preventing thromboxane A2 formation, which is necessary for platelet aggregation.

ii. **Clopidogrel:** An ADP receptor inhibitor that prevents platelet activation.

iii. **Ticagrelor:** A reversible inhibitor of the P2Y12 receptor on platelets.

5. Plasma Volume Expanders

a. **Definition:** Plasma volume expanders are intravenous solutions that increase the volume of plasma, aiding in the treatment of hypovolemia.

b. **Examples:**

i. **Normal Saline (0.9% NaCl):** A crystalloid solution that increases intravascular volume.

ii. **Albumin:** A natural colloid that maintains oncotic pressure and expands plasma volume.

iii. **Hydroxyethyl Starch (HES):** A synthetic colloid used to expand plasma volume in hypovolemia and shock.

Vitamin K:

A. Overview

1. **Vitamin K** is a fat-soluble vitamin that is essential for the synthesis of various clotting factors in the liver. It exists in two main forms:

    i. **Vitamin K1 (Phylloquinone):** Found in green leafy vegetables and is the primary form obtained through diet.

    ii. **Vitamin K2 (Menaquinone):** Produced by gut bacteria and is also found in fermented foods and animal products.

B. Mechanism of Action

1. **Role in Coagulation:** Vitamin K is a cofactor for the enzyme gamma-glutamyl carboxylase, which catalyzes the carboxylation of glutamic acid residues on certain proteins, including clotting factors II (prothrombin), VII, IX, and X, as well as proteins C and S. This carboxylation step is necessary for these clotting factors to bind calcium ions, which is essential for their activation and function in the coagulation cascade.

2. **Recycling:** Vitamin K undergoes a cycle of oxidation and reduction during its function. After participating in carboxylation, it is converted to an inactive form (Vitamin K epoxide), which is then reduced back to its active form by the enzyme Vitamin K epoxide reductase (VKOR). This recycling is important for the continued availability of Vitamin K in the body.

C. Clinical Uses

1. **Prevention and Treatment of Vitamin K Deficiency:** Administered to prevent bleeding in newborns (neonatal hemorrhagic disease) and in individuals with conditions leading to Vitamin K deficiency, such as malabsorption syndromes.

2. **Reversal of Anticoagulation:** Used to reverse the effects of warfarin, an oral anticoagulant that inhibits VKOR, leading to reduced levels of active Vitamin K and thus impaired synthesis of clotting factors.

3. **Management of Hypoprothrombinemia:** Administered in conditions where there is a deficiency in clotting factors due to impaired synthesis, such as in liver disease or after prolonged use of broad-spectrum antibiotics that disrupt gut bacteria.

D. Administration

1. **Oral:** Commonly used for routine supplementation and in mild deficiency.

2. **Intramuscular/Subcutaneous:** Preferred in newborns and in cases where oral absorption is impaired.

3. **Intravenous:** Used in emergencies for rapid reversal of anticoagulation or severe bleeding, though there is a risk of anaphylactoid reactions with IV administration.

E. Adverse Effects

1. **Hypersensitivity Reactions:** Rare but possible, particularly with intravenous administration.

2. **Hypercoagulability:** Overcorrection with high doses can lead to excessive clotting, especially in patients with underlying thrombotic disorders.

3. **Drug Interactions:** Warfarin, a Vitamin K antagonist, can have reduced effectiveness with increased Vitamin K intake.

Fibrinogen:

A. Overview

1. **Fibrinogen** is a glycoprotein produced by the liver and is the final substrate in the coagulation cascade that leads to the formation of a fibrin clot. It plays a central role in hemostasis by providing the structural framework for clot formation.

B. Mechanism of Action

1. **Conversion to Fibrin:** In the coagulation cascade, thrombin cleaves fibrinogen to form fibrin monomers, which then polymerize to form insoluble fibrin strands. These strands cross-link to form a stable clot that traps platelets and red blood cells, effectively sealing the site of injury and preventing further blood loss.

2. **Interaction with Platelets:** Fibrinogen also acts as a bridging molecule that binds to glycoprotein IIb/IIIa receptors on activated platelets, facilitating platelet aggregation and further stabilizing the clot.

C. Clinical Uses

1. **Treatment of Hypofibrinogenemia:** Administered in conditions where fibrinogen levels are critically low, such as in disseminated intravascular coagulation (DIC), liver disease, or following massive hemorrhage.

2. **Adjunct in Surgical Hemostasis:** Used during surgical procedures, particularly in cases involving extensive blood loss, to enhance clot formation and reduce bleeding.

3. **Inherited Fibrinogen Deficiencies:** Used in the management of congenital fibrinogen deficiencies such as afibrinogenemia and dysfibrinogenemia, where patients are unable to produce functional fibrinogen.

D. Administration

1. **Intravenous:** Fibrinogen is administered intravenously, typically as a concentrate derived from human plasma. The dose is determined based on the patient's fibrinogen levels and the clinical situation.

2. **Cryoprecipitate:** An alternative to fibrinogen concentrate, cryoprecipitate is a plasma product rich in fibrinogen and other clotting factors, used when fibrinogen concentrate is not available.

E. Adverse Effects

1. **Thrombosis:** There is a risk of thrombosis with fibrinogen administration, particularly if used in excess or in patients with a predisposition to thromboembolic events.

2. **Allergic Reactions:** Although rare, allergic reactions to fibrinogen concentrate can occur.

3. **Transfusion-Related Complications:** As a blood product, fibrinogen carries risks associated with transfusion, including transfusion-related acute lung injury (TRALI) and transmission of infections, though these risks are minimized with modern screening and processing techniques.

Heparin:

A. Overview

1. **Heparin** is a naturally occurring anticoagulant that is commonly used in medical practice to prevent and treat thromboembolic disorders. It is derived from animal tissues, such as porcine intestinal mucosa or bovine lung.

B. Mechanism of Action

1. **Antithrombin Activation:** Heparin exerts its anticoagulant effect primarily by binding to antithrombin III, a plasma protein that inhibits several enzymes in the coagulation cascade, most notably thrombin (Factor IIa) and Factor Xa.

    i. **Inhibition of Thrombin (Factor IIa):** The heparin-antithrombin complex inactivates thrombin, preventing the conversion of fibrinogen to fibrin, which is necessary for clot formation.

ii. **Inhibition of Factor Xa:** Heparin also enhances the inhibitory effect of antithrombin on Factor Xa, which is crucial for the conversion of prothrombin to thrombin.

2. **Immediate Action:** Heparin's anticoagulant effect is almost immediate when administered intravenously, making it useful in acute situations.

C. Clinical Uses

1. **Prevention and Treatment of Thrombosis:** Heparin is used in the prevention and treatment of deep vein thrombosis (DVT), pulmonary embolism (PE), and arterial thrombosis.

2. **Acute Coronary Syndromes (ACS):** Heparin is a key component in the management of unstable angina and myocardial infarction (MI), often used in conjunction with antiplatelet agents.

3. **Surgical Anticoagulation:** Heparin is frequently used during surgeries, particularly in cardiopulmonary bypass and vascular surgeries, to prevent clot formation.

4. **Prophylaxis:** It is used in lower doses for the prophylaxis of venous thromboembolism (VTE) in hospitalized patients who are at risk of clotting.

D. Administration

1. **Intravenous (IV):** For immediate anticoagulation, Heparin is administered as an IV bolus followed by a continuous infusion.

2. **Subcutaneous:** Used for prophylaxis against thrombosis, with a slower onset but longer duration of action compared to IV administration.

3. **Monitoring:** The anticoagulant effect of Heparin is monitored using the activated partial thromboplastin time (aPTT), which measures the efficacy of the intrinsic pathway of coagulation.

E. Adverse Effects

1. **Bleeding:** The most significant risk associated with Heparin is bleeding, ranging from minor bleeding to life-threatening hemorrhage.

2. **Heparin-Induced Thrombocytopenia (HIT):** A serious immune-mediated adverse effect where antibodies form against the heparin-platelet factor 4 complex, leading to a paradoxical increase in clotting despite the presence of Heparin.

3. **Osteoporosis:** Long-term use of Heparin can lead to osteoporosis and fractures due to its effect on bone metabolism.

4. **Hyperkalemia:** Heparin can inhibit aldosterone synthesis, leading to hyperkalemia.

Protamine Sulfate:

A. Overview

1. **Protamine Sulfate** is a medication used to reverse the anticoagulant effects of Heparin. It is a low-molecular-weight, highly cationic protein obtained from fish sperm or prepared synthetically.

B. Mechanism of Action

1. **Neutralization of Heparin:** Protamine sulfate works by binding to Heparin, forming a stable complex that neutralizes Heparin's anticoagulant activity.

   i. **Electrostatic Interaction:** Heparin is a strongly acidic (negatively charged) molecule, while Protamine sulfate is strongly basic (positively charged). When administered, Protamine sulfate binds to Heparin through electrostatic interactions, rendering it inactive.

   ii. **Immediate Reversal:** The neutralization of Heparin occurs rapidly, making Protamine sulfate highly effective in reversing the anticoagulant effect in cases of overdose or when rapid hemostasis is required.

C. Clinical Uses

1. **Reversal of Heparin:** Protamine sulfate is primarily used to reverse the anticoagulant effects of Heparin, particularly during surgical procedures or in cases of Heparin overdose.

i. **Cardiopulmonary Bypass Surgery:** After the use of Heparin during cardiac surgery, Protamine sulfate is administered to reverse its effects and restore normal coagulation.

ii. **Management of Heparin Overdose:** In cases where excessive bleeding occurs due to Heparin, Protamine sulfate is used as an emergency antidote.

2. **Neutralization of Low Molecular Weight Heparin (LMWH):** Protamine sulfate can partially neutralize the effects of LMWH, though it is less effective compared to its action on unfractionated Heparin.

D. Administration

1. **Intravenous (IV):** Protamine sulfate is administered via slow intravenous infusion. The dose is typically calculated based on the amount of Heparin to be neutralized.

   i. **Dose Calculation:** Approximately 1 mg of Protamine sulfate neutralizes 100 units of Heparin.

   ii. **Slow Infusion:** It is important to administer Protamine sulfate slowly to minimize the risk of adverse reactions.

E. Adverse Effects

1. **Hypotension:** Rapid infusion of Protamine sulfate can cause severe hypotension due to vasodilation and histamine release.

2. **Anaphylaxis:** Protamine sulfate has the potential to cause allergic reactions, including anaphylaxis, especially in patients with fish allergies or previous exposure to Protamine.

3. **Pulmonary Vasoconstriction:** Protamine can cause pulmonary vasoconstriction, leading to increased pulmonary artery pressure and, in severe cases, pulmonary hypertension.

4. **Bradycardia:** Protamine sulfate can induce bradycardia, especially when administered rapidly.

Warfarin:

A. Overview

1. **Warfarin** is an oral anticoagulant commonly used to prevent and treat thromboembolic events such as deep vein thrombosis (DVT), pulmonary embolism (PE), and to reduce the risk of stroke in patients with atrial fibrillation. It is derived from coumarin, a naturally occurring compound.

B. Mechanism of Action

1. **Vitamin K Antagonism:** Warfarin works by inhibiting Vitamin K epoxide reductase (VKOR), an enzyme crucial for the regeneration of active Vitamin K. This inhibition leads to decreased synthesis of Vitamin K-dependent clotting factors in their active forms.

    i.   **Clotting Factors Affected:** The clotting factors affected include Factor II (prothrombin), VII, IX, and X, as well as proteins C and S. These factors are essential for the coagulation cascade.

    ii. **Delayed Onset:** Warfarin does not affect the activity of existing clotting factors; rather, it prevents the synthesis of new ones. Therefore, its anticoagulant effect develops gradually and reaches its maximum effect after several days.

C. Clinical Uses

1. **Prevention of Thromboembolic Events:** Used to prevent stroke and systemic embolism in patients with atrial fibrillation, DVT, and PE.

2. **Post-Surgical Prophylaxis:** Prevents thromboembolic events following orthopedic surgeries (e.g., hip or knee replacement) and other high-risk surgeries.

3. **Treatment of Existing Thrombosis:** Treats existing thromboembolic conditions, including acute DVT and PE.

D. Administration

1. **Oral:** Warfarin is administered orally, with a typical dosing regimen adjusted based on individual patient needs and INR (International Normalized Ratio) levels.

2. **Monitoring:** Regular monitoring of INR is essential to ensure therapeutic efficacy and avoid bleeding complications. The target INR range depends on the indication but is generally between 2.0 and 3.0.

E. Adverse Effects

1. **Bleeding:** The most significant risk is bleeding, which can range from minor to life-threatening. Major bleeding events include gastrointestinal bleeding and intracranial hemorrhage.

2. **Teratogenicity:** Warfarin is contraindicated in pregnancy due to its teratogenic effects, which can cause birth defects and fetal bleeding.

3. **Drug Interactions:** Warfarin has numerous drug interactions due to its metabolism by cytochrome P450 enzymes (mainly CYP2C19). Other drugs or foods affecting these enzymes can alter Warfarin levels and INR, necessitating careful management.

F. Reversal

1. **Vitamin K:** Administered orally or intravenously to reverse Warfarin's effects, depending on the severity of bleeding.

2. **Prothrombin Complex Concentrate (PCC):** For urgent reversal in cases of major bleeding or rapid normalization of INR.

Dabigatran:

A. Overview

1. **Dabigatran** is an oral direct thrombin inhibitor used for the prevention and treatment of thromboembolic events. It is part of the newer class of anticoagulants known as direct oral anticoagulants (DOACs) or direct thrombin inhibitors.

B. Mechanism of Action

1. **Direct Thrombin Inhibition:** Dabigatran specifically inhibits thrombin (Factor IIa), which prevents the conversion of fibrinogen to fibrin and the activation of other clotting factors that are necessary for blood clot formation.

i. **Inhibition of Both Free and Clot-Bound Thrombin:** Dabigatran inhibits both free and fibrin-bound thrombin, which is significant for its anticoagulant effect.

ii. **Rapid Onset:** Unlike Warfarin, Dabigatran provides rapid onset of action, with peak plasma concentrations achieved within 1-2 hours after oral administration.

C. Clinical Uses

1. **Prevention of Stroke and Systemic Embolism:** Used in patients with non-valvular atrial fibrillation to reduce the risk of stroke and systemic embolism.

2. **Treatment of DVT and PE:** Used for the treatment and secondary prevention of deep vein thrombosis and pulmonary embolism.

3. **Post-Surgical Prophylaxis:** Administered for the prevention of venous thromboembolism following elective hip or knee replacement surgeries.

D. Administration

1. **Oral:** Dabigatran is administered orally as a capsule. It is typically taken twice daily, with the dosage adjusted based on the patient's renal function and other factors.

2. **No Routine Monitoring:** Unlike Warfarin, routine monitoring of coagulation parameters is not required with Dabigatran, although renal function should be monitored periodically.

E. Adverse Effects

1. **Bleeding:** Similar to other anticoagulants, Dabigatran can cause bleeding, including gastrointestinal bleeding and intracranial hemorrhage.

2. **Dyspepsia:** Commonly causes gastrointestinal symptoms such as dyspepsia, abdominal pain, and nausea.

3. **Renal Function:** Dose adjustments are required in patients with impaired renal function, as Dabigatran is primarily eliminated through the kidneys.

Alteplase (tPA):

A. Overview

1. **Alteplase** is a recombinant tissue plasminogen activator (tPA) used as a thrombolytic agent. It is employed in the management of acute myocardial infarction (MI), ischemic stroke, and pulmonary embolism.

B. Mechanism of Action

1. **Plasminogen Activation:** Alteplase is a tissue plasminogen activator that converts plasminogen, a proenzyme present in the blood, into plasmin. Plasmin is an enzyme that breaks down fibrin, the protein matrix of blood clots.

   i. **Fibrin-Specific:** Alteplase preferentially binds to fibrin in the clot, promoting localized fibrinolysis with minimal systemic effects.

   ii. **Rapid Onset:** The conversion of plasminogen to plasmin occurs rapidly, leading to the dissolution of the thrombus and restoration of blood flow.

C. Clinical Uses

1. **Acute Myocardial Infarction (MI):** Used to dissolve clots in the coronary arteries and restore blood flow to the heart muscle.

2. **Ischemic Stroke:** Administered to dissolve clots obstructing cerebral arteries and to reduce neurological damage if given within a specific time window (usually within 3-4.5 hours of symptom onset).

3. **Pulmonary Embolism:** Employed to break down clots obstructing pulmonary arteries and improve pulmonary circulation.

D. Administration

1. **Intravenous (IV):** Alteplase is administered via IV infusion. The dosage and infusion rate depend on the condition being treated and the patient's weight.

   i. **Acute MI:** A bolus dose is followed by a continuous infusion over several hours.

ii. **Ischemic Stroke:** Administered as an IV bolus followed by infusion, adhering to strict time constraints.

E. Adverse Effects

1. **Bleeding:** The most significant risk is bleeding, including gastrointestinal bleeding, intracranial hemorrhage, and bleeding at the site of injection.
2. **Allergic Reactions:** Rare but possible allergic reactions or hypersensitivity.
3. **Reperfusion Injury:** Rapid restoration of blood flow can sometimes lead to injury of the tissue previously affected by ischemia.

Streptokinase:

A. Overview

1. **Streptokinase** is a thrombolytic agent derived from the bacterium *Streptococcus*. It is used to dissolve blood clots in conditions such as acute myocardial infarction and pulmonary embolism.

B. Mechanism of Action

1. **Plasminogen Activation:** Streptokinase forms a complex with plasminogen, converting it into plasmin, which then breaks down fibrin clots.
   i. **Non-Fibrin-Specific:** Unlike Alteplase, Streptokinase is not specific to fibrin-bound plasminogen, leading to systemic activation of plasminogen and a greater potential for bleeding.
   ii. **Broad Effect:** This non-specific activation can lead to a more generalized fibrinolytic effect, affecting clots throughout the body.

C. Clinical Uses

1. **Acute Myocardial Infarction (MI):** Used to dissolve clots in coronary arteries and restore blood flow.
2. **Pulmonary Embolism:** Employed to break down clots in the pulmonary arteries.
3. **Deep Vein Thrombosis (DVT):** Used to treat thrombi in deep veins.

D. Administration

1. **Intravenous (IV):** Streptokinase is administered as an IV infusion. The dosing regimen involves an initial bolus followed by a continuous infusion for several hours.

    i. **Acute MI:** Typically involves a high-dose bolus followed by infusion.

    ii. **Pulmonary Embolism and DVT:** Dosing varies based on the clinical condition and patient response.

E. Adverse Effects

1. **Bleeding:** High risk of bleeding complications, including major bleeding events such as intracranial hemorrhage.

2. **Allergic Reactions:** As Streptokinase is derived from bacterial sources, it can cause allergic reactions or hypersensitivity, especially in patients with previous exposure.

3. **Fever:** Can induce fever as a side effect due to its antigenic properties.

Multiple Choice Questions (MCQs)

1. Which of the following is a vitamin K antagonist used as an oral anticoagulant?

    a) Heparin

    b) Dabigatran

    c) Warfarin

    d) Alteplase

2. What is the primary mechanism of action of Heparin?

    a) Inhibits vitamin K epoxide reductase

    b) Activates antithrombin III to inhibit thrombin and Factor Xa

    c) Directly inhibits thrombin

    d) Converts plasminogen to plasmin

3. Which drug is used to reverse the anticoagulant effects of Heparin?

    a) Vitamin K

    b) Protamine Sulfate

    c) Idarucizumab

    d) Streptokinase

4. What is the main therapeutic use of Alteplase (tPA)?

    a) Prevention of deep vein thrombosis

    b) Dissolution of existing blood clots in acute myocardial infarction

    c) Long-term anticoagulation

    d) Reduction of platelet aggregation

5. Which of the following drugs is a direct thrombin inhibitor?

    a) Warfarin

    b) Heparin

    c) Dabigatran

    d) Streptokinase

6. Which vitamin is essential for the synthesis of clotting factors II, VII, IX, and X?

    a) Vitamin D

    b) Vitamin C

    c) Vitamin K

    d) Vitamin B12

7. Which fibrinolytic agent is derived from Streptococcus bacteria?

    a) Alteplase

    b) Streptokinase

    c) Reteplase

    d) Urokinase

8. Which anticoagulant is primarily monitored using the International Normalized Ratio (INR)?

    a) Heparin

b) Warfarin

c) Dabigatran

d) Alteplase

9. What is the main adverse effect associated with the use of fibrinolytic agents like Alteplase?

    a) Hypertension

    b) Hyperkalemia

    c) Bleeding

    d) Hyperglycemia

10. Which plasma volume expander is a natural colloid made from human plasma?

    a) Normal Saline

    b) Hydroxyethyl Starch

    c) Albumin

    d) Dextran

11. What is the role of Vitamin K in the coagulation cascade?

    a) It directly activates thrombin

    b) It acts as a cofactor for gamma-glutamyl carboxylase in the synthesis of clotting factors

    c) It inhibits plasminogen activation

    d) It acts as an anticoagulant

12. Which anticoagulant is used as a low molecular weight heparin (LMWH)?

    a) Enoxaparin

    b) Warfarin

    c) Dabigatran

    d) Aspirin

13. Which drug is a recombinant tissue plasminogen activator (tPA) used in the management of acute ischemic stroke?

    a) Dabigatran

b) Heparin

c) Alteplase

d) Warfarin

14. Which antiplatelet drug inhibits cyclooxygenase-1 (COX-1) to reduce thromboxane A2 production?

a) Clopidogrel

b) Aspirin

c) Ticagrelor

d) Abciximab

15. Which of the following is a direct inhibitor of Factor Xa?

a) Warfarin

b) Heparin

c) Rivaroxaban

d) Dabigatran

16. Which drug is used for the rapid reversal of Warfarin-induced anticoagulation?

a) Protamine sulfate

b) Idarucizumab

c) Vitamin K

d) Streptokinase

17. What is the primary use of Protamine sulfate in clinical practice?

a) To prevent thromboembolic events

b) To reverse the effects of Heparin

c) To inhibit platelet aggregation

d) To dissolve existing blood clots

18. Which of the following drugs is a phosphodiesterase (PDE) inhibitor used as an antiplatelet agent?

a) Dipyridamole

b) Aspirin

c) Clopidogrel

d) Abciximab

19. Which anticoagulant is commonly used during surgeries, particularly in cardiopulmonary bypass and vascular surgeries?

   a) Warfarin

   b) Heparin

   c) Dabigatran

   d) Streptokinase

20. Which plasma volume expander is a synthetic colloid made from modified starches?

   a) Normal Saline

   b) Albumin

   c) Hydroxyethyl Starch (HES)

   d) Dextran

Short Answer Questions (SAQs)

1. Explain the role of Vitamin K in the synthesis of clotting factors.

2. What is the mechanism of action of Heparin in preventing blood clot formation?

3. Describe the clinical uses of Warfarin and how its effects are monitored.

4. How does Protamine sulfate reverse the anticoagulant effects of Heparin?

5. Discuss the therapeutic applications of Alteplase in the management of thromboembolic disorders.

6. What are the potential adverse effects of fibrinolytic therapy with Streptokinase?

7. How does Dabigatran differ from Warfarin in its mechanism of action and monitoring requirements?

8. What is the role of fibrinogen in the coagulation cascade, and when is fibrinogen concentrate used clinically?

9. Explain the pharmacological effects of aspirin as an antiplatelet agent.

10. Describe the mechanism of action and clinical indications of direct Factor Xa inhibitors.

11. What are the primary uses of plasma volume expanders in clinical practice?

12. How does Hydroxyethyl Starch (HES) function as a plasma volume expander, and what are its potential risks?

13. Discuss the use of Idarucizumab in the reversal of Dabigatran-induced anticoagulation.

14. What are the clinical indications for the use of thrombolytic agents like Alteplase?

15. How is the International Normalized Ratio (INR) used in the management of patients on Warfarin therapy?

16. Describe the adverse effects and contraindications of Heparin therapy.

17. Explain how P2Y12 ADP receptor inhibitors work as antiplatelet drugs and provide examples.

18. What are the advantages and disadvantages of using colloids versus crystalloids as plasma volume expanders?

19. Discuss the role of Vitamin K in reversing Warfarin overdose.

20. How do antiplatelet drugs differ from anticoagulants in their mechanisms and clinical uses?

Long Answer Questions (LAQs)

1. Discuss the classification, mechanisms of action, and clinical applications of anticoagulants, focusing on Heparin, Warfarin, and direct oral anticoagulants.

2. Describe the pharmacological management of thromboembolic disorders, including the roles of anticoagulants, antiplatelet agents, and fibrinolytics.

3. Explain the mechanisms of action, therapeutic uses, and monitoring requirements for Vitamin K antagonists and their role in managing thromboembolic diseases.

4. Discuss the pharmacology, clinical applications, and potential adverse effects of fibrinolytic agents, with a focus on Alteplase and Streptokinase.

5. Compare and contrast the uses, benefits, and risks of crystalloids and colloids as plasma volume expanders in the treatment of hypovolemia.

6. Explain the role of antiplatelet therapy in the prevention and treatment of cardiovascular diseases, highlighting the mechanisms and uses of aspirin, clopidogrel, and glycoprotein IIb/IIIa inhibitors.

7. Describe the role of thrombin inhibitors like Dabigatran in anticoagulation therapy and compare their use with that of traditional anticoagulants like Warfarin.

8. Discuss the pharmacological management of acute coronary syndromes (ACS), including the use of antiplatelet drugs, anticoagulants, and fibrinolytics.

9. Explain the clinical uses of plasma volume expanders in perioperative and critical care settings, focusing on their mechanisms, benefits, and potential risks.

10. Discuss the role of Vitamin K and its analogues in the treatment and prevention of bleeding disorders, including their use in reversing anticoagulation.

Answer Key for MCQs

1. c) Warfarin

2. b) Activates antithrombin III to inhibit thrombin and Factor Xa

3. b) Protamine Sulfate

4. b) Dissolution of existing blood clots in acute myocardial infarction

5. c) Dabigatran

6. c) Vitamin K

7. b) Streptokinase

8. b) Warfarin

9. c) Bleeding

10.c) Albumin

11.b) It acts as a cofactor for gamma-glutamyl carboxylase in the synthesis of clotting factors

12.a) Enoxaparin

13.c) Alteplase

14.b) Aspirin

15.c) Rivaroxaban

16.c) Vitamin K

17.b) To reverse the effects of Heparin

18.a) Dipyridamole

19.b) Heparin

20.c) Hydroxyethyl Starch (HES)

CHAPTER – 4

PHARMACOLOGY OF DRUGS ACTING ON URINARY SYSTEM

INTRODUCTION:

The pharmacology of drugs acting on the urinary system involves understanding how various medications interact with and affect the kidneys, ureters, bladder, and urethra. Here's a detailed introduction:

1. Overview of the Urinary System

The urinary system is responsible for the production, storage, and excretion of urine. Its main components are:

a. **Kidneys:** Filter blood to produce urine.

b. **Ureters:** Transport urine from the kidneys to the bladder.

c. **Bladder:** Stores urine until it is excreted.

d. **Urethra:** Conducts urine from the bladder to the outside of the body.

2. Classification of Drugs Acting on the Urinary System

A. Diuretics

a. **Thiazide Diuretics:** E.g., Hydrochlorothiazide. They act on the distal convoluted tubule, increasing sodium and water excretion.

b. **Loop Diuretics:** E.g., Furosemide, Bumetanide. They act on the loop of Henle, causing a significant increase in urine output.

c. **Potassium-Sparing Diuretics:** E.g., Spironolactone, Eplerenone. They act on the distal nephron, preventing potassium loss.

B. Antidiuretics

a. **Vasopressin Analogues:** E.g., Desmopressin. These mimic antidiuretic hormone (ADH) and help in conditions like diabetes insipidus.

C. Urinary Antiseptics and Antibiotics

a. **Nitrofurantoin:** Used for urinary tract infections (UTIs).

b. **Trimethoprim-Sulfamethoxazole:** A combination antibiotic effective against UTIs.

D. Urinary Analgesics

a. **Phenazopyridine:** Provides symptomatic relief from urinary tract pain, burning, and discomfort.

E. Urinary Acidifiers and Alkalinizers

a. **Methenamine:** Acidifies urine to prevent bacterial growth.

b. **Sodium Bicarbonate:** Alkalinizes urine to help with certain types of kidney stones.

3. Mechanisms of Action

Diuretics:

a. **Thiazides:** Inhibit the Na-Cl symporter in the distal convoluted tubule.

b. **Loop Diuretics:** Inhibit the Na-K-2Cl cotransporter in the thick ascending limb of the loop of Henle.

c. **Potassium-Sparing Diuretics:** Block aldosterone receptors or directly inhibit epithelial sodium channels.

Antidiuretics:

a. **Desmopressin:** Acts on V2 receptors in the kidneys to increase water reabsorption.

Antiseptics and Antibiotics:

a. **Nitrofurantoin:** Interferes with bacterial enzyme systems.

b. **Trimethoprim-Sulfamethoxazole:** Inhibits bacterial folic acid synthesis.

Analgesics:

a. **Phenazopyridine:** Exerts a local anesthetic effect on the urinary tract mucosa.

4. Clinical Uses

a. **Diuretics:** Used in conditions like hypertension, heart failure, and edema.

b. **Antidiuretics:** Used in managing diabetes insipidus and nocturnal enuresis.

c. **Antiseptics and Antibiotics:** Treat UTIs and prevent recurrent infections.

d. **Analgesics:** Alleviate discomfort associated with urinary tract infections and procedures.

5. Side Effects and Considerations

a. **Diuretics:** Electrolyte imbalances, dehydration, hypotension.

b. **Antidiuretics:** Risk of fluid overload, hyponatremia.

c. **Antiseptics and Antibiotics:** Allergic reactions, gastrointestinal disturbances.

d. **Analgesics:** May cause gastrointestinal upset or allergic reactions.

DIURETICS

Diuretics are a major class of drugs used to influence the urinary system, primarily to manage fluid balance and treat conditions like hypertension, heart failure, and edema. Here's a detailed look at diuretics, including their types, mechanisms of action, clinical uses, and side effects:

1. Types of Diuretics

A. Thiazide Diuretics

1. **Examples:** Hydrochlorothiazide, Chlorthalidone, Indapamide.

2. **Mechanism of Action:** These diuretics act on the distal convoluted tubule of the nephron. They inhibit the Na-Cl symporter, which decreases sodium and chloride reabsorption, leading to increased excretion of these ions along with water.

3. **Clinical Uses:** Hypertension, mild to moderate edema (e.g., heart failure, kidney disorders).

4. **Side Effects:** Hypokalemia, hyperuricemia (risk of gout), hyperglycemia, dehydration, and electrolyte imbalances.

B. Loop Diuretics

1. **Examples:** Furosemide, Bumetanide, Torsemide.

2. **Mechanism of Action:** These act on the thick ascending limb of the loop of Henle. They inhibit the Na-K-2Cl cotransporter, leading to a potent diuretic effect due to a significant reduction in sodium, potassium, and chloride reabsorption.

3. **Clinical Uses:** Severe edema (e.g., heart failure, liver cirrhosis, renal impairment), hypertension.

4. **Side Effects:** Hypokalemia, hypocalcemia, hypomagnesemia, dehydration, ototoxicity (especially with rapid intravenous administration).

C. Potassium-Sparing Diuretics

1. **Examples:** Spironolactone, Eplerenone, Triamterene, Amiloride.

2. **Mechanism of Action:**

   a. **Aldosterone Antagonists (e.g., Spironolactone, Eplerenone):** These inhibit the action of aldosterone in the distal nephron, reducing sodium reabsorption and potassium excretion.

   b. **Epithelial Sodium Channel Inhibitors (e.g., Triamterene, Amiloride):** Directly block sodium channels in the distal nephron, preventing sodium reabsorption without affecting potassium levels.

3. **Clinical Uses:** Hyperaldosteronism, heart failure, hypertension (often in combination with other diuretics), prevention of hypokalemia in other diuretic therapies.

4. **Side Effects:** Hyperkalemia, gynecomastia (especially with spironolactone), menstrual irregularities, and gastrointestinal disturbances.

D. Osmotic Diuretics

1. **Examples:** Mannitol, Urea.

2. **Mechanism of Action:** These diuretics act by increasing the osmolarity of the tubular fluid, which inhibits water reabsorption and enhances diuresis.

3. **Clinical Uses:** Acute renal failure, intracranial pressure reduction, and to facilitate the excretion of toxic substances.

4. **Side Effects:** Electrolyte imbalances, dehydration, nausea, headache, and risk of pulmonary edema.

2. Clinical Uses

a. **Hypertension:** Thiazide diuretics are commonly used as first-line treatment.

b. **Heart Failure:** Loop diuretics are often employed to manage fluid overload and reduce symptoms of congestion.

c. **Edema:** Diuretics are used to manage edema resulting from various conditions such as liver cirrhosis, kidney disease, and venous insufficiency.

d. **Renal Impairment:** Osmotic diuretics can help in managing acute renal failure and improving urine output.

3. Side Effects and Considerations

a. **Electrolyte Imbalances:** Diuretics can lead to imbalances in potassium, sodium, calcium, and magnesium levels.

b. **Dehydration:** Excessive use can cause significant fluid loss and dehydration.

c. **Kidney Function:** Monitoring kidney function is crucial, especially with loop diuretics and in patients with pre-existing renal conditions.

d. **Drug Interactions:** Diuretics may interact with other medications, including antihypertensives, anti-inflammatory drugs, and medications affecting electrolyte levels.

4. Monitoring and Management

a. **Regular Monitoring:** Blood electrolyte levels, renal function, and blood pressure should be monitored regularly.

b. **Dose Adjustment:** Dosages may need adjustment based on the patient's response and side effects.

c. **Patient Education:** Patients should be educated on recognizing signs of electrolyte imbalances and dehydration.

ANTI-DIURETICS

Anti-diuretics are medications that reduce the production of urine, often used to treat conditions like diabetes insipidus or nocturnal enuresis. Here's a detailed overview of anti-diuretics:

1. Types of Anti-diuretics

A. Vasopressin Analogues

a. **Examples:** Desmopressin, Vasopressin (also known as antidiuretic hormone (ADH)).

b. **Mechanism of Action:**

    i. **Desmopressin:** A synthetic analog of vasopressin, acts primarily on V2 receptors in the kidneys to enhance water reabsorption in the collecting ducts, reducing urine output.

    ii. **Vasopressin:** Acts on V1 and V2 receptors; V2 receptor stimulation increases water reabsorption, while V1 receptor stimulation affects vascular smooth muscle contraction.

c. **Clinical Uses:**

    i. **Desmopressin:** Treatment of central diabetes insipidus, nocturnal enuresis, and certain bleeding disorders (e.g., von Willebrand disease).

    ii. **Vasopressin:** Used in cases of vasodilatory shock and certain types of diabetes insipidus.

d. **Side Effects:** Headache, nausea, abdominal cramping, hyponatremia (especially with excessive use), and, in rare cases, water intoxication.

B. ADH Receptor Antagonists (Vaptans)

a. **Examples:** Tolvaptan, Conivaptan.

b. **Mechanism of Action:** These drugs are selective antagonists of the V2 vasopressin receptors. They inhibit the action of ADH, leading to increased water excretion by the kidneys.

c. **Clinical Uses:**

  i. **Tolvaptan:** Used to treat hyponatremia (low sodium levels) due to conditions like the Syndrome of Inappropriate Antidiuretic Hormone (SIADH) and certain types of kidney disease.

  ii. **Conivaptan:** Used for the treatment of euvolemic and hypervolemic hyponatremia.

d. **Side Effects:** Thirst, dry mouth, hypernatremia (high sodium levels), and liver enzyme abnormalities.

2. Mechanisms of Action

Vasopressin Analogues:

a. **Desmopressin:** Binds to V2 receptors in the kidney's collecting ducts, increasing the permeability of the tubular epithelium to water, thus allowing more water to be reabsorbed from the urine back into the bloodstream.

b. **Vasopressin:** Binds to both V1 receptors (causing vasoconstriction) and V2 receptors (enhancing water reabsorption).

ADH Receptor Antagonists:

a. **Tolvaptan and Conivaptan:** Block the V2 receptors, leading to decreased water reabsorption in the kidneys and increased urine output.

3. Clinical Uses

a. **Diabetes Insipidus:** Both central (caused by lack of ADH production) and nephrogenic (caused by the kidneys' inability to respond to ADH).

b. **Nocturnal Enuresis:** Desmopressin is commonly used to treat bedwetting in children and adults.

c. **Hyponatremia:** ADH receptor antagonists are used to manage conditions with excess water retention leading to low sodium levels.

d. **Vasodilatory Shock:** Vasopressin can be used to manage shock where blood pressure is low due to vasodilation.

4. Side Effects and Considerations

a. **Vasopressin Analogues:**

    i. **Desmopressin:** Risk of water intoxication, hyponatremia, and potential allergic reactions.

    ii. **Vasopressin:** Risk of excessive vasoconstriction, myocardial ischemia, and water intoxication.

b. **ADH Receptor Antagonists:**

    i. **Tolvaptan and Conivaptan:** Risk of electrolyte imbalances, especially hypernatremia, liver toxicity, and dehydration.

5. Monitoring and Management

a. **Electrolyte Levels:** Regular monitoring of sodium and other electrolytes is essential, especially with ADH receptor antagonists.

b. **Fluid Balance:** Monitoring fluid intake and output to prevent dehydration or water overload.

c. **Patient Education:** Patients should be informed about the signs of electrolyte imbalances and the importance of adhering to prescribed dosages.

CLASSIFICATION:

Drugs acting on the urinary system can be classified based on their primary effects and mechanisms of action. Here's a detailed classification with examples:

1. Diuretics

A. Thiazide Diuretics

a. **Examples:** Hydrochlorothiazide, Chlorthalidone, Indapamide.

b. **Mechanism of Action:** Inhibit sodium-chloride symporter in the distal convoluted tubule, leading to increased excretion of sodium and water.

B. Loop Diuretics

a. **Examples:** Furosemide, Bumetanide, Torsemide.

b. **Mechanism of Action:** Inhibit the Na-K-2Cl cotransporter in the thick ascending limb of the loop of Henle, leading to potent diuresis.

C. Potassium-Sparing Diuretics

a. **Examples:**

   i. **Aldosterone Antagonists:** Spironolactone, Eplerenone. Inhibit aldosterone, reducing sodium reabsorption and potassium excretion.

   ii. **Epithelial Sodium Channel Inhibitors:** Triamterene, Amiloride. Directly block sodium channels, preventing sodium reabsorption without affecting potassium levels.

D. Osmotic Diuretics

a. **Examples:** Mannitol, Urea.

b. **Mechanism of Action:** Increase osmolarity in the tubular fluid, preventing water reabsorption and enhancing diuresis.

2. Anti-diuretics

A. Vasopressin Analogues

a. **Examples:** Desmopressin, Vasopressin.

b. **Mechanism of Action:** Mimic antidiuretic hormone (ADH), enhancing water reabsorption in the kidneys.

B. ADH Receptor Antagonists (Vaptans)

a. **Examples:** Tolvaptan, Conivaptan.

b. **Mechanism of Action:** Block V2 vasopressin receptors, reducing water reabsorption and increasing urine output.

3. Urinary Antiseptics and Antibiotics

A. Urinary Antiseptics

    a. **Examples:** Nitrofurantoin, Methenamine.

    b. **Mechanism of Action:** Disrupt bacterial enzyme systems or acidify urine to prevent bacterial growth.

B. Urinary Antibiotics

    a. **Examples:** Trimethoprim-Sulfamethoxazole, Ciprofloxacin.

    b. **Mechanism of Action:** Inhibit bacterial folic acid synthesis or bacterial DNA gyrase, treating urinary tract infections (UTIs).

4. Urinary Analgesics

A. Urinary Analgesics

    a. **Examples:** Phenazopyridine.

    b. **Mechanism of Action:** Provides symptomatic relief from urinary tract pain and discomfort by exerting a local anesthetic effect.

5. Urinary Acidifiers and Alkalinizers

A. Urinary Acidifiers

    a. **Examples:** Methenamine.

    b. **Mechanism of Action:** Acidifies urine to prevent bacterial growth and help with certain types of kidney stones.

B. Urinary Alkalinizers

    a. **Examples:** Sodium Bicarbonate.

    b. **Mechanism of Action:** Alkalinizes urine to prevent the formation of uric acid and cystine stones.

6. Drugs for Overactive Bladder

A. Anticholinergics

    a. **Examples:** Oxybutynin, Tolterodine, Solifenacin.

    b. **Mechanism of Action:** Block muscarinic receptors in the bladder, reducing involuntary contractions and urgency.

B. Beta-3 Agonists

    a. **Examples:** Mirabegron.

b. **Mechanism of Action:** Stimulate beta-3 adrenergic receptors, relaxing the bladder muscle and increasing storage capacity.

7. Drugs for Benign Prostatic Hyperplasia (BPH)

A. Alpha-1 Adrenergic Blockers

a. **Examples:** Tamsulosin, Alfuzosin.

b. **Mechanism of Action:** Block alpha-1 adrenergic receptors in the prostate and bladder neck, improving urine flow.

B. 5-Alpha Reductase Inhibitors

a. **Examples:** Finasteride, Dutasteride.

b. **Mechanism of Action:** Inhibit the conversion of testosterone to dihydrotestosterone (DHT), reducing prostate size and improving symptoms.

Hydrochlorothiazide

A. Mechanism of Action

1. **Site of Action:** Distal convoluted tubule of the nephron.

2. **Mechanism:** Hydrochlorothiazide inhibits the sodium-chloride symporter (NCC) in the distal convoluted tubule, leading to decreased reabsorption of sodium and chloride. This results in increased excretion of sodium, chloride, and water, which reduces blood volume and lowers blood pressure.

B. Pharmacokinetics

1. **Absorption:** Well absorbed from the gastrointestinal tract.

2. **Distribution:** Widely distributed in the body; crosses the placenta and can enter breast milk.

3. **Metabolism:** Minimal metabolism; excreted mostly unchanged in the urine.

4. **Elimination:** Half-life is approximately 6-15 hours, depending on the patient's renal function.

C. Clinical Uses

1. **Hypertension:** Often used as a first-line treatment for high blood pressure.

2. **Edema:** Used in conditions such as heart failure, chronic kidney disease, and liver cirrhosis to manage fluid retention.

D. Side Effects

1. **Electrolyte Imbalances:** Hypokalemia, hyponatremia, hypomagnesemia, hypercalcemia.

2. **Metabolic Effects:** Hyperglycemia, hyperuricemia (risk of gout).

3. **Gastrointestinal:** Nausea, vomiting, loss of appetite.

4. **Allergic Reactions:** Rash, photosensitivity.

E. Monitoring and Management

1. **Electrolyte Levels:** Regular monitoring of potassium, sodium, and magnesium levels.

2. **Blood Glucose:** Monitor blood glucose levels in patients with diabetes or at risk of developing diabetes.

3. **Kidney Function:** Regular renal function tests to assess kidney health.

2. Chlorthalidone

A. Mechanism of Action

1. **Site of Action:** Distal convoluted tubule of the nephron.

2. **Mechanism:** Chlorthalidone also inhibits the sodium-chloride symporter (NCC) in the distal convoluted tubule. Similar to hydrochlorothiazide, it increases the excretion of sodium, chloride, and water, which lowers blood pressure and reduces fluid volume.

B. Pharmacokinetics

1. **Absorption:** Well absorbed orally, though absorption can be influenced by food.

2. **Distribution:** Similar distribution to hydrochlorothiazide; crosses the placenta and enters breast milk.

3. **Metabolism:** Minimal metabolism; excreted primarily unchanged in the urine.

4. **Elimination:** Longer half-life than hydrochlorothiazide, approximately 40-60 hours, which allows for once-daily dosing.

C. Clinical Uses

1. **Hypertension:** Effective in managing high blood pressure, often used as a first-line treatment.

2. **Edema:** Used to treat edema associated with conditions like heart failure and kidney disease.

D. Side Effects

1. **Electrolyte Imbalances:** Hypokalemia, hyponatremia, hypomagnesemia, hypercalcemia.

2. **Metabolic Effects:** Hyperglycemia, hyperuricemia.

3. **Gastrointestinal:** Similar to hydrochlorothiazide, with potential for nausea and appetite loss.

4. **Other:** Possible dizziness, headache, and fatigue.

E. Monitoring and Management

1. **Electrolyte Levels:** Regular monitoring of potassium, sodium, and magnesium.

2. **Blood Glucose:** Monitoring in diabetic patients or those at risk of developing diabetes.

3. **Kidney Function:** Regular assessment of kidney function.

Comparison Between Hydrochlorothiazide and Chlorthalidone

1. **Potency:** Chlorthalidone is often considered more potent and has a longer duration of action compared to hydrochlorothiazide.

2. **Half-Life:** Chlorthalidone has a longer half-life, which allows for once-daily dosing, while hydrochlorothiazide may require multiple doses.

3. **Clinical Preference:** Chlorthalidone is sometimes preferred for its longer duration and potentially greater antihypertensive efficacy.

Indapamide

A. Mechanism of Action

1. **Class:** Thiazide-like diuretic.

2. **Site of Action:** Distal convoluted tubule of the nephron.

3. **Mechanism:** Indapamide inhibits the sodium-chloride symporter (NCC) in the distal convoluted tubule, which reduces the reabsorption of sodium and chloride. This increases the excretion of these ions, along with water, leading to a reduction in blood volume and blood pressure.

B. Pharmacokinetics

1. **Absorption:** Well absorbed from the gastrointestinal tract.

2. **Distribution:** Widely distributed throughout the body; crosses the placenta and may enter breast milk.

3. **Metabolism:** Primarily metabolized in the liver.

4. **Elimination:** Excreted mostly via the kidneys. The half-life is approximately 14-24 hours, allowing for once-daily dosing.

C. Clinical Uses

1. **Hypertension:** Often used as a first-line treatment for high blood pressure.

2. **Edema:** Less commonly used for edema compared to loop diuretics, but can be effective for mild fluid retention.

D. Side Effects

1. **Electrolyte Imbalances:** Hypokalemia, hyponatremia, hypomagnesemia.

2. **Metabolic Effects:** Hyperglycemia, hyperuricemia (risk of gout).

3. **Gastrointestinal:** Nausea, vomiting.

4. **Other:** Dizziness, headache, and potential for allergic reactions like rash.

E. Monitoring and Management

1. **Electrolyte Levels:** Regular monitoring of potassium, sodium, and magnesium levels.

2. **Blood Glucose:** Monitor glucose levels in diabetic patients.

3. **Kidney Function:** Regular assessment of renal function.

2. Furosemide

A. Mechanism of Action

1. **Class:** Loop diuretic.

2. **Site of Action:** Thick ascending limb of the loop of Henle.

3. **Mechanism:** Furosemide inhibits the Na-K-2Cl cotransporter in the thick ascending limb of the loop of Henle. This action prevents the reabsorption of sodium, potassium, and chloride, leading to a significant increase in urine output and a reduction in fluid volume.

B. Pharmacokinetics

1. **Absorption:** Well absorbed from the gastrointestinal tract, though absorption can be variable.

2. **Distribution:** Widely distributed; crosses the placenta and enters breast milk.

3. **Metabolism:** Minimal metabolism in the liver.

4. **Elimination:** Excreted primarily in the urine. The half-life is approximately 1-2 hours, but the diuretic effect can last longer.

C. Clinical Uses

1. **Edema:** Used to treat severe edema associated with conditions like heart failure, liver cirrhosis, and renal impairment.

2. **Hypertension:** Used for hypertension, often when other diuretics are ineffective.

3. **Acute Renal Failure:** Can help manage fluid overload in acute renal failure.

D. Side Effects

1. **Electrolyte Imbalances:** Hypokalemia, hypomagnesemia, hypocalcemia.

2. **Metabolic Effects:** Hyperuricemia, potentially leading to gout.

3. **Gastrointestinal:** Nausea, vomiting.

4. **Other:** Ototoxicity (especially with rapid intravenous administration), dehydration, and hypotension.

E. Monitoring and Management

1. **Electrolyte Levels:** Regular monitoring of potassium, magnesium, calcium, and other electrolytes.
2. **Fluid Balance:** Monitor fluid intake and output to prevent dehydration.
3. **Kidney Function:** Regular renal function tests to monitor for potential renal impairment.

Comparison Between Indapamide and Furosemide

1. **Potency:** Furosemide is generally more potent than Indapamide, with a stronger diuretic effect.
2. **Duration of Action:** Indapamide has a longer duration of action compared to Furosemide, allowing for once-daily dosing.
3. **Use in Conditions:** Furosemide is preferred for managing severe edema and acute conditions requiring rapid diuresis, whereas Indapamide is more commonly used for chronic hypertension and mild fluid retention.

Bumetanide

A. Mechanism of Action

1. **Class:** Loop diuretic.
2. **Site of Action:** Thick ascending limb of the loop of Henle.
3. **Mechanism:** Bumetanide inhibits the Na-K-2Cl cotransporter (NKCC2) in the thick ascending limb of the loop of Henle. This inhibition prevents the reabsorption of sodium, potassium, and chloride, leading to a significant increase in urine production and a reduction in fluid volume.

B. Pharmacokinetics

1. **Absorption:** Rapidly absorbed from the gastrointestinal tract.
2. **Distribution:** Widely distributed; crosses the placenta and may enter breast milk.
3. **Metabolism:** Metabolized in the liver.

4. **Elimination:** Excreted primarily in the urine. The half-life is approximately 1-2 hours, but the diuretic effect can last up to 6-8 hours.

C. Clinical Uses

1. **Edema:** Effective in treating edema associated with heart failure, liver cirrhosis, and renal impairment.
2. **Hypertension:** Used when other diuretics are ineffective or in cases of severe hypertension.
3. **Acute Renal Failure:** Can be used to manage fluid overload in acute renal failure.

D. Side Effects

1. **Electrolyte Imbalances:** Hypokalemia, hypomagnesemia, hypocalcemia.
2. **Metabolic Effects:** Hyperuricemia (risk of gout).
3. **Gastrointestinal:** Nausea, vomiting.
4. **Other:** Ototoxicity (especially with rapid intravenous administration), dehydration, hypotension.

E. Monitoring and Management

1. **Electrolyte Levels:** Regular monitoring of potassium, magnesium, calcium, and other electrolytes.
2. **Fluid Balance:** Monitor fluid intake and output to prevent dehydration.
3. **Kidney Function:** Regular renal function tests to monitor for potential renal impairment.

2. Torsemide

A. Mechanism of Action

1. **Class:** Loop diuretic.
2. **Site of Action:** Thick ascending limb of the loop of Henle.
3. **Mechanism:** Torsemide inhibits the Na-K-2Cl cotransporter (NKCC2) in the thick ascending limb of the loop of Henle, similar to Bumetanide. This action leads to increased excretion of sodium, chloride, and water.

B. Pharmacokinetics

1. **Absorption:** Well absorbed from the gastrointestinal tract with high bioavailability.

2. **Distribution:** Widely distributed; crosses the placenta and enters breast milk.

3. **Metabolism:** Extensively metabolized in the liver.

4. **Elimination:** Excreted primarily in the urine. The half-life is approximately 3-4 hours, allowing for once-daily dosing in most cases.

C. Clinical Uses

1. **Edema:** Used to treat edema associated with heart failure, liver cirrhosis, and renal disease.

2. **Hypertension:** Can be used for hypertension, particularly in cases where other diuretics are insufficient.

3. **Chronic Kidney Disease:** Helps manage fluid overload in chronic kidney disease.

D. Side Effects

1. **Electrolyte Imbalances:** Similar to Bumetanide, including hypokalemia, hypomagnesemia, and hypocalcemia.

2. **Metabolic Effects:** Hyperuricemia.

3. **Gastrointestinal:** Nausea, diarrhea.

4. **Other:** Ototoxicity, dehydration, hypotension, and potential allergic reactions.

E. Monitoring and Management

1. **Electrolyte Levels:** Regular monitoring of potassium, magnesium, and calcium levels.

2. **Fluid Balance:** Monitor fluid intake and output to avoid dehydration.

3. **Kidney Function:** Regular assessment of renal function is necessary to avoid potential kidney issues.

Comparison Between Bumetanide and Torsemide

1. **Potency:** Both are potent loop diuretics, but Torsemide may have a longer duration of action compared to Bumetanide.

2. **Bioavailability:** Torsemide has higher oral bioavailability than Bumetanide, which can lead to more consistent therapeutic effects.

3. **Half-Life:** Torsemide has a longer half-life, allowing for once-daily dosing in most cases, while Bumetanide may require more frequent dosing.

4. **Clinical Preference:** The choice between these diuretics often depends on the specific clinical scenario, patient response, and side effect profile.

Spironolactone

A. Mechanism of Action

1. **Class:** Aldosterone antagonist.

2. **Site of Action:** Distal convoluted tubule and collecting duct of the nephron.

3. **Mechanism:** Spironolactone inhibits the action of aldosterone by binding to mineralocorticoid receptors in the distal nephron. Aldosterone normally promotes sodium reabsorption and potassium excretion; by blocking aldosterone, Spironolactone decreases sodium reabsorption and reduces potassium excretion, leading to increased potassium levels in the blood (potassium-sparing effect) and increased sodium and water excretion.

B. Pharmacokinetics

1. **Absorption:** Well absorbed from the gastrointestinal tract, though absorption can be affected by food.

2. **Distribution:** Widely distributed; crosses the placenta and enters breast milk.

3. **Metabolism:** Metabolized in the liver to active metabolites, such as canrenone.

4. **Elimination:** Excreted primarily in the urine. The half-life is approximately 1.4 hours, but the effects can last longer due to active metabolites.

C. Clinical Uses

1. **Hypertension:** Used for the treatment of high blood pressure, often in combination with other antihypertensives.
2. **Heart Failure:** Helps in managing symptoms of heart failure by reducing fluid overload and preventing remodeling.
3. **Edema:** Used for conditions associated with fluid retention, such as cirrhosis and nephrotic syndrome.
4. **Hyperaldosteronism:** Treats conditions caused by excessive aldosterone production, such as primary hyperaldosteronism.

D. Side Effects

1. **Electrolyte Imbalances:** Hyperkalemia (high potassium levels), hyponatremia (low sodium levels).
2. **Metabolic Effects:** Hyperuricemia, which may lead to gout.
3. **Endocrine Effects:** Gynecomastia (breast enlargement in men), menstrual irregularities, and sexual dysfunction.
4. **Gastrointestinal:** Nausea, vomiting, diarrhea.
5. **Other:** Dizziness, headache, rash.

E. Monitoring and Management

1. **Electrolyte Levels:** Regular monitoring of potassium and sodium levels is essential.
2. **Renal Function:** Regular assessment of kidney function to avoid potential complications.
3. **Endocrine Effects:** Monitoring for symptoms of hormonal imbalances and managing side effects accordingly.

2. Eplerenone

A. Mechanism of Action

1. **Class:** Aldosterone antagonist.

2. **Site of Action:** Distal convoluted tubule and collecting duct of the nephron.

3. **Mechanism:** Eplerenone also inhibits aldosterone by binding to mineralocorticoid receptors in the distal nephron, similar to Spironolactone. This inhibition reduces sodium reabsorption and potassium excretion, leading to a potassium-sparing effect and increased sodium and water excretion.

B. Pharmacokinetics

1. **Absorption:** Well absorbed from the gastrointestinal tract.

2. **Distribution:** Widely distributed; crosses the placenta and may enter breast milk.

3. **Metabolism:** Metabolized in the liver, primarily by CYP3A4.

4. **Elimination:** Excreted in the urine. The half-life is approximately 4-6 hours, allowing for once-daily or twice-daily dosing.

C. Clinical Uses

1. **Hypertension:** Used to manage high blood pressure, often in combination with other antihypertensives.

2. **Heart Failure:** Helps manage symptoms and improve outcomes in patients with heart failure, particularly post-myocardial infarction.

3. **Edema:** Can be used in conditions with fluid retention, although it is less commonly used for this purpose compared to Spironolactone.

D. Side Effects

1. **Electrolyte Imbalances:** Hyperkalemia, although less common than with Spironolactone.

2. **Metabolic Effects:** Hyperuricemia.

3. **Gastrointestinal:** Nausea, diarrhea.

4. **Other:** Dizziness, headache, and potential allergic reactions.

E. Monitoring and Management

1. **Electrolyte Levels:** Regular monitoring of potassium levels to prevent hyperkalemia.

2. **Renal Function:** Routine monitoring of kidney function to avoid potential issues.

3. **Drug Interactions:** Awareness of potential interactions with drugs that affect CYP3A4.

Comparison Between Spironolactone and Eplerenone

1. **Selectivity:** Eplerenone is more selective for mineralocorticoid receptors and has fewer endocrine side effects (e.g., less gynecomastia) compared to Spironolactone.

2. **Duration of Action:** Eplerenone has a longer half-life and more predictable pharmacokinetics, allowing for flexible dosing.

3. **Clinical Use:** Both drugs are used for hypertension and heart failure, but Eplerenone is often preferred in heart failure management due to its selectivity and reduced side effect profile.

Triamterene

A. Mechanism of Action

1. **Class:** Potassium-sparing diuretic.

2. **Site of Action:** Distal convoluted tubule and collecting duct of the nephron.

3. **Mechanism:** Triamterene inhibits epithelial sodium channels (ENaCs) in the distal convoluted tubule and collecting duct. By blocking these channels, Triamterene reduces sodium reabsorption and decreases potassium excretion, leading to increased sodium and water excretion while retaining potassium.

B. Pharmacokinetics

1. **Absorption:** Well absorbed from the gastrointestinal tract.

2. **Distribution:** Widely distributed in body tissues.

3. **Metabolism:** Metabolized in the liver to some extent.

4. **Elimination:** Excreted primarily in the urine. The half-life is approximately 6-10 hours, allowing for once or twice daily dosing.

C. Clinical Uses

1. **Hypertension:** Used to manage high blood pressure, often in combination with other antihypertensives.
2. **Edema:** Helps manage fluid retention, particularly when combined with thiazide diuretics to counteract potassium loss.
3. **Hypokalemia Prevention:** Often combined with thiazide diuretics to prevent hypokalemia.

D. Side Effects

1. **Electrolyte Imbalances:** Hyperkalemia (high potassium levels).
2. **Metabolic Effects:** Hyperuricemia (risk of gout).
3. **Gastrointestinal:** Nausea, vomiting, diarrhea.
4. **Other:** Dizziness, headache, rash.

2. Amiloride

A. Mechanism of Action

1. **Class:** Potassium-sparing diuretic.
2. **Site of Action:** Distal convoluted tubule and collecting duct of the nephron.
3. **Mechanism:** Amiloride directly blocks epithelial sodium channels (ENaCs) in the distal convoluted tubule and collecting duct. This decreases sodium reabsorption and reduces potassium excretion, resulting in increased sodium and water excretion while conserving potassium.

B. Pharmacokinetics

1. **Absorption:** Well absorbed from the gastrointestinal tract.
2. **Distribution:** Widely distributed; minimal protein binding.
3. **Metabolism:** Minimal metabolism; primarily excreted unchanged.
4. **Elimination:** Excreted mainly in the urine. The half-life is approximately 6-9 hours, allowing for once or twice daily dosing.

C. Clinical Uses

1. **Hypertension:** Used to treat high blood pressure, often in combination with other antihypertensives.
2. **Edema:** Effective for managing fluid retention, often used in combination with other diuretics.
3. **Hypokalemia Prevention:** Commonly used with thiazide diuretics to prevent potassium loss.

D. Side Effects

1. **Electrolyte Imbalances:** Hyperkalemia.
2. **Metabolic Effects:** Hyperuricemia.
3. **Gastrointestinal:** Nausea, vomiting.
4. **Other:** Headache, dizziness, and rash.

E. Monitoring and Management

1. **Electrolyte Levels:** Regular monitoring of potassium levels is crucial to prevent hyperkalemia.
2. **Renal Function:** Regular assessment of renal function is important.
3. **Drug Interactions:** Be aware of potential interactions with other drugs affecting potassium levels.

Comparison Between Triamterene and Amiloride

1. **Mechanism of Action:** Both drugs block epithelial sodium channels (ENaCs) but may have slightly different effects on sodium and potassium balance.
2. **Pharmacokinetics:** Both have similar half-lives and dosing schedules, but Triamterene has a broader distribution and potential for more pronounced side effects in some cases.
3. **Clinical Use:** Both are effective for hypertension and edema, often used in combination with thiazide diuretics to prevent hypokalemia.

4. **Side Effect Profile:** Both drugs can cause hyperkalemia, but Amiloride might have a slightly lower incidence of gastrointestinal side effects compared to Triamterene.

1. Mannitol

A. Mechanism of Action

1. **Class:** Osmotic diuretic.
2. **Site of Action:** Primarily the proximal convoluted tubule and the loop of Henle.
3. **Mechanism:** Mannitol is a non-absorbable solute that increases the osmolarity of the renal tubular fluid. This osmotic gradient prevents the reabsorption of water and electrolytes from the renal tubules, leading to an increased excretion of urine. Mannitol also reduces intracranial and intraocular pressure by drawing water out of the tissues into the vascular compartment.

B. Pharmacokinetics

1. **Absorption:** Not administered orally due to poor absorption; typically given intravenously.
2. **Distribution:** Distributed throughout the extracellular space; does not cross the blood-brain barrier.
3. **Metabolism:** Not metabolized; excreted unchanged.
4. **Elimination:** Excreted by the kidneys. The half-life is approximately 1-2 hours, but the diuretic effect lasts longer.

C. Clinical Uses

1. **Acute Renal Failure:** Used to maintain urine flow and prevent acute renal failure by promoting diuresis.
2. **Intracranial Pressure:** Helps reduce elevated intracranial pressure in conditions like brain edema or head trauma.
3. **Intraocular Pressure:** Used to decrease intraocular pressure in conditions such as acute glaucoma.

4. **Drug Overdose:** Can help in the excretion of certain toxins and drugs.

D. Side Effects

1. **Electrolyte Imbalances:** Can lead to dehydration, electrolyte imbalances, and hypovolemia.

2. **Renal:** Risk of renal impairment with high doses or rapid administration.

3. **Gastrointestinal:** Nausea, vomiting.

4. **Other:** Headache, dizziness, and potentially allergic reactions.

2. Urea

A. Mechanism of Action

1. **Class:** Osmotic diuretic.

2. **Site of Action:** Primarily the proximal convoluted tubule.

3. **Mechanism:** Urea increases the osmolarity of the renal tubular fluid, similar to Mannitol. By increasing osmotic pressure, Urea reduces the reabsorption of water and electrolytes in the kidneys, leading to increased urine output. It is also used to create hyperosmolar solutions for certain clinical situations.

B. Pharmacokinetics

1. **Absorption:** Typically administered intravenously as a hyperosmolar solution; not given orally due to poor absorption.

2. **Distribution:** Distributed throughout the extracellular fluid.

3. **Metabolism:** Urea is not metabolized in the body.

4. **Elimination:** Excreted by the kidneys in urine. The half-life varies based on the clinical situation and the volume of the solution used.

C. Clinical Uses

1. **Acute Renal Failure:** Used to promote diuresis and prevent further renal damage.

2. **Reduction of Intracranial Pressure:** Used to reduce intracranial pressure in some cases, although Mannitol is more commonly used for this purpose.

3. **Urea Cycle Disorders:** In certain rare conditions, urea can be used to manage urea cycle disorders.

D. Side Effects

1. **Electrolyte Imbalances:** Risk of dehydration and electrolyte imbalances.
2. **Renal:** Potential for renal impairment if not monitored carefully.
3. **Gastrointestinal:** Nausea, vomiting.
4. **Other:** Headache, dizziness, and possible allergic reactions.

E. Monitoring and Management

1. **Fluid Balance:** Monitor fluid intake and output to prevent dehydration.
2. **Electrolytes:** Regular assessment of electrolyte levels and renal function.
3. **Infusion Rate:** Administer carefully to avoid rapid changes in fluid and electrolyte balance.

Comparison Between Mannitol and Urea

1. **Mechanism:** Both are osmotic diuretics, but Mannitol is more commonly used for acute management of intracranial and intraocular pressure, while Urea is used in specific clinical situations and as part of urea cycle management.
2. **Administration:** Mannitol is typically administered intravenously and used for various acute conditions, while Urea is also administered intravenously and is used less frequently, often in specific cases such as urea cycle disorders.
3. **Side Effects:** Both can cause electrolyte imbalances and dehydration, but Mannitol has a broader range of uses and associated side effects due to its impact on intracranial and intraocular pressures.

Nitrofurantoin

A. Mechanism of Action

1. **Class:** Nitrofurantoin is an antibiotic with a broad spectrum of activity against many Gram-positive and Gram-negative bacteria.

2. **Mechanism:** Nitrofurantoin is reduced by bacterial nitrofurantoin reductase enzymes to reactive intermediates that damage bacterial DNA, proteins, and cell walls, leading to bacterial cell death. It works primarily in the urinary tract, where it achieves high concentrations.

B. Pharmacokinetics

1. **Absorption:** Well absorbed from the gastrointestinal tract.
2. **Distribution:** Distributed mainly in the urine, where it achieves high concentrations; poor distribution in tissues and serum.
3. **Metabolism:** Metabolized in the liver.
4. **Elimination:** Excreted primarily through the urine. The half-life is approximately 30-60 minutes.

C. Clinical Uses

1. **UTIs:** Used for the treatment and prophylaxis of uncomplicated urinary tract infections, particularly effective against E. coli and other common uropathogens.
2. **Chronic UTI Prophylaxis:** Can be used long-term in patients with recurrent UTIs to prevent future infections.

D. Side Effects

1. **Gastrointestinal:** Nausea, vomiting, diarrhea.
2. **Pulmonary:** Can cause pulmonary toxicity with chronic use, including cough and dyspnea.
3. **Hematological:** Risk of hemolytic anemia, especially in patients with G6PD deficiency.
4. **Neurological:** Headache, dizziness, peripheral neuropathy (rare but serious).

E. Monitoring and Management

1. **Renal Function:** Monitor renal function, especially in patients with preexisting renal impairment.

2. **Hematologic Monitoring:** Regular monitoring of blood counts, especially in long-term use.

3. **Pulmonary Symptoms:** Monitor for signs of pulmonary toxicity with prolonged use.

2. Methenamine

A. Mechanism of Action

1. **Class:** Methenamine is a urinary tract antiseptic.

2. **Mechanism:** Methenamine is metabolized in the acidic urine to formaldehyde, which is a potent bactericidal agent. The formaldehyde acts on bacterial proteins and nucleic acids, leading to bacterial cell death. Methenamine is most effective in acidic urine.

B. Pharmacokinetics

1. **Absorption:** Well absorbed from the gastrointestinal tract.

2. **Distribution:** Distributed throughout the body, but acts specifically in the urinary tract.

3. **Metabolism:** Methenamine is metabolized in the urine to formaldehyde.

4. **Elimination:** Excreted primarily in the urine. The half-life is approximately 1-2 hours.

C. Clinical Uses

1. **UTI Prophylaxis:** Used for the prophylaxis of recurrent urinary tract infections, especially in patients who have frequent infections.

2. **Chronic UTI Management:** Used in combination with other antibiotics or as an alternative in cases of recurrent infections.

D. Side Effects

1. **Gastrointestinal:** Nausea, vomiting, abdominal pain.

2. **Renal:** Can cause irritation in the urinary tract and may contribute to the formation of urinary crystals.

3. **Allergic Reactions:** Rash, itching, and other allergic responses.

4. **Urinary Symptoms:** Possible dysuria or urinary tract irritation.

E. Monitoring and Management

1. **Urine pH:** Ensure urine remains acidic for effective conversion of Methenamine to formaldehyde.
2. **Renal Function:** Regular monitoring, especially in patients with existing renal impairment.
3. **Side Effects:** Monitor for gastrointestinal and allergic reactions, and manage accordingly.

Comparison Between Nitrofurantoin and Methenamine

1. **Mechanism of Action:** Nitrofurantoin works through bacterial reduction mechanisms, while Methenamine works via formaldehyde production in acidic urine.
2. **Indications:** Nitrofurantoin is commonly used for active infections and prevention, while Methenamine is primarily used for prophylaxis.
3. **Side Effects:** Nitrofurantoin can cause more systemic effects, such as pulmonary and hematologic toxicity, while Methenamine's side effects are mostly related to gastrointestinal and urinary tract irritation.
4. **Renal Function Considerations:** Both drugs require consideration of renal function, but Methenamine's effectiveness is highly dependent on urine acidity.

Multiple Choice Questions (MCQs)

1. What is the primary site of action for thiazide diuretics like hydrochlorothiazide?

    a) Proximal convoluted tubule

    b) Distal convoluted tubule

    c) Loop of Henle

    d) Collecting duct

2. Which of the following is a potassium-sparing diuretic?

a) Furosemide

b) Hydrochlorothiazide

c) Spironolactone

d) Mannitol

3. Which diuretic is known for its ability to cause ototoxicity, especially with rapid intravenous administration?

a) Chlorthalidone

b) Spironolactone

c) Furosemide

d) Triamterene

4. Which drug is a vasopressin analogue used to treat central diabetes insipidus?

a) Triamterene

b) Desmopressin

c) Hydrochlorothiazide

d) Methenamine

5. What is the mechanism of action of loop diuretics like bumetanide?

a) Inhibition of Na-Cl symporter

b) Inhibition of Na-K-2Cl cotransporter

c) Aldosterone antagonism

d) Osmotic diuresis

6. Which drug is classified as a urinary analgesic?

a) Nitrofurantoin

b) Phenazopyridine

c) Methenamine

d) Furosemide

7. Which of the following diuretics is considered an aldosterone antagonist?

a) Hydrochlorothiazide

b) Eplerenone

c) Torsemide

d) Amiloride

8. Which osmotic diuretic is commonly used to reduce intracranial pressure?

   a) Urea

   b) Mannitol

   c) Furosemide

   d) Spironolactone

9. Which drug is used to alkalinize the urine to prevent uric acid stones?

   a) Methenamine

   b) Sodium Bicarbonate

   c) Nitrofurantoin

   d) Desmopressin

10. What is the primary clinical use of methenamine in the urinary system?

    a) Treating acute urinary tract infections

    b) Prophylaxis of recurrent urinary tract infections

    c) Reducing blood pressure

    d) Managing diabetes insipidus

11. Which drug is specifically used for the prophylaxis of recurrent UTIs due to its ability to acidify urine?

    a) Nitrofurantoin

    b) Phenazopyridine

    c) Methenamine

    d) Eplerenone

12. Which of the following is a potential side effect of hydrochlorothiazide?

    a) Hyperkalemia

    b) Hyperuricemia

    c) Ototoxicity

    d) Alkalosis

13. Which diuretic is known for having a longer half-life, allowing for once-daily dosing?

   a) Furosemide

   b) Hydrochlorothiazide

   c) Chlorthalidone

   d) Mannitol

14. Which of the following drugs is a potassium-sparing diuretic that inhibits epithelial sodium channels?

   a) Amiloride

   b) Torsemide

   c) Bumetanide

   d) Nitrofurantoin

15. Which drug is used to treat severe edema associated with heart failure and renal impairment?

   a) Hydrochlorothiazide

   b) Furosemide

   c) Triamterene

   d) Spironolactone

16. What is the main action of desmopressin in the kidneys?

   a) Increases sodium excretion

   b) Inhibits water reabsorption

   c) Enhances water reabsorption

   d) Promotes potassium excretion

17. Which of the following is a thiazide-like diuretic?

   a) Furosemide

   b) Indapamide

   c) Triamterene

   d) Spironolactone

18. Which drug acts by blocking the V2 receptors in the kidneys, leading to increased water excretion?

    a) Desmopressin

    b) Tolvaptan

    c) Eplerenone

    d) Mannitol

19. Which drug is a loop diuretic that acts on the thick ascending limb of the loop of Henle?

    a) Triamterene

    b) Spironolactone

    c) Torsemide

    d) Nitrofurantoin

20. Which diuretic is known to cause gynecomastia as a side effect?

    a) Furosemide

    b) Amiloride

    c) Spironolactone

    d) Hydrochlorothiazide

Short Answer Questions (SAQs)

1. Define diuretics and describe their general mechanism of action.

2. What are the clinical uses of loop diuretics like furosemide?

3. Explain how potassium-sparing diuretics prevent hypokalemia.

4. What is the mechanism of action of hydrochlorothiazide in treating hypertension?

5. Describe the potential side effects of spironolactone.

6. What are the differences between hydrochlorothiazide and chlorthalidone in terms of pharmacokinetics?

7. Explain the clinical use of desmopressin in treating diabetes insipidus.

8. How does methenamine work as a urinary antiseptic?

9. What is the role of mannitol in managing intracranial pressure?

10. Describe the monitoring required for patients on loop diuretics.

11. How does nitrofurantoin work against urinary tract infections?

12. What is the significance of aldosterone antagonism in the action of spironolactone?

13. Discuss the side effects associated with the use of osmotic diuretics like mannitol.

14. Explain the role of sodium bicarbonate as a urinary alkalinizer.

15. What are the advantages of using eplerenone over spironolactone?

16. Describe the potential complications of hyperkalemia in patients using potassium-sparing diuretics.

17. How do ADH receptor antagonists like tolvaptan work in managing hyponatremia?

18. What is the clinical relevance of using phenazopyridine in urinary tract infections?

19. How does the mechanism of action of indapamide differ from that of loop diuretics?

20. What are the key differences between triamterene and amiloride in their pharmacological effects?

Long Answer Questions (LAQs)

1. Discuss the classification, mechanisms of action, and clinical uses of different classes of diuretics.

2. Compare and contrast the pharmacokinetics, side effects, and clinical applications of loop diuretics and thiazide diuretics.

3. Explain the pharmacology of anti-diuretics, focusing on vasopressin analogues and ADH receptor antagonists. Include their mechanisms of action, clinical uses, and side effects.

4. Describe the role of diuretics in the management of hypertension, heart failure, and edema, with emphasis on the choice of specific diuretics for each condition.

5. Discuss the pharmacological management of urinary tract infections, including the role of antibiotics, urinary antiseptics, and analgesics.

6. Explain the mechanisms, clinical applications, and potential side effects of potassium-sparing diuretics, comparing aldosterone antagonists with sodium channel inhibitors.

7. Describe the use of osmotic diuretics in clinical practice, including their mechanisms of action, indications, and potential complications.

8. Compare the pharmacology of hydrochlorothiazide, chlorthalidone, and indapamide, focusing on their differences in efficacy, side effects, and clinical applications.

9. Discuss the pharmacological management of conditions like diabetes insipidus and hyponatremia using vasopressin analogues and ADH receptor antagonists.

10. Explain the importance of monitoring electrolyte levels and renal function in patients using diuretics, with examples from different classes of diuretics.

Answer Key for MCQs

1. b) Distal convoluted tubule
2. c) Spironolactone
3. c) Furosemide
4. b) Desmopressin
5. b) Inhibition of Na-K-2Cl cotransporter
6. b) Phenazopyridine
7. b) Eplerenone
8. b) Mannitol
9. b) Sodium Bicarbonate

10.b) Prophylaxis of recurrent urinary tract infections

11.c) Methenamine

12.b) Hyperuricemia

13.c) Chlorthalidone

14.a) Amiloride

15.b) Furosemide

16.c) Enhances water reabsorption

17.b) Indapamide

18.b) Tolvaptan

19.c) Torsemide

20.c) Spironolactone

CHAPTER – 5

AUTOCOIDS AND RELATED DRUGS – I

INTRODUCTION:

Autocoids are a diverse group of biological molecules that act as local hormones. They are synthesized and released by various tissues and exert their effects on nearby cells, playing crucial roles in inflammation, pain, allergic reactions, and other physiological processes. Unlike systemic hormones, autocoids typically have a short duration of action and work in a localized manner.

Key Types of Autocoids:

1. **Histamine**
   a. **Role**: Involved in allergic reactions, gastric acid secretion, and neurotransmission.
   b. **Receptors**: H1, H2, H3, and H4 receptors.
   c. **Drugs**: Antihistamines (H1 blockers like diphenhydramine, H2 blockers like ranitidine).

2. **Serotonin (5-HT)**
   a. **Role**: Regulates mood, appetite, sleep, and pain.
   b. **Receptors**: 5-HT1 to 5-HT7 receptors.
   c. **Drugs**: SSRIs, 5-HT3 antagonists (e.g., ondansetron), triptans for migraine.

3. **Eicosanoids**
   a. **Includes**: Prostaglandins, thromboxanes, leukotrienes.
   b. **Role**: Involved in inflammation, fever, blood clotting, and smooth muscle contraction.
   c. **Drugs**: NSAIDs (inhibit prostaglandin synthesis), leukotriene inhibitors (e.g., montelukast).

4. **Kinins**
    a. **Includes**: Bradykinin, kallidin.
    b. **Role**: Mediate inflammation, pain, and vasodilation.
    c. **Drugs**: Kinin receptor antagonists, ACE inhibitors (indirectly affect bradykinin levels).

Overview of Autocoid-Related Drugs:
1. **Antihistamines**: Block histamine receptors, reducing allergic symptoms and gastric acid secretion.
2. **Serotonin Modulators**: Affect serotonin levels or receptors, treating conditions like depression, anxiety, and migraines.
3. **Eicosanoid Modulators**: Inhibit the synthesis or action of eicosanoids, providing anti-inflammatory and analgesic effects.
4. **Kinin Antagonists**: Inhibit the effects of kinins, used in conditions like hereditary angioedema.

INTRODUCTION TO AUTACOIDS AND CLASSIFICATION

Autocoids are a diverse group of biological molecules that act as local hormones. They are synthesized and released by various tissues and exert their effects on nearby cells, playing crucial roles in inflammation, pain, allergic reactions, and other physiological processes. Unlike systemic hormones, autocoids typically have a short duration of action and work in a localized manner.

Key Types of Autocoids:
1. **Histamine**
    a. **Role**: Involved in allergic reactions, gastric acid secretion, and neurotransmission.
    b. **Receptors**: H1, H2, H3, and H4 receptors.
    c. **Drugs**: Antihistamines (H1 blockers like diphenhydramine, H2 blockers like ranitidine).
2. **Serotonin (5-HT)**

a. **Role**: Regulates mood, appetite, sleep, and pain.

b. **Receptors**: 5-HT1 to 5-HT7 receptors.

c. **Drugs**: SSRIs, 5-HT3 antagonists (e.g., ondansetron), triptans for migraine.

3. **Eicosanoids**

a. **Includes**: Prostaglandins, thromboxanes, leukotrienes.

b. **Role**: Involved in inflammation, fever, blood clotting, and smooth muscle contraction.

c. **Drugs**: NSAIDs (inhibit prostaglandin synthesis), leukotriene inhibitors (e.g., montelukast).

4. **Kinins**

a. **Includes**: Bradykinin, kallidin.

b. **Role**: Mediate inflammation, pain, and vasodilation.

c. **Drugs**: Kinin receptor antagonists, ACE inhibitors (indirectly affect bradykinin levels).

Overview of Autocoid-Related Drugs:

1. **Antihistamines**: Block histamine receptors, reducing allergic symptoms and gastric acid secretion.

2. **Serotonin Modulators**: Affect serotonin levels or receptors, treating conditions like depression, anxiety, and migraines.

3. **Eicosanoid Modulators**: Inhibit the synthesis or action of eicosanoids, providing anti-inflammatory and analgesic effects.

4. **Kinin Antagonists**: Inhibit the effects of kinins, used in conditions like hereditary angioedema.

Introduction to Autocoids

Autocoids are biologically active substances that are synthesized and released by cells in response to specific stimuli. Unlike endocrine hormones, which are secreted into the bloodstream and act on distant target organs, autocoids generally act locally near their site of synthesis and release. These substances are involved in a variety of physiological and pathological processes, including inflammation, pain, allergy, hemostasis, and smooth muscle contraction.

Key Characteristics of Autocoids:

1. **Local Action**: Autocoids typically act close to where they are produced, making their effects highly localized.

2. **Short Duration of Action**: They are often rapidly metabolized or inactivated, which limits their action to a short time frame.

3. **Varied Functions**: Autocoids can have multiple roles depending on the tissue and the receptors they interact with.

Classification of Autocoids

Autocoids can be broadly classified based on their chemical nature and the types of receptors they act on:

1. Biogenic Amines

a. **Histamine**

  i. **Synthesis**: Derived from the amino acid histidine.

  ii. **Functions**: Mediates allergic reactions, regulates gastric acid secretion, and acts as a neurotransmitter.

  iii. **Receptors**: H1, H2, H3, and H4 receptors.

  iv. **Drugs**: Antihistamines (e.g., diphenhydramine, ranitidine).

b. **Serotonin (5-Hydroxytryptamine or 5-HT)**

  i. **Synthesis**: Synthesized from the amino acid tryptophan.

  ii. **Functions**: Regulates mood, appetite, sleep, pain perception, and vasoconstriction.

  iii. **Receptors**: 5-HT1 to 5-HT7 receptors.

  iv. **Drugs**: SSRIs (e.g., fluoxetine), 5-HT3 antagonists (e.g., ondansetron), triptans for migraines.

2. Lipid-Derived Autocoids

a. **Eicosanoids**

  i. **Prostaglandins**

1. **Functions**: Involved in inflammation, fever, pain, vasodilation, and regulation of blood flow.
        2. **Drugs**: NSAIDs (e.g., aspirin, ibuprofen), COX-2 inhibitors (e.g., celecoxib).

   ii. **Thromboxanes**
        1. **Functions**: Promote platelet aggregation and vasoconstriction.
        2. **Drugs**: Aspirin (inhibits thromboxane synthesis).

   iii. **Leukotrienes**
        1. **Functions**: Mediate inflammation, bronchoconstriction, and allergic responses.
        2. **Drugs**: Leukotriene receptor antagonists (e.g., montelukast).

3. Polypeptides

a. **Kinins**

   i. **Bradykinin**
        1. **Functions**: Causes vasodilation, increases vascular permeability, and induces pain.
        2. **Drugs**: Kinin receptor antagonists, ACE inhibitors (indirectly increase bradykinin levels).

   ii. **Angiotensin**
        1. **Functions**: Regulates blood pressure and fluid balance.
        2. **Drugs**: ACE inhibitors (e.g., enalapril), angiotensin receptor blockers (e.g., losartan).

b. **Substance P**

   i. **Functions**: A neuropeptide involved in pain transmission and inflammatory responses.
   ii. **Drugs**: NK1 receptor antagonists (e.g., aprepitant).

4. Gaseous Autocoids

a. **Nitric Oxide (NO)**

i. **Functions**: Acts as a vasodilator, neurotransmitter, and immune regulator.

ii. **Drugs**: Nitroglycerin (releases NO), phosphodiesterase inhibitors (e.g., sildenafil).

HISTAMINE, 5-HT AND THEIR ANTAGONISTS

Histamine

Histamine is a biogenic amine synthesized from the amino acid histidine by the enzyme histidine decarboxylase. It plays a significant role in immune responses, gastric acid secretion, and neurotransmission.

Functions of Histamine:

a. **Immune Response**: Released by mast cells and basophils during allergic reactions, histamine increases vascular permeability, leading to swelling and redness.

b. **Gastric Secretion**: Histamine stimulates the secretion of gastric acid by acting on H2 receptors in the stomach.

c. **Neurotransmission**: In the central nervous system, histamine acts as a neurotransmitter, influencing wakefulness and appetite.

Histamine Receptors:

a. **H1 Receptors**: Found in smooth muscles, endothelium, and the central nervous system. Stimulation leads to vasodilation, bronchoconstriction, and increased vascular permeability.

b. **H2 Receptors**: Located primarily in the stomach lining, where they mediate gastric acid secretion.

c. **H3 Receptors**: Present in the central nervous system, where they regulate the release of other neurotransmitters.

d. **H4 Receptors**: Found mainly in the bone marrow and white blood cells, involved in immune response regulation.

Histamine Antagonists:

a. **H1 Antagonists (Antihistamines)**: Used to treat allergic reactions by blocking H1 receptors, reducing symptoms like itching, swelling, and redness.

   1. **First-Generation Antihistamines**: Diphenhydramine, Chlorpheniramine.

      1. **Characteristics**: Cross the blood-brain barrier, causing sedation and drowsiness.

   2. **Second-Generation Antihistamines**: Loratadine, Cetirizine, Fexofenadine.

      1. **Characteristics**: Less likely to cause sedation as they do not readily cross the blood-brain barrier.

b. **H2 Antagonists**: Used to reduce gastric acid secretion, treating conditions like peptic ulcers and gastroesophageal reflux disease (GERD).

   1. **Examples**: Ranitidine, Famotidine, Cimetidine.

c. **H3 Antagonists**: Primarily in research and under development for various neurological conditions.

d. **H4 Antagonists**: Potential therapeutic agents in inflammatory and autoimmune diseases, currently under research.

Serotonin (5-HT)

Serotonin (5-Hydroxytryptamine, 5-HT) is another crucial biogenic amine, synthesized from the amino acid tryptophan. It is predominantly found in the gastrointestinal tract, platelets, and the central nervous system. Serotonin has a wide range of functions, including mood regulation, appetite control, sleep regulation, and modulation of pain perception.

Functions of Serotonin:

1. **Mood Regulation**: Serotonin is a key neurotransmitter involved in the regulation of mood, anxiety, and happiness.

2. **Gastrointestinal Motility**: In the GI tract, serotonin regulates bowel movements and secretion.

3. **Vasoconstriction**: Serotonin causes the constriction of blood vessels, playing a role in hemostasis.

4. **Pain Perception**: It modulates pain sensitivity and is involved in the body's pain control mechanisms.

Serotonin Receptors:

1. **5-HT1 Receptors**: Involved in the inhibition of neurotransmitter release and vasoconstriction.

2. **5-HT2 Receptors**: Mediate platelet aggregation, smooth muscle contraction, and vasoconstriction.

3. **5-HT3 Receptors**: Involved in nausea and vomiting, especially in chemotherapy-induced nausea.

4. **5-HT4, 5-HT5, 5-HT6, 5-HT7 Receptors**: Involved in various functions including mood regulation, cognition, and GI motility.

Serotonin Antagonists:

1. **5-HT1 Antagonists**: Limited therapeutic use, primarily in research.

2. **5-HT2 Antagonists**: Used in the treatment of schizophrenia and migraine.

    i. **Examples**: Ketanserin (antihypertensive), Risperidone (antipsychotic).

3. **5-HT3 Antagonists**: Primarily used to prevent nausea and vomiting, particularly in chemotherapy or surgery.

    i. **Examples**: Ondansetron, Granisetron.

4. **5-HT4 Antagonists**: Under investigation for use in gastrointestinal disorders.

Serotonin Modulators:

1. **Selective Serotonin Reuptake Inhibitors (SSRIs)**: These drugs increase serotonin levels in the brain by inhibiting its reuptake into presynaptic

cells, commonly used to treat depression, anxiety, and other mood disorders.

    i.   **Examples**: Fluoxetine, Sertraline, Paroxetine.

2. **Serotonin-Norepinephrine Reuptake Inhibitors (SNRIs)**: Increase levels of both serotonin and norepinephrine, used for depression and chronic pain management.

    i.   **Examples**: Venlafaxine, Duloxetine.

PROSTAGLANDINS

Prostaglandins are a group of lipid-derived autocoids belonging to the broader class of eicosanoids, which are synthesized from arachidonic acid, a polyunsaturated fatty acid present in cell membranes. Prostaglandins play vital roles in various physiological and pathological processes, including inflammation, pain, fever, and the regulation of blood flow and clotting.

Biosynthesis of Prostaglandins

Prostaglandins are synthesized via the **cyclooxygenase (COX) pathway**, which involves the following steps:

1. **Release of Arachidonic Acid**: Phospholipase A2 enzyme liberates arachidonic acid from the phospholipid membrane.

2. **Conversion by Cyclooxygenase Enzymes**: Arachidonic acid is converted into prostaglandin G2 (PGG2) and then into prostaglandin H2 (PGH2) by the action of cyclooxygenase enzymes (COX-1 and COX-2).

    i.   **COX-1**: Constitutively expressed in most tissues, responsible for maintaining normal physiological functions such as protecting the stomach lining and regulating platelet aggregation.

    ii.   **COX-2**: Inducible enzyme, expressed in response to inflammatory stimuli, leading to increased production of prostaglandins involved in inflammation and pain.

3. **Formation of Specific Prostaglandins**: PGH2 is further metabolized by specific synthases to produce various prostaglandins (e.g., PGE2, PGI2, PGD2, PGF2α) and thromboxanes.

Functions of Prostaglandins

Prostaglandins have diverse and often opposing roles depending on the specific prostaglandin and the tissue involved:

1. **PGE2 (Prostaglandin E2)**
   a. **Functions**:
      i. Mediates fever by acting on the hypothalamus.
      ii. Promotes inflammation and pain by sensitizing nerve endings.
      iii. Causes vasodilation, leading to redness and swelling in inflamed tissues.
      iv. Stimulates gastric mucus secretion and inhibits gastric acid secretion, protecting the stomach lining.
   b. **Clinical Relevance**: Targeted by NSAIDs to reduce fever, pain, and inflammation.

2. **PGI2 (Prostacyclin)**
   a. **Functions**:
      i. Inhibits platelet aggregation, preventing blood clot formation.
      ii. Causes vasodilation, lowering blood pressure and improving blood flow.
      iii. Protects the endothelium from injury.
   b. **Clinical Relevance**: Prostacyclin analogs (e.g., epoprostenol) are used in the treatment of pulmonary arterial hypertension.

3. **PGD2 (Prostaglandin D2)**
   a. **Functions**:
      i. Involved in sleep regulation and allergic responses.

ii.   Causes bronchoconstriction and plays a role in asthma and allergic rhinitis.

b. **Clinical Relevance**: Potential target for treating allergic conditions.

4. **PGF2α (Prostaglandin F2α)**

   a. **Functions**:

      i.   Causes contraction of the uterine smooth muscle, involved in labor and menstruation.

      ii. Induces bronchoconstriction.

   b. **Clinical Relevance**: Used therapeutically to induce labor (e.g., dinoprostone) and in the management of postpartum hemorrhage.

5. **TXA2 (Thromboxane A2)**

   a. **Functions**:

      i.   Promotes platelet aggregation, leading to blood clot formation.

      ii. Causes vasoconstriction, increasing blood pressure.

   b. **Clinical Relevance**: Aspirin irreversibly inhibits COX-1, reducing thromboxane A2 production and thus preventing blood clots.

Prostaglandin-Related Drugs

1. **Nonsteroidal Anti-Inflammatory Drugs (NSAIDs)**

   a. **Mechanism**: Inhibit the COX enzymes (COX-1 and COX-2), reducing the production of prostaglandins involved in inflammation, pain, and fever.

   b. **Examples**: Aspirin, Ibuprofen, Naproxen.

   c. **Clinical Use**: Used for the treatment of pain, inflammation, and fever. Aspirin, in low doses, is also used for its antiplatelet effects to prevent heart attacks and strokes.

2. **COX-2 Inhibitors**

a. **Mechanism**: Selectively inhibit the COX-2 enzyme, reducing inflammation and pain while minimizing gastrointestinal side effects associated with COX-1 inhibition.

b. **Examples**: Celecoxib, Etoricoxib.

c. **Clinical Use**: Used in the management of osteoarthritis, rheumatoid arthritis, and acute pain conditions.

3. **Prostaglandin Analogues**

a. **Examples:**

i. **Misoprostol (PGE1 analogue)**: Used to prevent NSAID-induced gastric ulcers and to induce labor or abortion.

ii. **Latanoprost (PGF2α analogue)**: Used to reduce intraocular pressure in glaucoma.

iii. **Epoprostenol (PGI2 analogue)**: Used in the treatment of pulmonary arterial hypertension.

b. **Clinical Use**: Prostaglandin analogues are used for a variety of conditions, including gastric protection, glaucoma management, induction of labor, and treatment of pulmonary hypertension.

THROMBOXANES

Thromboxanes are a subgroup of eicosanoids, lipid compounds derived from arachidonic acid, and are closely related to prostaglandins. Thromboxanes play a critical role in hemostasis and thrombosis, primarily by promoting platelet aggregation and vasoconstriction.

Biosynthesis of Thromboxanes

Thromboxanes are synthesized through the following process:

1. **Release of Arachidonic Acid**: Arachidonic acid is liberated from membrane phospholipids by the enzyme phospholipase A2.

2. **Conversion by Cyclooxygenase (COX) Enzymes**: Arachidonic acid is metabolized by cyclooxygenase (COX-1 and COX-2) to form prostaglandin H2 (PGH2).

3. **Formation of Thromboxanes**: PGH2 is then converted to thromboxane A2 (TXA2) by thromboxane synthase, an enzyme predominantly found in platelets.

Functions of Thromboxane A2 (TXA2)

Thromboxane A2 (TXA2) is the most important and well-studied thromboxane, and it plays several critical roles in the cardiovascular system:

1. **Platelet Aggregation**: TXA2 is a potent promoter of platelet aggregation, which is crucial for the formation of blood clots. When vascular injury occurs, TXA2 is released from platelets, stimulating other platelets to aggregate and form a clot to prevent excessive bleeding.

2. **Vasoconstriction**: TXA2 causes constriction of blood vessels, which reduces blood flow and helps maintain blood pressure. This vasoconstriction also aids in reducing blood loss during injury by minimizing the flow of blood to the affected area.

3. **Smooth Muscle Contraction**: TXA2 contributes to the contraction of smooth muscle in blood vessels, further supporting its role in hemostasis.

Thromboxane Receptors

Thromboxanes exert their effects by binding to thromboxane receptors (TP receptors), which are G-protein-coupled receptors (GPCRs). These receptors are found on platelets, smooth muscle cells, and various other tissues.

1. **TPα and TPβ Isoforms**: The TP receptor exists in two isoforms, TPα and TPβ, which are derived from alternative splicing of the TP gene. Both isoforms mediate similar functions but may differ in their regulatory mechanisms.

Thromboxane-Related Drugs

The regulation of thromboxane activity is crucial in managing cardiovascular diseases, particularly those related to thrombosis and atherosclerosis. Several drugs target the thromboxane pathway:

1. **Aspirin (Acetylsalicylic Acid)**

a. **Mechanism**: Aspirin irreversibly inhibits the COX-1 enzyme in platelets, leading to a reduction in thromboxane A2 production. This effect prevents platelet aggregation and thrombus formation.

b. **Clinical Use**: Low-dose aspirin is widely used for the prevention of cardiovascular events such as myocardial infarction (heart attack) and stroke in high-risk patients. Its antiplatelet effect makes it a cornerstone in the management of atherosclerotic cardiovascular diseases.

2. **Thromboxane Receptor Antagonists**

a. **Examples**: Drugs like ifetroban and terutroban are thromboxane receptor antagonists that block the action of TXA2 on its receptors, thus preventing platelet aggregation and vasoconstriction.

b. **Clinical Use**: These agents are under investigation for use in conditions like atherosclerosis, pulmonary hypertension, and other thrombotic disorders, but they are not yet widely available in clinical practice.

3. **Thromboxane Synthase Inhibitors**

a. **Examples**: Drugs like dazoxiben and ozagrel inhibit thromboxane synthase, reducing the production of TXA2. These agents prevent platelet aggregation and reduce the risk of thrombus formation.

b. **Clinical Use**: Although thromboxane synthase inhibitors have been studied, they are not commonly used due to mixed results in clinical trials and potential side effects.

Clinical Significance

Thromboxanes, particularly TXA2, are key mediators in the pathogenesis of various cardiovascular diseases, including heart attacks and strokes. Their role in promoting platelet aggregation and vasoconstriction makes them a target for therapeutic intervention to prevent thrombotic events. The use of antiplatelet agents like aspirin has been well-established in reducing the risk of these events, demonstrating the importance of modulating thromboxane activity in clinical practice.

LEUKOTRIENES

Leukotrienes are a group of biologically active lipid mediators that belong to the eicosanoid family, like prostaglandins and thromboxanes. They are derived from arachidonic acid and play a critical role in the inflammatory response, particularly in conditions such as asthma, allergic rhinitis, and other hypersensitivity reactions.

Biosynthesis of Leukotrienes

Leukotrienes are synthesized through the **lipoxygenase pathway**, involving the following steps:

1. **Release of Arachidonic Acid**: Phospholipase A2 enzyme liberates arachidonic acid from the phospholipid membrane, similar to the prostaglandin and thromboxane pathways.

2. **Action of 5-Lipoxygenase**: Arachidonic acid is converted into 5-hydroperoxyeicosatetraenoic acid (5-HPETE) by the enzyme 5-lipoxygenase (5-LOX).

3. **Formation of Leukotrienes**:
   a. 5-HPETE is further converted into leukotriene A4 (LTA4), a key intermediate.
   b. LTA4 can be metabolized into two primary leukotrienes:
      i. **Leukotriene B4 (LTB4)**: Formed by the action of LTA4 hydrolase.
      ii. **Leukotriene C4 (LTC4)**: Formed by the conjugation of LTA4 with glutathione, catalyzed by LTC4 synthase. LTC4 is further metabolized to leukotriene D4 (LTD4) and leukotriene E4 (LTE4).

Types and Functions of Leukotrienes

Leukotrienes are divided into two main types, based on their structure and biological activity:

1. **Leukotriene B4 (LTB4)**
   a. **Functions**:
      i. LTB4 is a potent chemoattractant, recruiting neutrophils and other immune cells to sites of inflammation.
      ii. It promotes the adhesion of these cells to the endothelium and their migration into tissues.
      iii. LTB4 enhances the release of lysosomal enzymes and reactive oxygen species (ROS) from neutrophils, contributing to the inflammatory response.
   b. **Clinical Relevance**: LTB4 is involved in the pathogenesis of various inflammatory diseases, including arthritis, inflammatory bowel disease, and psoriasis.

2. **Cysteinyl Leukotrienes (LTC4, LTD4, LTE4)**
   a. **Functions**:
      i. These leukotrienes are potent bronchoconstrictors, causing the narrowing of the airways in the lungs, which is a key feature of asthma.
      ii. They increase vascular permeability, leading to edema and mucus secretion in the respiratory tract.
      iii. Cysteinyl leukotrienes are involved in allergic reactions, contributing to symptoms such as wheezing, shortness of breath, and nasal congestion.
   b. **Clinical Relevance**: Cysteinyl leukotrienes are major contributors to the pathophysiology of asthma and allergic rhinitis. Blocking their effects can help control these conditions.

Leukotriene Receptors

Leukotrienes exert their effects by binding to specific receptors on target cells:

1. **BLT Receptors**: LTB4 primarily acts through BLT1 and BLT2 receptors, which are G-protein-coupled receptors found on leukocytes. BLT1 is the high-affinity receptor mediating the chemotactic and inflammatory effects of LTB4.

2. **Cysteinyl Leukotriene Receptors (CysLT Receptors)**: LTC4, LTD4, and LTE4 bind to CysLT1 and CysLT2 receptors, which are also G-protein-coupled receptors. CysLT1 is the main receptor mediating bronchoconstriction and other pro-inflammatory actions of cysteinyl leukotrienes.

Leukotriene-Related Drugs

The understanding of leukotrienes has led to the development of drugs that target their synthesis or block their receptors, particularly for the treatment of asthma and allergic conditions.

1. **Leukotriene Receptor Antagonists (LTRAs)**

   a. **Mechanism**: LTRAs block the CysLT1 receptor, preventing leukotrienes from binding and exerting their bronchoconstrictive and pro-inflammatory effects.

   b. **Examples**:

      i. **Montelukast**: Widely used for the prevention and treatment of asthma and allergic rhinitis. It helps reduce airway inflammation, bronchoconstriction, and mucus secretion.

      ii. **Zafirlukast**: Another CysLT1 receptor antagonist with similar indications as montelukast.

   c. **Clinical Use**: LTRAs are particularly useful in the management of chronic asthma, exercise-induced bronchoconstriction, and allergic rhinitis. They are often used as an adjunct to inhaled corticosteroids.

2. **5-Lipoxygenase Inhibitors**

a. **Mechanism**: These drugs inhibit the enzyme 5-lipoxygenase, reducing the production of leukotrienes from arachidonic acid.

b. **Example**:

    i. **Zileuton**: A selective 5-lipoxygenase inhibitor that decreases the formation of all leukotrienes, including LTB4 and the cysteinyl leukotrienes.

c. **Clinical Use**: Zileuton is used for the long-term management of asthma. It is particularly beneficial in patients whose symptoms are not adequately controlled by other therapies.

3. **Leukotriene Modifiers in Development**

a. Ongoing research is focused on developing new leukotriene modifiers, including more potent and selective 5-lipoxygenase inhibitors, as well as novel leukotriene receptor antagonists that target both CysLT1 and CysLT2 receptors.

ANGIOTENSIN

Angiotensin is a key component of the renin-angiotensin system (RAS), a hormone system that regulates blood pressure, fluid balance, and electrolyte balance. Angiotensin plays a critical role in cardiovascular physiology and pathophysiology, especially in conditions like hypertension, heart failure, and chronic kidney disease.

The Renin-Angiotensin System (RAS)

The RAS involves a cascade of biochemical reactions that lead to the production of angiotensin II, a potent vasoconstrictor. The main components of this system include:

1. **Renin**: An enzyme produced by the juxtaglomerular cells of the kidneys in response to low blood pressure, low sodium levels, or sympathetic nervous system activation. Renin cleaves angiotensinogen to form angiotensin I.

2. **Angiotensinogen**: A precursor protein produced mainly by the liver. It is cleaved by renin to form angiotensin I.

3. **Angiotensin I**: An inactive decapeptide formed by the action of renin on angiotensinogen. Angiotensin I is then converted to the active form, angiotensin II, by the enzyme angiotensin-converting enzyme (ACE).

4. **Angiotensin-Converting Enzyme (ACE)**: A key enzyme located primarily in the lungs, ACE converts angiotensin I to angiotensin II. It also degrades bradykinin, a vasodilator, thus contributing to its overall pressor effect.

5. **Angiotensin II**: The primary active product of the RAS, angiotensin II exerts multiple effects on the cardiovascular system, kidneys, and adrenal glands.

Functions of Angiotensin II

Angiotensin II is a potent vasoconstrictor and has several physiological effects:

1. **Vasoconstriction**: Angiotensin II causes constriction of arterioles, leading to an increase in systemic vascular resistance and blood pressure.

2. **Aldosterone Secretion**: Angiotensin II stimulates the adrenal cortex to release aldosterone, a hormone that increases sodium and water reabsorption in the kidneys, thereby increasing blood volume and pressure.

3. **Stimulation of Antidiuretic Hormone (ADH)**: Angiotensin II promotes the release of ADH (vasopressin) from the posterior pituitary gland, which enhances water reabsorption by the kidneys.

4. **Cardiac and Vascular Hypertrophy**: Angiotensin II contributes to the remodeling of the heart and blood vessels, leading to hypertrophy, which is associated with chronic hypertension and heart failure.

5. **Thirst Stimulation**: Angiotensin II stimulates the thirst center in the hypothalamus, leading to increased water intake, which helps restore blood volume.

Angiotensin Receptors

Angiotensin II exerts its effects through two main types of receptors:

1. **AT1 Receptors**: These are the primary receptors mediating the classical effects of angiotensin II, including vasoconstriction, aldosterone release, and sympathetic activation.

2. **AT2 Receptors**: These receptors are less well understood but are thought to counteract some of the effects of AT1 receptors. They may be involved in vasodilation, anti-proliferative effects, and apoptosis.

Angiotensin-Related Drugs

The RAS is a major target for pharmacological intervention in the treatment of hypertension, heart failure, and other cardiovascular diseases. Key classes of drugs targeting this system include:

1. **Angiotensin-Converting Enzyme Inhibitors (ACE Inhibitors)**

    a. **Mechanism**: ACE inhibitors block the conversion of angiotensin I to angiotensin II by inhibiting ACE. This leads to reduced levels of angiotensin II, decreased vasoconstriction, and reduced aldosterone secretion.

    b. **Examples**: Enalapril, Lisinopril, Ramipril.

    c. **Clinical Use**: ACE inhibitors are used to treat hypertension, heart failure, chronic kidney disease, and to prevent cardiovascular events in high-risk patients.

2. **Angiotensin II Receptor Blockers (ARBs)**

    a. **Mechanism**: ARBs selectively block the AT1 receptors, preventing angiotensin II from exerting its effects. This leads to vasodilation, reduced aldosterone levels, and decreased blood pressure.

    b. **Examples**: Losartan, Valsartan, Telmisartan.

    c. **Clinical Use**: ARBs are used for similar indications as ACE inhibitors, including hypertension, heart failure, and chronic kidney disease. They are often preferred in patients who cannot tolerate ACE inhibitors due to side effects like cough.

3. **Renin Inhibitors**

    a. **Mechanism**: Renin inhibitors directly inhibit the activity of renin, thereby reducing the production of angiotensin I and subsequently angiotensin II.

    b. **Example**: Aliskiren.

    c. **Clinical Use**: Aliskiren is used to treat hypertension, though it is not as widely prescribed as ACE inhibitors or ARBs.

4. **Aldosterone Antagonists**

    a. **Mechanism**: Although not direct angiotensin pathway inhibitors, aldosterone antagonists block the effects of aldosterone, reducing sodium and water retention, and lowering blood pressure.

    b. **Examples**: Spironolactone, Eplerenone.

    c. **Clinical Use**: These are used in heart failure, hypertension, and conditions with hyperaldosteronism.

BRADYKININ

Bradykinin is a potent vasoactive peptide that belongs to the kallikrein-kinin system, another autacoid system involved in various physiological and pathological processes. It plays a significant role in vasodilation, increased vascular permeability, pain, and inflammation.

Synthesis of Bradykinin

Bradykinin is produced through the following steps:

1. **Prekallikrein Activation**:

    a. Bradykinin is generated from kininogen, a precursor protein, by the action of enzymes called kallikreins.

    b. Plasma prekallikrein is activated to kallikrein by factor XIIa (a component of the coagulation cascade) or by other proteolytic enzymes.

2. **Formation from Kininogen**:
   a. Kallikrein cleaves high-molecular-weight kininogen (HMWK) to release bradykinin, a nonapeptide (9 amino acids long).
   b. Similarly, tissue kallikrein cleaves low-molecular-weight kininogen (LMWK) to produce kallidin (lysyl-bradykinin), which can be converted to bradykinin by the removal of a lysine residue.

Functions of Bradykinin

Bradykinin exerts its effects through the activation of specific receptors on target cells. The primary functions include:

1. **Vasodilation**:
   a. Bradykinin is a powerful vasodilator, causing relaxation of vascular smooth muscle and leading to a decrease in blood pressure.
   b. This vasodilation is mediated through the release of nitric oxide (NO), prostacyclin, and endothelium-derived hyperpolarizing factors (EDHF) from endothelial cells.

2. **Increased Vascular Permeability**:
   a. Bradykinin increases the permeability of blood vessels, leading to leakage of plasma proteins and fluids into tissues.
   b. This contributes to the formation of edema, a hallmark of inflammation.

3. **Pain and Inflammation**:
   a. Bradykinin is a potent mediator of pain (algesic agent). It directly stimulates sensory nerve endings, causing pain and hyperalgesia.
   b. It also contributes to inflammation by promoting the release of pro-inflammatory cytokines and chemokines.

4. **Smooth Muscle Contraction**:
   a. Bradykinin can cause contraction of smooth muscles in various organs, including the gastrointestinal tract, uterus, and airways.

b. In the respiratory system, bradykinin can induce bronchoconstriction, which is relevant in conditions like asthma.

5. **Renal Effects**:

a. Bradykinin has diuretic and natriuretic effects in the kidneys. It increases renal blood flow and promotes the excretion of sodium and water.

Bradykinin Receptors

Bradykinin exerts its biological effects through two main types of receptors:

1. **B2 Receptors**:

a. B2 receptors are constitutively expressed on most cells and are the primary receptors mediating the effects of bradykinin under normal physiological conditions.

b. Activation of B2 receptors leads to vasodilation, increased vascular permeability, pain, and other inflammatory responses.

2. **B1 Receptors**:

a. B1 receptors are inducible and are upregulated in response to tissue injury, inflammation, and other pathological conditions.

b. B1 receptors are involved in chronic inflammation and pain, particularly in conditions like rheumatoid arthritis and neuropathic pain.

Bradykinin-Related Drugs

Bradykinin and its pathway are targeted by certain therapeutic agents, particularly in the context of conditions associated with excessive bradykinin activity.

1. **Angiotensin-Converting Enzyme Inhibitors (ACE Inhibitors)**

a. **Mechanism**: ACE inhibitors, such as enalapril and lisinopril, block the enzyme ACE, which not only converts angiotensin I to angiotensin II but also degrades bradykinin.

b. **Effect on Bradykinin**: By inhibiting ACE, these drugs increase bradykinin levels, contributing to their vasodilatory and antihypertensive effects.

c. **Clinical Relevance**: The accumulation of bradykinin is partly responsible for the beneficial effects of ACE inhibitors, but it also contributes to side effects like a persistent dry cough and, in rare cases, angioedema.

2. **Bradykinin Receptor Antagonists**

a. **Mechanism**: These drugs block the bradykinin receptors (B1 or B2), thereby inhibiting the actions of bradykinin.

b. **Example**: Icatibant is a selective B2 receptor antagonist used in the treatment of hereditary angioedema, a condition characterized by excessive bradykinin production leading to episodes of severe swelling.

c. **Clinical Use**: Bradykinin receptor antagonists are primarily used in conditions where bradykinin is implicated in pathological processes, such as hereditary angioedema.

3. **Kallikrein Inhibitors**

a. **Mechanism**: Kallikrein inhibitors, such as ecallantide, inhibit the activity of kallikrein, thereby reducing the production of bradykinin.

b. **Clinical Use**: Ecallantide is used to treat acute attacks of hereditary angioedema.

SUBSTANCE P

Substance P is a neuropeptide and an important member of the tachykinin family of peptides. It is widely distributed in the central and peripheral nervous systems and plays a crucial role in pain transmission, inflammation, and various neurogenic functions. Substance P is considered both a neurotransmitter and a neuromodulator, and it is heavily involved in the body's response to stress, injury, and inflammation.

Synthesis and Distribution

1. **Synthesis**: Substance P is synthesized as part of a larger precursor protein known as preprotachykinin A (PPT-A), which is then cleaved to form Substance P and other tachykinins like neurokinin A.
2. **Distribution**: Substance P is found throughout the body, particularly in the brain (especially in regions associated with pain processing such as the spinal cord, hypothalamus, and amygdala), gastrointestinal tract, skin, and respiratory tract.

Functions of Substance P

Substance P exerts a wide range of physiological and pathological effects, particularly in the context of pain, inflammation, and neurogenic functions:

1. **Pain Transmission (Nociception)**:
   a. Substance P is a key player in the transmission of pain signals from peripheral sensory neurons to the central nervous system (CNS). It is released from the terminals of sensory neurons in response to noxious stimuli.
   b. In the spinal cord, Substance P binds to neurokinin-1 (NK1) receptors on second-order neurons, facilitating the transmission of pain signals to the brain.
2. **Inflammation**:
   a. Substance P is a pro-inflammatory mediator. It can induce the release of inflammatory cytokines and chemokines, increase vascular permeability, and promote the recruitment of immune cells to sites of injury or infection.
   b. It also contributes to neurogenic inflammation, a process where nerve fibers release neuropeptides like Substance P, leading to local inflammation independent of the immune system.

3. **Vasodilation**:

    a. Substance P causes vasodilation by inducing the release of nitric oxide (NO) from endothelial cells. This leads to increased blood flow to affected areas, which is a critical aspect of the inflammatory response.

4. **Bronchoconstriction**:

    a. In the respiratory system, Substance P can cause bronchoconstriction and is implicated in conditions such as asthma, where it contributes to airway inflammation and hyperresponsiveness.

5. **Gastrointestinal Effects**:

    a. Substance P is involved in the regulation of gastrointestinal motility and secretion. It can stimulate smooth muscle contraction, influencing peristalsis and the overall function of the digestive system.

6. **Stress Response**:

    a. In the CNS, Substance P is involved in the body's response to stress. It affects mood, anxiety, and depression, and is linked to stress-induced disorders.

Substance P Receptors

The effects of Substance P are primarily mediated through its interaction with neurokinin-1 (NK1) receptors:

1. **NK1 Receptors**:

    a. These are G-protein-coupled receptors that have a high affinity for Substance P. They are widely distributed in the CNS and peripheral tissues, including the brain, spinal cord, lungs, and gastrointestinal tract.

    b. Activation of NK1 receptors by Substance P leads to a variety of cellular responses, including the activation of signaling pathways that mediate pain transmission, inflammation, and other neurogenic effects.

Substance P-Related Drugs

The clinical significance of Substance P has led to the development of various drugs targeting its receptor, particularly in the context of pain management and psychiatric disorders:

1. **NK1 Receptor Antagonists**:
   a. **Mechanism**: NK1 receptor antagonists block the binding of Substance P to its receptor, thereby inhibiting its effects on pain transmission, inflammation, and stress responses.
   b. **Examples**: Aprepitant, Fosaprepitant.
   c. **Clinical Use**:
      i. **Chemotherapy-Induced Nausea and Vomiting (CINV)**: Aprepitant and other NK1 receptor antagonists are used to prevent nausea and vomiting associated with chemotherapy. By blocking Substance P in the brain, these drugs reduce the emetic reflex.
      ii. **Depression and Anxiety**: Research is ongoing to explore the role of NK1 receptor antagonists in treating mood disorders such as depression and anxiety. While initial studies were promising, further research is needed to fully understand their efficacy in this context.
      iii. **Pain Management**: Although the role of NK1 receptor antagonists in pain management has been explored, their clinical use in this area remains limited due to inconsistent efficacy.

2. **Tachykinin Receptor Antagonists**:
   a. These drugs target multiple receptors of the tachykinin family, including NK1, NK2, and NK3 receptors. They are being

investigated for various therapeutic applications, including pain, respiratory diseases, and psychiatric disorders.

Multiple Choice Questions (MCQs)

1. Which of the following is a key characteristic of autocoids?
   a) Long duration of action
   b) Systemic circulation
   c) Localized action
   d) High molecular weight

2. Histamine plays a role in all of the following functions except:
   a) Gastric acid secretion
   b) Neurotransmission
   c) Vasoconstriction
   d) Allergic reactions

3. Which histamine receptor is primarily involved in allergic reactions?
   a) H1
   b) H2
   c) H3
   d) H4

4. Which drug class is used to reduce gastric acid secretion by blocking H2 receptors?
   a) Antihistamines
   b) SSRIs
   c) Proton pump inhibitors
   d) H2 blockers

5. Serotonin is synthesized from which amino acid?
   a) Tyrosine
   b) Histidine

c) Tryptophan

d) Phenylalanine

6. Which serotonin receptor subtype is involved in chemotherapy-induced nausea and vomiting?

a) 5-HT1

b) 5-HT2

c) 5-HT3

d) 5-HT4

7. Which of the following is a function of prostaglandin E2 (PGE2)?

a) Promotes platelet aggregation

b) Causes vasodilation

c) Inhibits smooth muscle contraction

d) Reduces inflammation

8. Which enzyme is responsible for the synthesis of leukotrienes from arachidonic acid?

a) Cyclooxygenase

b) 5-Lipoxygenase

c) Phospholipase A2

d) Thromboxane synthase

9. Which of the following drugs is a leukotriene receptor antagonist?

a) Montelukast

b) Aspirin

c) Ondansetron

d) Enalapril

10. Angiotensin II primarily exerts its effects through which receptor?

a) AT1

b) AT2

c) AT3

d) AT4

11. Bradykinin causes which of the following effects?

    a) Vasoconstriction

    b) Vasodilation

    c) Decreased vascular permeability

    d) Platelet aggregation

12. Which drug class inhibits the degradation of bradykinin?

    a) ACE inhibitors

    b) ARBs

    c) NSAIDs

    d) SSRIs

13. Substance P is primarily involved in which of the following processes?

    a) Blood clotting

    b) Pain transmission

    c) Blood pressure regulation

    d) Hormone secretion

14. Which receptor does Substance P primarily bind to?

    a) NK1

    b) H1

    c) AT1

    d) CysLT1

15. Which of the following is a function of thromboxane A2 (TXA2)?

    a) Inhibits platelet aggregation

    b) Causes vasodilation

    c) Promotes platelet aggregation

    d) Reduces blood pressure

16. Which drug is known for irreversibly inhibiting thromboxane A2 production?

    a) Aspirin

    b) Ibuprofen

c) Montelukast

d) Enalapril

17. Which of the following is a key function of prostacyclin (PGI2)?

a) Promotes blood clot formation

b) Causes vasoconstriction

c) Inhibits platelet aggregation

d) Induces uterine contraction

18. Which of the following drugs is a selective 5-lipoxygenase inhibitor?

a) Zileuton

b) Montelukast

c) Ifetroban

d) Epoprostenol

19. Which prostaglandin is involved in the regulation of sleep and allergic responses?

a) PGE2

b) PGF2α

c) PGD2

d) PGI2

20. Which of the following drugs is a bradykinin receptor antagonist used in hereditary angioedema?

a) Icatibant

b) Cimetidine

c) Aliskiren

d) Zafirlukast

Short Answer Type Questions (Subjective)

1. Define autocoids and explain their general characteristics.

2. Describe the role of histamine in allergic reactions and its related receptors.

3. Explain the mechanism of action of H1 antihistamines and their clinical uses.

4. What are the functions of serotonin in the central nervous system?

5. How do nonsteroidal anti-inflammatory drugs (NSAIDs) affect prostaglandin synthesis?

6. Describe the biosynthesis of leukotrienes and their role in asthma.

7. Explain the physiological effects of angiotensin II and its role in blood pressure regulation.

8. How do ACE inhibitors affect the renin-angiotensin system and what are their clinical uses?

9. Describe the role of bradykinin in inflammation and pain.

10. What is the mechanism of action of Substance P in pain transmission?

11. Discuss the clinical significance of thromboxane A2 in cardiovascular diseases.

12. Explain how COX-2 inhibitors differ from nonselective NSAIDs in their mechanism and effects.

13. What are leukotriene receptor antagonists, and how are they used in the treatment of asthma?

14. How does thromboxane A2 contribute to platelet aggregation and vasoconstriction?

15. Describe the role of prostacyclin in the cardiovascular system.

16. Explain the therapeutic uses of bradykinin receptor antagonists.

17. Discuss the potential side effects of increasing bradykinin levels in the body.

18. What are the clinical applications of NK1 receptor antagonists in chemotherapy-induced nausea?

19. Explain the role of 5-HT3 antagonists in preventing nausea and vomiting.

20. How does Substance P contribute to neurogenic inflammation?

Long Answer Type Questions (Subjective)

1. Discuss the classification of autocoids, providing examples and their physiological roles.

2. Explain the role of histamine in gastric acid secretion and how H2 blockers are used in treating related conditions.

3. Describe the biosynthesis, functions, and clinical relevance of prostaglandins, including the role of NSAIDs.

4. Discuss the renin-angiotensin system in detail and the pharmacological interventions targeting this pathway.

5. Explain the synthesis, functions, and therapeutic modulation of bradykinin in the treatment of cardiovascular diseases.

6. Discuss the role of leukotrienes in asthma and the therapeutic strategies targeting their pathway.

7. Describe the role of Substance P in pain transmission, inflammation, and its potential as a therapeutic target.

8. Explain the role of thromboxanes in hemostasis and how their inhibition is used in preventing cardiovascular diseases.

9. Discuss the clinical significance of serotonin in mood regulation and the pharmacological approaches to modulate its levels.

10. Explain the role of prostaglandins and thromboxanes in inflammation and how drugs like NSAIDs and COX-2 inhibitors modulate these pathways.

Answer Key for MCQs

1. c) Localized action

2. c) Vasoconstriction

3. d) H2 blockers

4. a) Antihistamines

5. c) Tryptophan

6. c) 5-HT3

7. b) Causes vasodilation

8. b) 5-Lipoxygenase

9. a) Montelukast

10.a) AT1

11.b) Vasodilation

12.a) ACE inhibitors

13.b) Pain transmission

14.a) NK1

15.c) Promotes platelet aggregation

16.a) Aspirin

17.c) Inhibits platelet aggregation

18.a) Zileuton

19.c) PGD2

20.a) Icatibant

CHAPTER – 6

AUTOCOIDS AND RELATED DRUGS – II

INTRODUCTION:

Autocoids are biological factors that act like local hormones, functioning near the site of synthesis and release, and are rapidly degraded. The study of autocoids includes various endogenous substances such as histamines, prostaglandins, leukotrienes, serotonin, and kinins. While the first part of the topic might cover histamines and their antagonists, prostaglandins, and leukotrienes, the second part delves into more specialized areas, such as serotonin (5-HT), kinins (bradykinin and kallidin), and specific peptide autocoids like angiotensin and endothelins.

Key Areas of Focus in Autocoids and Related Drugs-II:

1. **Serotonin (5-HT) and Its Receptors:**

    a. **Synthesis and Release:** Understanding how serotonin is synthesized from tryptophan, stored, and released in the body.

    b. **Receptors:** Detailed study of the different types of serotonin receptors (5-HT1 to 5-HT7) and their specific roles in various physiological functions, including mood regulation, vascular tone, and gastrointestinal motility.

    c. **Pharmacological Actions:** Focus on the physiological and pathological roles of serotonin, particularly in the central nervous system (CNS) and cardiovascular system.

    d. **Drugs Acting on Serotonin Pathways:** This includes selective serotonin reuptake inhibitors (SSRIs), serotonin receptor agonists and antagonists, and their therapeutic applications in conditions like depression, anxiety, migraine, and gastrointestinal disorders.

2. **Kinins:**

a. **Bradykinin and Kallidin:** Study of the synthesis, release, and actions of these potent vasodilator peptides, particularly their role in inflammation, pain, and blood pressure regulation.

b. **Receptors:** Detailed understanding of bradykinin receptors (B1 and B2), their distribution, and the signaling pathways they activate.

c. **Pharmacological Modulation:** Exploration of kinin receptor antagonists and their potential therapeutic uses in conditions such as hereditary angioedema, hypertension, and chronic pain.

3. **Peptide Autocoids:**

a. **Angiotensin:** Study of the renin-angiotensin-aldosterone system (RAAS), focusing on the role of angiotensin II in blood pressure regulation and fluid balance. This includes drugs like ACE inhibitors, angiotensin receptor blockers (ARBs), and their uses in hypertension and heart failure.

b. **Endothelins:** These potent vasoconstrictor peptides are examined in the context of their role in vascular homeostasis and pathophysiological conditions like pulmonary hypertension. Endothelin receptor antagonists and their therapeutic implications are also discussed.

c. **Vasoactive Intestinal Peptide (VIP) and Substance P:** These neuropeptides are studied for their roles in smooth muscle relaxation, neurotransmission, and inflammation.

4. **Clinical Applications:**

a. **Drug Development:** Understanding the challenges and strategies in developing drugs targeting these autocoid systems, with an emphasis on specificity, side effects, and therapeutic efficacy.

b. **Disease Associations:** A look at how dysregulation of autocoid systems contributes to various diseases, including cardiovascular disorders, gastrointestinal diseases, psychiatric conditions, and chronic pain syndromes.

NON-STEROIDAL ANTI-INFLAMMATORY AGENTS

Non-Steroidal Anti-Inflammatory Drugs (NSAIDs) are a class of medications widely used to reduce inflammation, relieve pain, and decrease fever. In the context of Autocoids and Related Drugs-II, NSAIDs are particularly significant because they modulate the activity of certain autocoids, such as prostaglandins, which play a key role in inflammation, pain, and fever.

Mechanism of Action:

NSAIDs primarily exert their effects by inhibiting the enzyme cyclooxygenase (COX), which is responsible for the synthesis of prostaglandins from arachidonic acid. There are two main isoforms of this enzyme:

1. **COX-1:** This isoform is constitutively expressed in most tissues and is involved in the production of prostaglandins that protect the gastric mucosa, regulate platelet aggregation, and maintain renal blood flow.

2. **COX-2:** This isoform is inducible and is primarily involved in the production of prostaglandins that mediate inflammation, pain, and fever in response to tissue injury or infection.

Classification of NSAIDs:

NSAIDs can be classified based on their chemical structure and selectivity for COX enzymes:

1. **Non-selective COX Inhibitors:**

    a. **Aspirin:** The prototypical NSAID, which irreversibly inhibits COX-1 and COX-2. It is used for its anti-inflammatory, analgesic, antipyretic, and antiplatelet effects.

    b. **Ibuprofen and Naproxen:** These are reversible inhibitors of both COX-1 and COX-2, widely used for their analgesic and anti-inflammatory properties.

c. **Indomethacin:** A potent non-selective COX inhibitor used in the treatment of acute gout and rheumatoid arthritis.

2. **COX-2 Selective Inhibitors (Coxibs):**
   a. **Celecoxib:** A selective COX-2 inhibitor designed to reduce inflammation and pain with a lower risk of gastrointestinal side effects compared to non-selective NSAIDs.
   b. **Etoricoxib and Parecoxib:** Other examples of COX-2 selective inhibitors used for conditions like osteoarthritis and postoperative pain.

3. **Preferential COX-2 Inhibitors:**
   a. **Diclofenac:** Although it inhibits both COX-1 and COX-2, it has a slightly higher affinity for COX-2, making it a preferred option for reducing inflammation and pain with a somewhat reduced risk of gastrointestinal side effects compared to other non-selective NSAIDs.

Therapeutic Uses:

NSAIDs are used in a variety of clinical conditions, including:

1. **Inflammatory Conditions:** Rheumatoid arthritis, osteoarthritis, ankylosing spondylitis, and other inflammatory joint disorders.
2. **Pain Relief:** NSAIDs are effective in managing mild to moderate pain, including headaches, dysmenorrhea (menstrual pain), and musculoskeletal pain.
3. **Fever Reduction:** NSAIDs like ibuprofen are commonly used as antipyretics.
4. **Cardiovascular Protection:** Low-dose aspirin is used for its antiplatelet effects in the prevention of cardiovascular events such as myocardial infarction and stroke.

Side Effects:

The inhibition of COX-1 by NSAIDs leads to a range of side effects due to the reduction of protective prostaglandins:

1. **Gastrointestinal Toxicity:** This includes gastritis, peptic ulcers, and gastrointestinal bleeding, particularly with non-selective NSAIDs.
2. **Renal Toxicity:** NSAIDs can reduce renal blood flow, leading to acute kidney injury, especially in patients with pre-existing renal impairment or dehydration.
3. **Cardiovascular Risk:** COX-2 inhibitors, while reducing gastrointestinal toxicity, have been associated with an increased risk of cardiovascular events, such as myocardial infarction and stroke, due to the imbalance between pro-thrombotic and anti-thrombotic prostaglandins.
4. **Hypersensitivity Reactions:** Some patients may experience allergic reactions, including asthma exacerbations, particularly with aspirin.

Pharmacokinetics:

1. **Absorption:** NSAIDs are generally well-absorbed orally and reach peak plasma concentrations within 1-2 hours.
2. **Distribution:** They are highly protein-bound and widely distributed throughout the body.
3. **Metabolism:** Most NSAIDs are metabolized in the liver by cytochrome P450 enzymes.
4. **Excretion:** NSAIDs are excreted mainly by the kidneys, with some biliary excretion.

Drug Interactions:

1. **Anticoagulants:** NSAIDs can increase the risk of bleeding when taken with anticoagulants like warfarin.
2. **Antihypertensives:** NSAIDs may reduce the effectiveness of antihypertensive drugs, particularly ACE inhibitors and diuretics.
3. **Lithium:** NSAIDs can increase lithium levels, leading to toxicity.

ANTI-GOUT DRUGS

Gout is a type of inflammatory arthritis characterized by the deposition of monosodium urate (MSU) crystals in joints and tissues, leading to intense pain, swelling, and redness. It is caused by hyperuricemia (elevated levels of uric acid in the blood), which can result from overproduction or underexcretion of uric acid. The management of gout involves the use of anti-gout drugs that either relieve acute attacks, prevent recurrent episodes, or reduce hyperuricemia.

Classification of Anti-Gout Drugs:

1. **Drugs for Acute Gout Attacks:**
   a. Colchicine
   b. Non-Steroidal Anti-Inflammatory Drugs (NSAIDs)
   c. Corticosteroids

2. **Drugs for Chronic Management (Urate-Lowering Therapy):**
   a. Xanthine Oxidase Inhibitors
      i. Allopurinol
      ii. Febuxostat
   b. Uricosuric Agents
      i. Probenecid
      ii. Lesinurad
   c. Uricase (Urate Oxidase) Agents
      i. Pegloticase
   d. Interleukin-1 Inhibitors

1. Drugs for Acute Gout Attacks:

These drugs are used to manage the intense inflammation and pain associated with acute gouty arthritis.

a. **Colchicine:**
   i. **Mechanism of Action:** Colchicine disrupts microtubule formation by binding to tubulin, inhibiting the migration of leukocytes to the site of inflammation, thereby reducing phagocytosis of urate

crystals and subsequent release of inflammatory mediators such as cytokines and prostaglandins.

    ii. **Therapeutic Use:** Colchicine is effective in reducing pain and inflammation during an acute gout attack when administered early. It can also be used in low doses for prophylaxis.

    iii. **Side Effects:** Common side effects include gastrointestinal disturbances like nausea, vomiting, and diarrhea. Long-term use can lead to bone marrow suppression and myopathy.

    iv. **Pharmacokinetics:** Colchicine is well absorbed orally, metabolized in the liver, and excreted mainly through the bile and feces.

b. **Non-Steroidal Anti-Inflammatory Drugs (NSAIDs):**

    i. **Mechanism of Action:** NSAIDs inhibit the cyclooxygenase (COX) enzymes, thereby reducing the synthesis of prostaglandins, which play a significant role in the inflammatory response to urate crystals.

    ii. **Therapeutic Use:** NSAIDs like indomethacin, naproxen, and ibuprofen are commonly used to alleviate pain and inflammation in acute gout attacks.

    iii. **Side Effects:** Gastrointestinal disturbances, including ulcers and bleeding, renal toxicity, and cardiovascular risks.

    iv. **Pharmacokinetics:** NSAIDs are generally well absorbed orally, metabolized in the liver, and excreted by the kidneys.

c. **Corticosteroids:**

    i. **Mechanism of Action:** Corticosteroids exert their anti-inflammatory effects by inhibiting the release of inflammatory mediators such as prostaglandins, leukotrienes, and cytokines, and by suppressing leukocyte migration and activation.

ii. **Therapeutic Use:** Corticosteroids, such as prednisone, are used in patients who cannot tolerate NSAIDs or colchicine. They can be administered orally, intravenously, or via intra-articular injection.

iii. **Side Effects:** Long-term use can lead to systemic effects such as immunosuppression, hyperglycemia, osteoporosis, and adrenal suppression.

iv. **Pharmacokinetics:** Corticosteroids are well absorbed, metabolized in the liver, and excreted by the kidneys.

2. Drugs for Chronic Management (Urate-Lowering Therapy):

These drugs are used to prevent recurrent gout attacks by lowering serum uric acid levels.

a. **Xanthine Oxidase Inhibitors:**

i. **Allopurinol:**

1. **Mechanism of Action:** Allopurinol is a purine analog that inhibits xanthine oxidase, the enzyme responsible for converting hypoxanthine and xanthine into uric acid. This results in decreased production of uric acid.

2. **Therapeutic Use:** Allopurinol is used for long-term management of hyperuricemia in patients with chronic gout, especially in those who are overproducers of uric acid.

3. **Side Effects:** Rash, gastrointestinal disturbances, and, rarely, allopurinol hypersensitivity syndrome, which can be life-threatening.

4. **Pharmacokinetics:** Allopurinol is well absorbed orally, metabolized to an active metabolite (oxypurinol), and excreted by the kidneys.

ii. **Febuxostat:**

1. **Mechanism of Action:** Similar to allopurinol, febuxostat is a non-purine selective inhibitor of xanthine oxidase, reducing uric acid production.

2. **Therapeutic Use:** Febuxostat is an alternative to allopurinol, particularly in patients with renal impairment or those intolerant to allopurinol.

3. **Side Effects:** Increased liver enzymes, rash, and cardiovascular events.

4. **Pharmacokinetics:** Febuxostat is well absorbed, metabolized in the liver, and excreted through both urine and feces.

b. **Uricosuric Agents:**

i. **Probenecid:**

1. **Mechanism of Action:** Probenecid increases the excretion of uric acid by inhibiting its reabsorption in the renal tubules, thus lowering serum uric acid levels.

2. **Therapeutic Use:** Probenecid is used in patients with underexcretion of uric acid. It is often combined with other drugs for effective urate-lowering therapy.

3. **Side Effects:** Gastrointestinal upset, renal stones, and hypersensitivity reactions.

4. **Pharmacokinetics:** Probenecid is well absorbed, metabolized by the liver, and excreted by the kidneys.

ii. **Lesinurad:**

1. **Mechanism of Action:** Lesinurad is a selective uric acid reabsorption inhibitor (SURI) that works by inhibiting the urate transporter 1 (URAT1) in the kidneys, promoting uric acid excretion.

2. **Therapeutic Use:** It is used in combination with xanthine oxidase inhibitors for the treatment of hyperuricemia in gout patients.

3. **Side Effects:** Increased risk of renal impairment, headache, and cardiovascular events.

4. **Pharmacokinetics:** Lesinurad is well absorbed, metabolized in the liver, and excreted mainly by the kidneys.

c. **Uricase (Urate Oxidase) Agents:**

   i. **Pegloticase:**

      1. **Mechanism of Action:** Pegloticase is a recombinant uricase enzyme that converts uric acid into allantoin, a more soluble and easily excreted metabolite.

      2. **Therapeutic Use:** It is used in patients with severe, refractory gout who have not responded to conventional urate-lowering therapies.

      3. **Side Effects:** Infusion reactions, anaphylaxis, and gout flares.

      4. **Pharmacokinetics:** Pegloticase is administered intravenously and has a long half-life, allowing for infrequent dosing.

d. **Interleukin-1 (IL-1) Inhibitors:**

   i. **Anakinra:** An IL-1 receptor antagonist used off-label for treating acute gout flares, especially in patients who are unresponsive to standard therapies.

   ii. **Canakinumab:** A monoclonal antibody against IL-1β, used for treating gout flares in patients who cannot tolerate NSAIDs, colchicine, or corticosteroids.

ANTIRHEUMATIC DRUGS

Rheumatoid arthritis (RA) is a chronic, systemic autoimmune disease characterized by inflammation of the synovial joints, leading to pain, swelling, and eventually joint destruction. The pathogenesis involves immune system dysregulation, where autocoids like cytokines (e.g., TNF-α, IL-1, IL-6) and other inflammatory mediators play a significant role. Antirheumatic drugs are used to modify the disease process, reduce symptoms, and prevent joint damage.

Classification of Antirheumatic Drugs:

1. Non-Steroidal Anti-Inflammatory Drugs (NSAIDs)
2. Glucocorticoids
3. Disease-Modifying Antirheumatic Drugs (DMARDs)
    a. Conventional DMARDs
    b. Biologic DMARDs
    c. Targeted Synthetic DMARDs

1. Non-Steroidal Anti-Inflammatory Drugs (NSAIDs):

a. **Mechanism of Action:** NSAIDs inhibit the cyclooxygenase (COX) enzymes (COX-1 and COX-2), reducing the synthesis of prostaglandins, which are key mediators of inflammation, pain, and fever.

b. **Therapeutic Use:** NSAIDs provide symptomatic relief in RA by reducing pain, stiffness, and inflammation. However, they do not alter the disease progression or prevent joint damage.

c. **Common NSAIDs:** Ibuprofen, Naproxen, Diclofenac, Indomethacin, Celecoxib (selective COX-2 inhibitor).

d. **Side Effects:** Gastrointestinal ulcers, renal impairment, cardiovascular risks, and increased bleeding tendency.

e. **Pharmacokinetics:** NSAIDs are generally well absorbed orally, metabolized in the liver, and excreted by the kidneys.

2. Glucocorticoids:

a. **Mechanism of Action:** Glucocorticoids (e.g., Prednisone, Prednisolone) exert potent anti-inflammatory and immunosuppressive effects by inhibiting multiple inflammatory pathways. They reduce the production of cytokines, prostaglandins, and leukotrienes, and suppress immune cell activation and proliferation.

b. **Therapeutic Use:** Glucocorticoids are used in RA to rapidly control inflammation and symptoms, particularly during acute flare-ups. They can be administered orally, intravenously, or intra-articularly.

c. **Side Effects:** Long-term use can lead to significant side effects, including osteoporosis, hyperglycemia, hypertension, weight gain, and increased risk of infections.

d. **Pharmacokinetics:** Glucocorticoids are well absorbed, metabolized primarily in the liver, and excreted by the kidneys.

3. Disease-Modifying Antirheumatic Drugs (DMARDs):

DMARDs are the cornerstone of RA treatment, as they can slow down disease progression, prevent joint damage, and maintain long-term function. They can be divided into conventional synthetic DMARDs, biologic DMARDs, and targeted synthetic DMARDs.

a. Conventional Synthetic DMARDs:

i. **Methotrexate:**

    1. **Mechanism of Action:** Methotrexate inhibits dihydrofolate reductase, reducing DNA synthesis and cell proliferation. It also has anti-inflammatory effects by increasing adenosine levels, which dampen immune responses.

    2. **Therapeutic Use:** Methotrexate is the most commonly used DMARD in RA due to its efficacy in reducing symptoms, slowing disease progression, and its relatively favorable safety profile.

    3. **Side Effects:** Gastrointestinal disturbances, hepatotoxicity, bone marrow suppression, and pulmonary toxicity.

4. **Pharmacokinetics:** Methotrexate is absorbed orally or administered subcutaneously, metabolized in the liver, and excreted by the kidneys.

ii. **Sulfasalazine:**

1. **Mechanism of Action:** Sulfasalazine is metabolized into 5-aminosalicylic acid and sulfapyridine, which have anti-inflammatory effects by inhibiting cytokine production and immune cell activation.

2. **Therapeutic Use:** It is used in mild to moderate RA, often in combination with other DMARDs like methotrexate.

3. **Side Effects:** Gastrointestinal upset, rash, leukopenia, and hepatotoxicity.

4. **Pharmacokinetics:** Sulfasalazine is well absorbed orally, metabolized in the liver, and excreted by the kidneys.

iii. **Hydroxychloroquine:**

1. **Mechanism of Action:** Hydroxychloroquine interferes with lysosomal activity and antigen processing, thereby reducing immune cell activation and inflammation.

2. **Therapeutic Use:** It is used in mild RA and is often combined with other DMARDs. It is also effective in managing lupus and other autoimmune conditions.

3. **Side Effects:** Retinopathy (rare but serious), gastrointestinal upset, and skin reactions.

4. **Pharmacokinetics:** Hydroxychloroquine is well absorbed orally, metabolized in the liver, and excreted by the kidneys.

iv. **Leflunomide:**

1. **Mechanism of Action:** Leflunomide inhibits dihydroorotate dehydrogenase, reducing pyrimidine synthesis and thereby limiting lymphocyte proliferation and inflammation.

2. **Therapeutic Use:** Used in moderate to severe RA, often as an alternative to methotrexate.

3. **Side Effects:** Hepatotoxicity, gastrointestinal disturbances, hypertension, and teratogenicity.

4. **Pharmacokinetics:** Leflunomide is well absorbed orally, metabolized in the liver, and has a long half-life due to enterohepatic recirculation.

b. Biologic DMARDs:

Biologic DMARDs are engineered proteins that target specific components of the immune system, such as cytokines or their receptors, to reduce inflammation and prevent joint damage in RA. They are often used in patients who do not respond adequately to conventional DMARDs.

i. **Tumor Necrosis Factor (TNF) Inhibitors:**

1. **Examples:** Etanercept, Infliximab, Adalimumab, Certolizumab, Golimumab.

2. **Mechanism of Action:** TNF inhibitors block the activity of TNF-α, a key cytokine involved in the inflammatory process of RA.

3. **Therapeutic Use:** These drugs are highly effective in reducing disease activity and preventing joint damage. They are often combined with methotrexate.

4. **Side Effects:** Increased risk of infections (e.g., tuberculosis), injection site reactions, and potential malignancy risk.

5. **Pharmacokinetics:** TNF inhibitors are administered subcutaneously or intravenously, with varying half-lives and dosing regimens.

ii. **Interleukin-1 (IL-1) Inhibitors:**

1. **Anakinra:**

a. **Mechanism of Action:** Anakinra is an IL-1 receptor antagonist that inhibits the inflammatory effects of IL-1 in RA.

b. **Therapeutic Use:** Less commonly used than TNF inhibitors, it is an option for patients who do not respond to other biologics.

c. **Side Effects:** Injection site reactions, increased infection risk, and neutropenia.

d. **Pharmacokinetics:** Administered subcutaneously daily.

iii. **Interleukin-6 (IL-6) Inhibitors:**

1. **Tocilizumab:**

a. **Mechanism of Action:** Tocilizumab blocks the IL-6 receptor, reducing the inflammatory cascade in RA.

b. **Therapeutic Use:** Effective in patients with moderate to severe RA, especially those who have not responded to TNF inhibitors.

c. **Side Effects:** Increased infection risk, elevated liver enzymes, and gastrointestinal perforation.

d. **Pharmacokinetics:** Administered intravenously or subcutaneously.

iv. **B-Cell Depleting Agents:**

1. **Rituximab:**

a. **Mechanism of Action:** Rituximab targets CD20 on B cells, leading to their depletion and subsequent reduction in autoantibody production and inflammation.

b. **Therapeutic Use:** Used in patients with moderate to severe RA, especially those who do not respond to TNF inhibitors.

c. **Side Effects:** Infusion reactions, infections, and potential reactivation of hepatitis B.

d. **Pharmacokinetics:** Administered intravenously, with effects lasting for months.

v. **T-Cell Costimulation Modulators:**

1. **Abatacept:**

   a. **Mechanism of Action:** Abatacept interferes with T-cell activation by blocking the CD28-CD80/86 interaction, reducing the immune response in RA.

   b. **Therapeutic Use:** Used in patients with moderate to severe RA who have not responded to other biologics.

   c. **Side Effects:** Increased infection risk, infusion reactions, and possible exacerbation of chronic obstructive pulmonary disease (COPD).

   d. **Pharmacokinetics:** Administered intravenously or subcutaneously.

c. Targeted Synthetic DMARDs:

i. **Janus Kinase (JAK) Inhibitors:**

1. **Examples:** Tofacitinib, Baricitinib, Upadacitinib.

2. **Mechanism of Action:** JAK inhibitors block the JAK-STAT signaling pathway, which is involved in the inflammatory response in RA.

3. **Therapeutic Use:** Effective in moderate to severe RA, especially in patients who have not responded to other DMARDs.

4. **Side Effects:** Increased infection risk (including herpes zoster), elevated liver enzymes, and potential risk of thromboembolic events.

5. **Pharmacokinetics:** Administered orally, providing an alternative to injectable biologics.

CLASSIFICATION:

The topic "Autocoids and Related Drugs-II" primarily focuses on the pharmacological agents that modulate the action of autocoids, which are locally acting biological factors involved in various physiological and pathological processes. These drugs are classified based on their therapeutic use and the specific autocoids they target. Below is a classification of Autocoids and Related Drugs-II along with examples:

1. Non-Steroidal Anti-Inflammatory Drugs (NSAIDs):

a. **Examples:**

   i. Ibuprofen

   ii. Naproxen

   iii. Diclofenac

   iv. Celecoxib (selective COX-2 inhibitor)

2. Anti-Gout Drugs:

a. **Examples:**

   i. Allopurinol (Xanthine oxidase inhibitor)

   ii. Febuxostat (Xanthine oxidase inhibitor)

   iii. Colchicine (Microtubule inhibitor)

   iv. Probenecid (Uricosuric agent)

   v. Pegloticase (Urate oxidase enzyme)

3. Antirheumatic Drugs:

a. **Non-Steroidal Anti-Inflammatory Drugs (NSAIDs):**

   i. **Examples:** Ibuprofen, Naproxen

b. **Glucocorticoids:**

   i. **Examples:** Prednisone, Methylprednisolone

c. **Disease-Modifying Antirheumatic Drugs (DMARDs):**

   i. **Conventional Synthetic DMARDs:**

      a. **Examples:** Methotrexate, Sulfasalazine, Hydroxychloroquine, Leflunomide

   ii. **Biologic DMARDs:**

a. **TNF Inhibitors:** Etanercept, Infliximab

b. **IL-1 Inhibitors:** Anakinra

c. **IL-6 Inhibitors:** Tocilizumab

d. **B-Cell Depleting Agents:** Rituximab

e. **T-Cell Costimulation Modulators:** Abatacept

iii. **Targeted Synthetic DMARDs:**

a. **Examples:** Tofacitinib, Baricitinib (JAK inhibitors)

4. Analgesics:

a. **Examples:**

i. Morphine (Opioid analgesic)

ii. Codeine (Opioid analgesic)

iii. Paracetamol/Acetaminophen (Non-opioid analgesic)

5. Anti-Migraine Drugs:

a. **Examples:**

i. Sumatriptan (5-HT1 receptor agonist)

ii. Rizatriptan (5-HT1 receptor agonist)

iii. Ergotamine (Ergot alkaloid)

6. Antihistamines:

a. **H1 Receptor Antagonists:**

i. **Examples:** Diphenhydramine, Loratadine, Cetirizine

b. **H2 Receptor Antagonists:**

i. **Examples:** Ranitidine, Famotidine, Cimetidine

7. Serotonin Receptor Modulators:

a. **Examples:**

i. Ondansetron (5-HT3 receptor antagonist)

ii. Buspirone (5-HT1A receptor partial agonist)

8. Leukotriene Modifiers:

a. **Examples:**

i. Montelukast (Leukotriene receptor antagonist)

ii.   Zafirlukast (Leukotriene receptor antagonist)

iii.   Zileuton (5-lipoxygenase inhibitor)

9. Bradykinin Receptor Antagonists:

a. **Examples:**

i.   Icatibant (Bradykinin B2 receptor antagonist)

10. Angiotensin Receptor Blockers (ARBs):

a. **Examples:**

i.   Losartan

ii.   Valsartan

iii.   Irbesartan

11. Prostaglandin Analogues:

a. **Examples:**

i.   Misoprostol (PGE1 analogue)

ii.   Latanoprost (PGF2α analogue)

A. Ibuprofen:

1. Mechanism of Action:

a. **Cyclooxygenase Inhibition:**

i.   Ibuprofen works by non-selectively inhibiting the enzyme cyclooxygenase (COX), which exists in two main forms: COX-1 and COX-2.

ii.   **COX-1 Inhibition:** Leads to decreased production of prostaglandins that protect the stomach lining and maintain platelet function, which can cause gastrointestinal side effects and affect blood clotting.

iii.   **COX-2 Inhibition:** Reduces the production of prostaglandins that mediate inflammation, pain, and fever, providing therapeutic effects.

2. Pharmacokinetics:

a. **Absorption:**

   i. Ibuprofen is well absorbed from the gastrointestinal tract, with peak plasma concentrations occurring approximately 1-2 hours after oral administration.

b. **Distribution:**

   i. It is extensively bound to plasma proteins (about 99%), which limits its distribution to tissues.

c. **Metabolism:**

   i. Ibuprofen undergoes hepatic metabolism primarily via cytochrome P450 enzymes, particularly CYP2C9, to form inactive metabolites.

d. **Excretion:**

   i. The drug and its metabolites are primarily excreted via the kidneys. The half-life of ibuprofen is relatively short, approximately 2-4 hours.

3. Therapeutic Uses:

a. **Pain Relief:**

   i. Used to relieve mild to moderate pain, including headaches, toothaches, menstrual pain, muscle aches, and arthritis.

b. **Anti-Inflammatory:**

   i. Commonly used in the treatment of inflammatory conditions such as osteoarthritis and rheumatoid arthritis.

c. **Antipyretic:**

   i. Effective in reducing fever.

4. Side Effects:

a. **Gastrointestinal:**

   i. Nausea, vomiting, dyspepsia, and potential for peptic ulceration and gastrointestinal bleeding.

b. **Cardiovascular:**

i. Increased risk of hypertension, myocardial infarction, and stroke with long-term use.

c. **Renal:**

i. May cause renal impairment, especially in patients with pre-existing kidney conditions.

d. **Hematologic:**

i. Prolonged bleeding time due to inhibition of platelet aggregation.

B. Naproxen:

1. Mechanism of Action:

a. **Cyclooxygenase Inhibition:**

i. Naproxen also non-selectively inhibits COX-1 and COX-2 enzymes, similar to ibuprofen.

ii. The inhibition of COX enzymes results in decreased synthesis of prostaglandins, leading to reduced inflammation, pain, and fever.

b. **Prolonged Action:**

i. Naproxen has a longer half-life compared to ibuprofen, allowing for less frequent dosing.

2. Pharmacokinetics:

a. **Absorption:**

i. Naproxen is well absorbed from the gastrointestinal tract, with peak plasma levels occurring 2-4 hours after oral administration.

b. **Distribution:**

i. It is highly bound to plasma proteins (about 99%), which affects its distribution and free drug availability.

c. **Metabolism:**

i. Naproxen undergoes hepatic metabolism, primarily through demethylation and conjugation with glucuronic acid to form inactive metabolites.

d. **Excretion:**

i. The drug is mainly excreted in the urine, with a half-life of about 12-17 hours, allowing for twice-daily dosing in most cases.

3. Therapeutic Uses:

a. Pain Relief:

i. Effective in treating mild to moderate pain such as dental pain, headache, and menstrual cramps.

b. Anti-Inflammatory:

i. Commonly used in the treatment of chronic inflammatory conditions like osteoarthritis, rheumatoid arthritis, and ankylosing spondylitis.

c. Antipyretic:

i. Used to reduce fever, although less commonly compared to ibuprofen.

4. Side Effects:

a. Gastrointestinal:

i. Similar to ibuprofen, Naproxen can cause nausea, vomiting, dyspepsia, peptic ulceration, and gastrointestinal bleeding.

b. Cardiovascular:

i. Naproxen has a lower cardiovascular risk compared to some other NSAIDs but may still increase the risk of myocardial infarction and stroke, especially with long-term use.

c. Renal:

i. May cause renal impairment, particularly in patients with pre-existing kidney conditions.

d. Hematologic:

i. Prolonged bleeding time due to its effect on platelet function.

Comparison of Ibuprofen and Naproxen:

a. **Duration of Action:** Naproxen has a longer duration of action due to its longer half-life, which allows for less frequent dosing compared to ibuprofen.

b. **Gastrointestinal Tolerability:** Both drugs have similar gastrointestinal side effects, though the risk may vary slightly depending on the dose and duration of use.

c. **Cardiovascular Risk:** Naproxen is generally considered to have a lower cardiovascular risk compared to ibuprofen, particularly in long-term use.

C. Diclofenac:

1. Mechanism of Action:

a. **Non-Selective COX Inhibition:**

  i. Diclofenac inhibits both COX-1 and COX-2 enzymes, though it has a slightly higher affinity for COX-2.

  ii. **COX-1 Inhibition:** Reduces the synthesis of prostaglandins that protect the gastric mucosa and are involved in platelet aggregation, leading to potential gastrointestinal side effects and bleeding risks.

  iii. **COX-2 Inhibition:** Reduces the production of prostaglandins that mediate inflammation, pain, and fever, providing its primary therapeutic effects.

2. Pharmacokinetics:

a. **Absorption:**

  i. Diclofenac is rapidly and completely absorbed after oral administration, with peak plasma concentrations typically occurring within 1-2 hours.

b. **Distribution:**

  i. It is extensively bound to plasma proteins (more than 99%) and is widely distributed throughout the body, including inflamed tissues.

c. **Metabolism:**

i. Diclofenac is metabolized primarily in the liver through cytochrome P450 enzymes, particularly CYP2C9, and undergoes extensive first-pass metabolism.

d. **Excretion:**

i. The drug and its metabolites are primarily excreted in the urine (about 65%) and bile (about 35%). The half-life of diclofenac is approximately 1-2 hours, but its effects can last longer due to accumulation in inflamed tissues.

3. Therapeutic Uses:

a. **Anti-Inflammatory:**

i. Commonly used to treat inflammatory conditions such as osteoarthritis, rheumatoid arthritis, and ankylosing spondylitis.

b. **Analgesic:**

i. Effective in managing acute pain, including postoperative pain, dental pain, and musculoskeletal pain.

c. **Antipyretic:**

i. Diclofenac is used to reduce fever, though this is not its primary indication.

4. Side Effects:

a. **Gastrointestinal:**

i. Common side effects include dyspepsia, nausea, vomiting, and a significant risk of gastrointestinal ulceration and bleeding, especially with long-term use.

b. **Cardiovascular:**

i. Increased risk of cardiovascular events, such as myocardial infarction and stroke, particularly with long-term use.

c. **Hepatic:**

i. Potential for hepatotoxicity, particularly with prolonged use or in patients with pre-existing liver conditions.

d. **Renal:**

   i. May cause renal impairment or exacerbate pre-existing kidney conditions due to its effects on renal blood flow.

e. **Dermatologic:**

   i. Rarely, diclofenac can cause photosensitivity reactions and skin rashes.

D. Celecoxib:

1. Mechanism of Action:

a. **Selective COX-2 Inhibition:**

   i. Celecoxib selectively inhibits the COX-2 enzyme, which is primarily expressed during inflammation and pain, thereby reducing the production of pro-inflammatory prostaglandins.

   ii. **Reduced COX-1 Activity:** Because celecoxib has minimal impact on COX-1, it has a lower risk of gastrointestinal side effects and does not significantly affect platelet function.

2. Pharmacokinetics:

a. **Absorption:**

   i. Celecoxib is well absorbed after oral administration, with peak plasma concentrations reached within 2-4 hours.

b. **Distribution:**

   i. It is highly protein-bound (approximately 97%) and is widely distributed throughout the body.

c. **Metabolism:**

   i. Celecoxib is metabolized in the liver primarily by the cytochrome P450 enzyme CYP2C9 to inactive metabolites.

d. **Excretion:**

   i. The drug and its metabolites are excreted primarily through the feces (57%) and urine (27%). The half-life of celecoxib is approximately 11 hours, allowing for once or twice-daily dosing.

3. Therapeutic Uses:

a. **Anti-Inflammatory:**

    i.   Used to treat chronic inflammatory conditions like osteoarthritis, rheumatoid arthritis, and ankylosing spondylitis.

b. **Analgesic:**

    i.   Effective in managing acute pain, including postoperative pain and menstrual pain.

c. **Fewer GI Complications:**

    i.   Due to its COX-2 selectivity, celecoxib is preferred in patients who require long-term NSAID therapy but are at risk for gastrointestinal complications.

4. Side Effects:

a. **Cardiovascular:**

    i.   Celecoxib is associated with an increased risk of cardiovascular events such as myocardial infarction and stroke, especially with long-term use or in patients with pre-existing cardiovascular conditions.

b. **Gastrointestinal:**

    i.   Compared to non-selective NSAIDs like diclofenac, celecoxib has a lower incidence of gastrointestinal side effects, though risks still exist, particularly at higher doses or with prolonged use.

c. **Renal:**

    i.   Similar to other NSAIDs, celecoxib may cause renal impairment, particularly in patients with pre-existing kidney conditions.

d. **Hepatic:**

    i.   Potential for hepatotoxicity, although this is less common.

e. **Allergic Reactions:**

    i.   Celecoxib contains a sulfonamide moiety, so patients with sulfonamide allergies may be at risk for allergic reactions, including skin rashes and, rarely, severe reactions like Stevens-Johnson syndrome.

Comparison of Diclofenac and Celecoxib:

a. **COX Selectivity:**

   i. Diclofenac is a non-selective COX inhibitor, while celecoxib is a selective COX-2 inhibitor.

b. **Gastrointestinal Tolerability:**

   i. Celecoxib has a better gastrointestinal safety profile due to its selectivity for COX-2, whereas diclofenac poses a higher risk of gastrointestinal complications.

c. **Cardiovascular Risk:**

   i. Both drugs are associated with cardiovascular risks, but the risks may be slightly different due to their COX selectivity.

d. **Use in Specific Populations:**

   i. Celecoxib is often preferred in patients who require long-term NSAID therapy and are at risk for gastrointestinal complications, while diclofenac may be chosen for its potent anti-inflammatory effects.

E. Allopurinol:

1. Mechanism of Action:

a. **Xanthine Oxidase Inhibition:**

   i. Allopurinol is a structural analog of hypoxanthine and acts as a competitive inhibitor of xanthine oxidase, an enzyme responsible for converting hypoxanthine to xanthine and xanthine to uric acid.

   ii. By inhibiting xanthine oxidase, allopurinol reduces the production of uric acid, leading to lower serum and urinary uric acid levels, which helps prevent gout attacks and complications such as urate nephropathy and tophi.

2. Pharmacokinetics:

a. **Absorption:**

    i. Allopurinol is well absorbed orally, with peak plasma concentrations occurring within 1-2 hours after administration.

b. **Distribution:**

    i. It is moderately bound to plasma proteins and is widely distributed throughout the body.

c. **Metabolism:**

    i. Allopurinol is metabolized in the liver to oxypurinol (also known as alloxanthine), an active metabolite that also inhibits xanthine oxidase.

d. **Excretion:**

    i. The drug and its metabolites are primarily excreted via the kidneys. Allopurinol has a short half-life of approximately 1-2 hours, but oxypurinol has a much longer half-life of 18-30 hours, allowing for sustained inhibition of xanthine oxidase.

3. Therapeutic Uses:

a. **Chronic Gout:**

    i. Allopurinol is used as a first-line treatment for the long-term management of chronic gout, particularly in patients with recurrent attacks, tophi, or urate nephropathy.

b. **Hyperuricemia:**

    i. It is also used to manage hyperuricemia in patients with conditions such as cancer undergoing chemotherapy, which can cause tumor lysis syndrome and lead to elevated uric acid levels.

4. Side Effects:

a. **Gastrointestinal:**

    i. Common side effects include nausea, diarrhea, and abdominal pain.

b. **Skin Reactions:**

i. Allopurinol can cause a range of skin reactions, from mild rashes to severe hypersensitivity reactions like Stevens-Johnson syndrome (SJS) and toxic epidermal necrolysis (TEN).

c. **Hepatotoxicity:**

i. Liver function abnormalities may occur, though this is rare.

d. **Renal:**

i. Patients with pre-existing renal impairment need dose adjustments due to the risk of drug accumulation.

e. **Hypersensitivity Syndrome:**

i. A rare but serious condition known as allopurinol hypersensitivity syndrome (AHS) can occur, characterized by fever, rash, eosinophilia, and multi-organ involvement.

F. Febuxostat:

1. Mechanism of Action:

a. **Selective Xanthine Oxidase Inhibition:**

i. Febuxostat is a non-purine selective inhibitor of xanthine oxidase. It inhibits both the oxidized and reduced forms of xanthine oxidase, effectively reducing uric acid production.

ii. Unlike allopurinol, febuxostat is more selective for xanthine oxidase and does not inhibit other enzymes involved in purine and pyrimidine metabolism, potentially leading to fewer off-target effects.

2. Pharmacokinetics:

a. **Absorption:**

i. Febuxostat is well absorbed after oral administration, with peak plasma levels occurring within 1-1.5 hours.

b. **Distribution:**

i. It is highly bound to plasma proteins (about 99%) and has a large volume of distribution.

c. **Metabolism:**

    i.   Febuxostat is extensively metabolized in the liver primarily by conjugation and oxidation via cytochrome P450 enzymes (CYP1A2, CYP2C8, and CYP2C9).

d. **Excretion:**

    i.   The drug is excreted through both renal and fecal routes. The half-life of febuxostat is approximately 5-8 hours, allowing for once-daily dosing.

3. Therapeutic Uses:

a. **Chronic Gout:**

    i.   Febuxostat is used for the long-term management of hyperuricemia in patients with chronic gout, especially in those who are intolerant to or inadequately treated with allopurinol.

b. **Hyperuricemia:**

    i.   It is also indicated for the management of hyperuricemia associated with gout, but it is not recommended for use in asymptomatic hyperuricemia.

4. Side Effects:

a. **Cardiovascular:**

    i.   Febuxostat has been associated with an increased risk of cardiovascular events such as myocardial infarction, stroke, and cardiovascular death, particularly in patients with pre-existing cardiovascular conditions.

b. **Liver Function Abnormalities:**

    i.   Elevations in liver enzymes may occur, so regular monitoring of liver function is recommended.

c. **Gastrointestinal:**

    i.   Common side effects include nausea, diarrhea, and abdominal pain.

d. **Skin Reactions:**

i. Similar to allopurinol, febuxostat can cause skin reactions, although severe reactions like SJS and TEN are less common.

e. **Arthralgia:**

i. Joint pain is a reported side effect in some patients.

Comparison of Allopurinol and Febuxostat:

a. **Mechanism of Action:**

i. Both drugs inhibit xanthine oxidase, but febuxostat is a more selective inhibitor, which may lead to a different side effect profile.

b. **Efficacy:**

i. Febuxostat may be more effective in lowering serum uric acid levels in some patients, particularly those who do not achieve target uric acid levels with allopurinol.

c. **Tolerability:**

i. Allopurinol has been associated with a broader range of hypersensitivity reactions, while febuxostat has raised concerns about cardiovascular safety.

d. **Dosing:**

i. Allopurinol requires dose adjustment in patients with renal impairment, whereas febuxostat does not require as significant dose adjustments for mild to moderate renal impairment.

e. **Cost:**

i. Allopurinol is generally less expensive and more widely available compared to febuxostat, which may influence treatment decisions.

G. Colchicine:

1. Mechanism of Action:

a. **Microtubule Inhibition:**

i. Colchicine works by binding to tubulin, a protein that is a key component of microtubules in cells. This binding disrupts microtubule polymerization, preventing the formation of microtubules.

    ii. By inhibiting microtubule formation, colchicine impairs the function of neutrophils, a type of white blood cell that plays a major role in the inflammatory response to uric acid crystals. Specifically, it inhibits neutrophil migration, chemotaxis, adhesion, and phagocytosis.

    iii. This reduction in neutrophil activity leads to decreased inflammation and pain during acute gout attacks.

2. Pharmacokinetics:

a. Absorption:

    i. Colchicine is rapidly absorbed from the gastrointestinal tract after oral administration. Peak plasma concentrations are usually reached within 0.5 to 2 hours.

b. Distribution:

    i. The drug is widely distributed throughout the body, including into leukocytes, where it exerts its anti-inflammatory effects. Colchicine is highly bound to plasma proteins.

c. Metabolism:

    i. Colchicine is metabolized primarily in the liver by the cytochrome P450 enzyme CYP3A4, and it undergoes significant enterohepatic recirculation.

d. Excretion:

    i. The drug and its metabolites are excreted mainly through the feces, with a smaller portion excreted in the urine. The half-life of colchicine ranges from 9 to 16 hours.

3. Therapeutic Uses:

a. Acute Gout Attacks:

i. Colchicine is used to relieve pain and inflammation in acute gout attacks. It is most effective when taken at the first sign of an attack.

b. **Prophylaxis:**

i. Colchicine is also used at low doses as a prophylactic treatment to prevent recurrent gout attacks, particularly during the initiation of urate-lowering therapy (e.g., allopurinol or febuxostat).

c. **Familial Mediterranean Fever:**

i. In addition to gout, colchicine is indicated for the prevention of acute attacks of familial Mediterranean fever (FMF).

4. Side Effects:

a. **Gastrointestinal:**

i. The most common side effects are gastrointestinal disturbances, including nausea, vomiting, diarrhea, and abdominal pain. These side effects are dose-dependent and may limit the use of colchicine.

b. **Hematologic:**

i. Prolonged use or high doses of colchicine can lead to bone marrow suppression, resulting in leukopenia, thrombocytopenia, and aplastic anemia.

c. **Neuromuscular:**

i. Myopathy and neuropathy are rare but serious side effects, particularly in patients with renal impairment or those taking concomitant medications that interact with colchicine.

d. **Toxicity:**

i. Colchicine has a narrow therapeutic index, and overdose can be fatal, leading to multi-organ failure and death.

H. Probenecid:

1. Mechanism of Action:

a. **Uricosuric Effect:**

i.   Probenecid is a uricosuric agent, meaning it increases the excretion of uric acid in the urine. It works by inhibiting the reabsorption of uric acid in the proximal tubules of the kidneys.

ii.   Specifically, probenecid blocks the urate transporter 1 (URAT1) and organic anion transporter (OAT) proteins, which are responsible for the reabsorption of uric acid from the urine back into the bloodstream.

iii.   By inhibiting these transporters, probenecid reduces serum uric acid levels and increases the clearance of uric acid, thus preventing the formation of uric acid crystals in joints and tissues.

2. Pharmacokinetics:

a. Absorption:

i.   Probenecid is well absorbed after oral administration, with peak plasma levels reached within 2-4 hours.

b. Distribution:

i.   The drug is highly protein-bound and has a large volume of distribution.

c. Metabolism:

i.   Probenecid is partially metabolized in the liver, and its metabolites are pharmacologically active.

d. Excretion:

i.   The drug and its metabolites are excreted primarily in the urine. Probenecid has a half-life of approximately 5-8 hours, depending on the dose.

3. Therapeutic Uses:

a. Chronic Gout:

i.   Probenecid is used in the long-term management of chronic gout in patients who have normal renal function and are under-excretors of uric acid.

b. **Prolongation of Antibiotic Action:**

  i.   Probenecid is also used to prolong the plasma levels and duration of action of certain antibiotics, such as penicillin and cephalosporins, by inhibiting their renal tubular secretion.

4. Side Effects:

a. **Gastrointestinal:**

  i.   Common side effects include gastrointestinal disturbances such as nausea, vomiting, and anorexia.

b. **Renal:**

  i.   Probenecid can cause kidney stones (uric acid nephrolithiasis) due to increased urinary uric acid excretion. Patients should be advised to drink plenty of fluids and alkalinize their urine to prevent stone formation.

c. **Hematologic:**

  i.   Hemolytic anemia may occur, particularly in patients with glucose-6-phosphate dehydrogenase (G6PD) deficiency.

d. **Hypersensitivity Reactions:**

  i.   Allergic reactions, including rash and anaphylaxis, have been reported.

e. **Drug Interactions:**

  i.   Probenecid can interact with a variety of drugs, including NSAIDs, antibiotics, and other gout medications, by altering their renal excretion.

Comparison of Colchicine and Probenecid:

a. **Mechanism of Action:**

  i.   Colchicine primarily acts by reducing inflammation during acute gout attacks, while Probenecid reduces serum uric acid levels by increasing uric acid excretion.

b. **Therapeutic Use:**

i. Colchicine is used for both acute attacks and prophylaxis of gout, whereas Probenecid is mainly used for the long-term management of hyperuricemia in gout.

c. **Side Effects:**

i. Colchicine's side effects are mainly gastrointestinal and hematologic, with the potential for severe toxicity, while Probenecid's side effects are largely renal and include the risk of kidney stones.

d. **Efficacy:**

i. Colchicine is effective in reducing inflammation during acute gout attacks, but it does not lower uric acid levels. Probenecid effectively lowers uric acid levels but is not used for acute inflammation.

I. Pegloticase:

1. Mechanism of Action:

a. **Pegylated Recombinant Uricase:**

i. Pegloticase is a pegylated form of recombinant uricase (also known as pegylated uricase), an enzyme that catalyzes the conversion of uric acid to allantoin.

ii. Allantoin is a more soluble and easily excreted metabolite compared to uric acid. By increasing the breakdown of uric acid to allantoin, Pegloticase effectively lowers serum uric acid levels.

iii. The pegylation process prolongs the half-life of the enzyme and reduces its immunogenicity, allowing for less frequent dosing.

2. Pharmacokinetics:

a. **Absorption:**

i. Pegloticase is administered intravenously. Its pharmacokinetics are influenced by its pegylated form, which extends its duration of action.

b. **Distribution:**

   i. The distribution of Pegloticase is limited to the bloodstream as it is not administered orally. It is distributed in the vascular compartment.

c. **Metabolism:**

   i. Pegloticase is metabolized in the liver and tissues by proteolytic enzymes. The pegylation extends the enzyme's activity and half-life, reducing the frequency of administration.

d. **Excretion:**

   i. The enzyme and its metabolites are primarily excreted via the kidneys. The half-life of Pegloticase is approximately 7 to 10 days, allowing for a biweekly dosing schedule.

3. **Therapeutic Uses:**

a. **Chronic Gout:**

   i. Pegloticase is indicated for the treatment of chronic gout in patients who have not responded adequately to conventional urate-lowering therapy (e.g., allopurinol or febuxostat) or who have severe, refractory gout.

b. **Refractory Gout:**

   i. It is particularly useful for patients with tophaceous gout, where uric acid crystals have formed deposits in tissues.

4. **Side Effects:**

a. **Allergic Reactions:**

   i. Infusion reactions are common, including symptoms such as rash, fever, and chills. Severe allergic reactions like anaphylaxis can occur.

b. **Gout Flare-ups:**

   i. Acute gout flares may occur during the initial treatment period, as the rapid reduction in uric acid levels can precipitate attacks.

c. **Urate Lowering:**

    i. While effective in lowering uric acid levels, Pegloticase can also lead to the development of antibodies against the enzyme, reducing its effectiveness over time.

d. **Renal:**

    i. Rarely, Pegloticase can cause renal impairment due to the rapid breakdown of uric acid.

J. Methylprednisolone:

1. Mechanism of Action:

a. **Glucocorticoid Receptor Agonist:**

    i. Methylprednisolone is a synthetic glucocorticoid that binds to glucocorticoid receptors in cells, resulting in anti-inflammatory and immunosuppressive effects.

    ii. It works by inhibiting the expression of inflammatory cytokines and enzymes involved in the inflammatory response, including phospholipase A2 and cyclooxygenase-2 (COX-2).

    iii. Additionally, methylprednisolone stabilizes cellular membranes and reduces capillary permeability, contributing to its anti-inflammatory effects.

2. Pharmacokinetics:

a. **Absorption:**

    i. Methylprednisolone is well absorbed from the gastrointestinal tract when taken orally. It can also be administered intramuscularly or intravenously for faster onset.

b. **Distribution:**

    i. It is widely distributed throughout the body and crosses the blood-brain barrier. The drug is highly bound to plasma proteins.

c. **Metabolism:**

i. Methylprednisolone is metabolized in the liver by the cytochrome P450 enzyme system, primarily to inactive metabolites.

d. **Excretion:**

i. The drug and its metabolites are excreted mainly via the kidneys. The half-life of methylprednisolone varies depending on the route of administration and dosage, ranging from 2 to 4 hours for oral forms to longer durations for depot injections.

3. Therapeutic Uses:

a. **Acute Gout Flares:**

i. Methylprednisolone is used for the management of acute gout attacks, particularly in patients who cannot tolerate NSAIDs or colchicine.

b. **Chronic Gout Management:**

i. It is used as a short-term intervention to control severe symptoms and inflammation during chronic gout or in cases of tophaceous gout.

c. **Other Conditions:**

i. Methylprednisolone is also used for various inflammatory and autoimmune conditions, including rheumatoid arthritis, lupus, and allergic reactions.

4. Side Effects:

a. **Gastrointestinal:**

i. Common side effects include gastrointestinal disturbances such as dyspepsia, nausea, and ulcers.

b. **Endocrine:**

i. Long-term use can lead to adrenal suppression, Cushing's syndrome, and osteoporosis.

c. **Metabolic:**

i. Weight gain, hyperglycemia, and increased risk of diabetes mellitus may occur.

d. **Infectious:**

i. Increased susceptibility to infections due to immunosuppressive effects.

e. **Psychiatric:**

i. Mood swings, insomnia, and, rarely, psychosis.

Comparison of Pegloticase and Methylprednisolone:

a. **Mechanism of Action:**

i. Pegloticase directly lowers uric acid levels by converting uric acid to allantoin, whereas Methylprednisolone works through anti-inflammatory and immunosuppressive effects.

b. **Therapeutic Use:**

i. Pegloticase is specifically used for chronic gout and refractory cases, while Methylprednisolone is used for managing acute inflammation and severe gout flares.

c. **Administration:**

i. Pegloticase is administered intravenously and has a long duration of action, while Methylprednisolone can be given orally, intramuscularly, or intravenously, depending on the clinical situation.

d. **Side Effects:**

i. Pegloticase can cause allergic reactions and acute gout flares, while Methylprednisolone has a broader range of side effects including metabolic, endocrine, and gastrointestinal issues.

K. Methotrexate:

1. Mechanism of Action:

a. **Antimetabolite:**

i. Methotrexate is a folate antagonist that inhibits the enzyme dihydrofolate reductase (DHFR), which is crucial for the synthesis of tetrahydrofolate. Tetrahydrofolate is essential for the synthesis of nucleic acids, including purines and thymidine.

ii. By inhibiting DHFR, methotrexate disrupts DNA and RNA synthesis, leading to decreased proliferation of rapidly dividing cells such as lymphocytes. This action contributes to its immunosuppressive effects.

b. **Anti-inflammatory Effects:**

i. Methotrexate also exerts anti-inflammatory effects by inhibiting the production of inflammatory cytokines and downregulating the expression of adhesion molecules on leukocytes.

2. Pharmacokinetics:

a. **Absorption:**

i. Methotrexate is well absorbed orally, but absorption can be variable. Intramuscular or subcutaneous routes can be used for better control of absorption.

b. **Distribution:**

i. The drug is widely distributed throughout the body and enters the central nervous system and other tissues. It is approximately 50% bound to plasma proteins.

c. **Metabolism:**

i. Methotrexate is metabolized in the liver to various metabolites, including the active metabolite 7-hydroxymethotrexate.

d. **Excretion:**

i. It is primarily excreted unchanged in the urine. The half-life of methotrexate is dose-dependent, ranging from 3 to 10 hours for low doses and longer for high doses.

3. Therapeutic Uses:

a. **Rheumatoid Arthritis:**

   i. Methotrexate is the first-line disease-modifying anti-rheumatic drug (DMARD) used in rheumatoid arthritis to reduce disease activity and prevent joint damage.

b. **Psoriasis:**

   i. It is used in the treatment of severe psoriasis due to its immunosuppressive effects.

c. **Other Conditions:**

   i. Methotrexate is also used in the treatment of certain cancers (e.g., leukemia, lymphoma) and other autoimmune diseases like systemic lupus erythematosus (SLE).

4. Side Effects:

a. **Hematologic:**

   i. Bone marrow suppression leading to anemia, leukopenia, and thrombocytopenia.

b. **Gastrointestinal:**

   i. Common side effects include nausea, vomiting, mucositis, and stomatitis.

c. **Hepatic:**

   i. Liver toxicity, including elevated liver enzymes and hepatic fibrosis with long-term use.

d. **Renal:**

   i. Risk of nephrotoxicity, particularly at high doses.

e. **Pulmonary:**

   i. Methotrexate can cause interstitial pneumonitis and pulmonary fibrosis.

L. Sulfasalazine:

1. Mechanism of Action:

a. **Sulfonamide and 5-Aminosalicylic Acid:**

i. Sulfasalazine is a prodrug that is metabolized in the colon to sulfapyridine and 5-aminosalicylic acid (5-ASA). Both metabolites contribute to its therapeutic effects.

b. **Anti-inflammatory Effects:**

i. 5-ASA has direct anti-inflammatory effects on the colonic mucosa, primarily by scavenging free radicals and inhibiting the production of inflammatory cytokines.

c. **Immunomodulatory Effects:**

i. Sulfapyridine, a metabolite, has immunosuppressive effects by inhibiting T-cell proliferation and altering the function of B-cells.

2. **Pharmacokinetics:**

a. **Absorption:**

i. Sulfasalazine itself is not well absorbed from the gastrointestinal tract. It is primarily broken down into its active metabolites within the colon.

b. **Distribution:**

i. The metabolites, sulfapyridine and 5-ASA, are distributed throughout the body. Sulfapyridine is more widely distributed, whereas 5-ASA acts locally in the gut.

c. **Metabolism:**

i. Sulfasalazine is metabolized in the colon by intestinal bacteria. Sulfapyridine and 5-ASA are absorbed and further metabolized in the liver.

d. **Excretion:**

i. Both sulfapyridine and 5-ASA are excreted in the urine. The half-life of sulfapyridine is approximately 6 hours, while 5-ASA has a half-life of about 6 to 8 hours.

3. **Therapeutic Uses:**

a. **Rheumatoid Arthritis:**

i. Sulfasalazine is used as a DMARD for the treatment of rheumatoid arthritis, particularly in patients who cannot tolerate methotrexate.

b. **Inflammatory Bowel Disease (IBD):**

i. It is effective in the treatment of ulcerative colitis and, to a lesser extent, Crohn's disease due to its local anti-inflammatory effects in the colon.

c. **Other Conditions:**

i. Sulfasalazine is sometimes used off-label for other autoimmune conditions, such as ankylosing spondylitis.

4. Side Effects:

a. **Gastrointestinal:**

i. Common side effects include nausea, vomiting, abdominal pain, and diarrhea.

b. **Hematologic:**

i. Can cause bone marrow suppression, leading to anemia, leukopenia, and thrombocytopenia.

c. **Dermatologic:**

i. Rash and hypersensitivity reactions, including Steven-Johnson syndrome, have been reported.

d. **Hepatic:**

i. Liver toxicity, including elevated liver enzymes and hepatic dysfunction.

e. **Renal:**

i. Rarely, sulfasalazine can cause renal impairment or crystalluria.

Comparison of Methotrexate and Sulfasalazine:

a. **Mechanism of Action:**

i. Methotrexate is a folate antagonist with broad immunosuppressive effects, while Sulfasalazine has a dual mechanism involving anti-inflammatory effects in the gut and immunosuppressive effects through its metabolites.

b. **Therapeutic Use:**

   i.   Methotrexate is a first-line DMARD for rheumatoid arthritis and is also used for psoriasis and certain cancers. Sulfasalazine is primarily used for rheumatoid arthritis and inflammatory bowel diseases.

c. **Side Effects:**

   i.   Methotrexate is associated with significant hematologic and hepatic toxicity, while Sulfasalazine's side effects are primarily gastrointestinal and dermatologic.

d. **Administration:**

   i.   Methotrexate is administered orally or parenterally, whereas Sulfasalazine is typically administered orally.

Multiple Choice Questions (MCQs)

1. Which serotonin receptor is primarily involved in the regulation of mood and anxiety?

   a) 5-HT1

   b) 5-HT2

   c) 5-HT3

   d) 5-HT4

2. Which drug is a selective serotonin reuptake inhibitor (SSRI) commonly used to treat depression?

   a) Fluoxetine

   b) Amitriptyline

   c) Sertraline

   d) Diazepam

3. Which of the following is a kinin receptor antagonist used in the treatment of hereditary angioedema?

   a) Icatibant

   b) Losartan

   c) Celecoxib

   d) Sumatriptan

4. Which enzyme is inhibited by NSAIDs to reduce inflammation?

   a) Cyclooxygenase (COX)

   b) Lipoxygenase

   c) Phospholipase A2

   d) Thromboxane synthase

5. Which NSAID is known for its selective inhibition of COX-2?

   a) Aspirin

   b) Naproxen

   c) Ibuprofen

   d) Celecoxib

6. Which drug is used in the long-term management of chronic gout by inhibiting xanthine oxidase?

   a) Colchicine

   b) Indomethacin

   c) Allopurinol

   d) Probenecid

7. Which drug class does methotrexate belong to?

   a) NSAIDs

   b) Biologic DMARDs

   c) Conventional synthetic DMARDs

   d) Glucocorticoids

8. What is the primary mechanism of action of colchicine in treating acute gout?

a) Inhibits xanthine oxidase

b) Inhibits microtubule formation

c) Blocks cyclooxygenase enzymes

d) Increases uric acid excretion

9. Which biologic DMARD targets tumor necrosis factor (TNF) in the treatment of rheumatoid arthritis?

a) Tocilizumab

b) Rituximab

c) Etanercept

d) Abatacept

10. Which drug is used to convert uric acid to allantoin in the management of refractory gout?

a) Febuxostat

b) Pegloticase

c) Lesinurad

d) Methylprednisolone

11. Which enzyme is primarily responsible for the metabolism of ibuprofen?

a) CYP1A2

b) CYP2C9

c) CYP3A4

d) CYP2D6

12. What is the main adverse effect of long-term NSAID use related to the gastrointestinal system?

a) Peptic ulceration

b) Renal impairment

c) Hepatotoxicity

d) Hypertension

13. Which drug is a leukotriene receptor antagonist used in the management of asthma?

a) Montelukast

b) Celecoxib

c) Aspirin

d) Ibuprofen

14. Which serotonin receptor is primarily involved in the treatment of migraine?

a) 5-HT1

b) 5-HT2

c) 5-HT3

d) 5-HT4

15. Which kinin is most associated with pain and inflammation?

a) Angiotensin II

b) Bradykinin

c) Substance P

d) Serotonin

16. Which drug is a uricosuric agent that increases uric acid excretion?

a) Allopurinol

b) Febuxostat

c) Probenecid

d) Colchicine

17. Which prostaglandin analogue is used to protect the gastric mucosa?

a) Misoprostol

b) Latanoprost

c) Aspirin

d) Ibuprofen

18. Which class of drugs is primarily used to inhibit TNF-α in rheumatoid arthritis?

a) NSAIDs

b) Biologic DMARDs

c) Glucocorticoids

d) Conventional DMARDs

19. Which NSAID has a prolonged half-life, allowing for twice-daily dosing?

    a) Ibuprofen

    b) Naproxen

    c) Diclofenac

    d) Celecoxib

20. Which drug is a selective inhibitor of the enzyme xanthine oxidase and is used to treat gout?

    a) Colchicine

    b) Allopurinol

    c) Probenecid

    d) Pegloticase

Short Answer Questions (SAQs)

1. What is the role of serotonin in mood regulation, and how do SSRIs affect this process?

2. Explain the mechanism of action of ibuprofen in reducing inflammation.

3. Describe the clinical uses of colchicine in the management of gout.

4. What are the common side effects associated with long-term NSAID use?

5. How does methotrexate help in the treatment of rheumatoid arthritis?

6. Discuss the therapeutic applications of kinin receptor antagonists.

7. What is the significance of COX-2 selectivity in NSAIDs like celecoxib?

8. How does pegloticase work in the management of refractory gout?

9. What are the pharmacokinetic properties of allopurinol that contribute to its effectiveness in gout management?

10. Explain the role of TNF inhibitors in the treatment of rheumatoid arthritis.

11. How does probenecid increase uric acid excretion in patients with gout?

12. What are the advantages and risks of using biologic DMARDs in rheumatoid arthritis?

13. Discuss the use of leukotriene receptor antagonists in asthma management.

14. How does colchicine inhibit inflammation during an acute gout attack?

15. Explain the potential cardiovascular risks associated with COX-2 inhibitors.

16. What is the role of bradykinin in inflammation and pain?

17. How does misoprostol help in preventing NSAID-induced gastric ulcers?

18. What are the differences between allopurinol and febuxostat in managing hyperuricemia?

19. Discuss the role of serotonin receptor modulators in the treatment of migraines.

20. What are the common drug interactions associated with NSAIDs?

Long Answer Questions (LAQs)

1. Discuss the classification, mechanisms of action, and clinical applications of NSAIDs, with a focus on their role in managing inflammation, pain, and fever.

2. Explain the pharmacological management of gout, including the roles of colchicine, allopurinol, febuxostat, and uricosuric agents.

3. Describe the use of DMARDs in the treatment of rheumatoid arthritis, including conventional synthetic, biologic, and targeted synthetic DMARDs.

4. Discuss the role of serotonin in the central nervous system and the therapeutic implications of drugs that modulate serotonin pathways, including SSRIs and receptor antagonists.

5. Explain the mechanisms of action, therapeutic uses, and side effects of prostaglandin analogues in clinical practice.

6. Discuss the therapeutic applications and risks associated with COX-2 selective inhibitors in the management of pain and inflammation.

7. Describe the pharmacology of biologic DMARDs, including TNF inhibitors, IL-1 inhibitors, and IL-6 inhibitors, in the treatment of autoimmune diseases.

8. Explain the role of pegloticase in the management of refractory gout and compare it with other urate-lowering therapies.

9. Discuss the pharmacological actions of kinins, including bradykinin, and their role in inflammatory and cardiovascular diseases.

10. Describe the pharmacokinetics, mechanisms of action, and clinical applications of methotrexate in the treatment of autoimmune diseases and cancer.

Answer Key for MCQs

1. a) 5-HT1
2. a) Fluoxetine
3. a) Icatibant
4. a) Cyclooxygenase (COX)
5. d) Celecoxib
6. c) Allopurinol
7. c) Conventional synthetic DMARDs
8. b) Inhibits microtubule formation
9. c) Etanercept
10. b) Pegloticase
11. b) CYP2C9
12. a) Peptic ulceration
13. a) Montelukast
14. a) 5-HT1
15. b) Bradykinin
16. c) Probenecid
17. a) Misoprostol
18. b) Biologic DMARDs
19. b) Naproxen
20. b) Allopurinol

CHAPTER – 7

PHARMACOLOGY OF DRUGS ACTING ON ENDOCRINE SYSTEM–I

INTRODUCTION:

The endocrine system plays a critical role in maintaining homeostasis by regulating various physiological processes through hormone secretion. Drugs targeting the endocrine system can be broadly classified into those affecting the hypothalamic-pituitary-adrenal (HPA) axis, thyroid gland, and reproductive hormones. Here's a detailed introduction to these drugs:

1. Hypothalamic-Pituitary-Adrenal (HPA) Axis Drugs:

Glucocorticoids:

Mechanism of Action: Glucocorticoids bind to the glucocorticoid receptor, influencing gene expression to exert anti-inflammatory and immunosuppressive effects.

a. **Examples:** Hydrocortisone, Prednisolone, Dexamethasone, Betamethasone.

b. **Uses:** Treatment of inflammatory conditions, autoimmune disorders, and adrenal insufficiency.

c. **Adverse Effects:** Long-term use can lead to osteoporosis, hyperglycemia, and adrenal suppression.

Mineralocorticoids:

a. **Mechanism of Action:** Mineralocorticoids bind to the mineralocorticoid receptor, affecting electrolyte balance and blood pressure.

b. **Example:** Fludrocortisone.

c. **Uses:** Management of adrenal insufficiency and orthostatic hypotension.

d. **Adverse Effects:** Sodium retention, hypertension, and hypokalemia.

2. Thyroid Hormone Drugs:

Thyroid Hormones:

a. **Mechanism of Action:** Thyroid hormones (T3 and T4) bind to nuclear receptors, affecting transcription and influencing metabolism.

b. **Examples:** Levothyroxine (L-T4), Liothyronine (L-T3).

c. **Uses:** Replacement therapy in hypothyroidism and to manage certain types of thyroid cancer.

d. **Adverse Effects:** Hyperthyroidism symptoms such as tachycardia, weight loss, and tremors.

Antithyroid Drugs:

a. **Mechanism of Action:** These drugs inhibit thyroid hormone synthesis by blocking the enzyme thyroid peroxidase.

b. **Examples:** Methimazole, Propylthiouracil (PTU).

c. **Uses:** Treatment of hyperthyroidism and Graves' disease.

d. **Adverse Effects:** Agranulocytosis, liver toxicity, and rash.

3. Reproductive Hormone Drugs:

Estrogens:

a. **Mechanism of Action:** Estrogens bind to estrogen receptors, influencing reproductive tissue development and maintaining bone density.

b. **Examples:** Ethinyl estradiol, Estradiol.

c. **Uses:** Hormone replacement therapy, contraception, and treatment of menopausal symptoms.

d. **Adverse Effects:** Increased risk of thromboembolism, breast tenderness, and nausea.

Progestogens:

a. **Mechanism of Action:** Progestogens bind to progesterone receptors, regulating menstrual cycles and maintaining pregnancy.

b. **Examples:** Progesterone, Norgestrel, Levonorgestrel.

c. **Uses:** Contraception, management of menstrual disorders, and hormone replacement therapy.

d. **Adverse Effects:** Weight gain, mood changes, and breakthrough bleeding.

Antiandrogens:

a. **Mechanism of Action:** Antiandrogens block the effects of androgens by binding to androgen receptors.

b. **Examples:** Finasteride, Spironolactone.

c. **Uses:** Treatment of conditions like benign prostatic hyperplasia (BPH) and androgenic alopecia.

d. **Adverse Effects:** Sexual dysfunction, gynecomastia, and liver function alterations.

BASIC CONCEPTS IN ENDOCRINE PHARMACOLOGY

Endocrine pharmacology focuses on how drugs interact with the endocrine system, which regulates various physiological processes through hormone release. Here are the fundamental concepts:

1. Hormone Receptors and Signal Transduction

a. **Receptor Types:**

   i. **Cell-Surface Receptors:** These include G-protein-coupled receptors (GPCRs), receptor tyrosine kinases (RTKs), and ion channel receptors. They mediate the effects of hormones like insulin and adrenaline.

   ii. **Intracellular Receptors:** These include nuclear hormone receptors (e.g., steroid hormone receptors) that directly interact with DNA to influence gene expression.

b. **Signal Transduction Pathways:**

   i. **cAMP Pathway:** Involves GPCRs and adenylyl cyclase, leading to increased cyclic AMP (cAMP) and activation of protein kinase A (PKA).

ii. **Phosphatidylinositol (PI) Pathway:** Involves phospholipase C, leading to the production of inositol triphosphate (IP3) and diacylglycerol (DAG), which activate protein kinase C (PKC).

iii. **Receptor Tyrosine Kinase Pathway:** Involves autophosphorylation of tyrosine residues on the receptor, activating downstream signaling pathways like the MAPK pathway.

2. Hormone Mechanisms of Action

a. **Endocrine Action:** Hormones are released into the bloodstream and act on distant target organs. For example, thyroid hormones influence metabolic rate in various tissues.

b. **Paracrine Action:** Hormones act locally on adjacent cells. For instance, local growth factors influence nearby cells' behavior.

c. **Autocrine Action:** Hormones act on the same cell that produced them. For example, certain growth factors act on the cells that secrete them.

3. Pharmacokinetics and Pharmacodynamics of Hormone Drugs

a. **Absorption:** Hormones can be administered orally, parenterally (injections), or transdermally. For example, thyroid hormones are often administered orally, while insulin is injected.

b. **Distribution:** Hormones are distributed in the blood and tissues. Many hormones are bound to plasma proteins (e.g., thyroid hormones bound to thyroid-binding globulin).

c. **Metabolism:** Hormones are metabolized primarily in the liver and kidneys. For instance, corticosteroids are metabolized in the liver before excretion.

d. **Excretion:** Hormones are excreted in urine or feces. For example, estrogens are metabolized and excreted in urine.

4. Endocrine Disorders and Pharmacotherapy

a. **Hypothyroidism:** Treated with thyroid hormone replacements like levothyroxine.

b. **Hyperthyroidism:** Managed with antithyroid drugs like methimazole or propylthiouracil.

c. **Adrenal Insufficiency:** Treated with glucocorticoids such as hydrocortisone or prednisolone.

d. **Diabetes Mellitus:** Managed with insulin or oral hypoglycemics like metformin.

5. Drug Interactions and Side Effects

a. **Drug Interactions:** Hormone drugs can interact with other medications, affecting their efficacy. For example, corticosteroids can alter the metabolism of other drugs.

b. **Side Effects:** Each hormone drug class has specific side effects. For instance, glucocorticoids can lead to osteoporosis, while thyroid hormones can cause hyperthyroidism symptoms if overdosed.

ANTERIOR PITUITARY HORMONES

The anterior pituitary gland secretes several key hormones that regulate various physiological processes. Here's a detailed look at the analogues and inhibitors of these hormones:

1. Growth Hormone (GH) and Its Analogues

a. **Growth Hormone (GH):** Stimulates growth and cell reproduction by promoting protein synthesis and cell division.

    i. **Analogues:**

    1. **Somatropin:** Recombinant human GH used for growth hormone deficiency in children and adults. It mimics the action of endogenous GH.

    2. **Somatrem:** Similar to somatropin, but differs slightly in its amino acid sequence. Used for the same indications as somatropin.

    ii. **Inhibitors:**

1. **Octreotide:** A somatostatin analogue that inhibits GH secretion. Used to manage acromegaly (excess GH production) and certain types of neuroendocrine tumors.

2. **Lanreotide:** Another somatostatin analogue with similar effects as octreotide, used in acromegaly and neuroendocrine tumors.

2. Adrenocorticotropic Hormone (ACTH) and Its Analogues

a. **Adrenocorticotropic Hormone (ACTH):** Stimulates the adrenal cortex to produce cortisol and other adrenal steroids.

    i. **Analogues:**

        1. **Cosyntropin:** A synthetic form of ACTH used for diagnostic purposes in assessing adrenal gland function. It stimulates cortisol release in response to ACTH.

    ii. **Inhibitors:**

        1. **Metyrapone:** Inhibits cortisol synthesis by blocking 11β-hydroxylase, used in the diagnosis and treatment of Cushing's syndrome.

        2. **Ketoconazole:** An antifungal agent that also inhibits adrenal steroid synthesis, used in the treatment of Cushing's syndrome.

        3. **Etomidate:** An anesthetic agent that inhibits adrenal steroid synthesis, used in the acute management of severe Cushing's syndrome.

3. Thyroid-Stimulating Hormone (TSH) and Its Analogues

a. **Thyroid-Stimulating Hormone (TSH):** Stimulates the thyroid gland to produce thyroid hormones (T3 and T4).

    i. **Analogues:**

        1. **Thyrotropin Alfa:** A recombinant form of TSH used as an adjunct in the diagnosis of thyroid cancer and to stimulate iodine uptake in thyroid scans.

ii. **Inhibitors:**

1. **No direct TSH inhibitors** are used clinically; however, drugs affecting thyroid hormone synthesis or action (e.g., antithyroid drugs like methimazole) can indirectly influence TSH levels by altering thyroid hormone feedback.

4. Follicle-Stimulating Hormone (FSH) and Luteinizing Hormone (LH) Analogues

a. **Follicle-Stimulating Hormone (FSH):** Stimulates follicle development in females and spermatogenesis in males.

b. **Luteinizing Hormone (LH):** Triggers ovulation in females and testosterone production in males.

i. **Analogues:**

1. **Follitropin Alfa and Beta (rFSH):** Recombinant FSH used in assisted reproductive technologies (ART) to stimulate follicle development.

2. **Lutropin Alfa (rLH):** Recombinant LH used in combination with FSH in ART for stimulating gonadal function.

3. **Menotropins (hMG):** Contain both FSH and LH, used in ART for stimulating follicle development and ovulation.

ii. **Inhibitors:**

1. **GnRH Analogues:**

a. **GnRH Agonists:** Initially stimulate FSH and LH release but eventually cause downregulation of GnRH receptors, reducing gonadotropin release. Examples include leuprolide and goserelin, used in treating hormone-dependent cancers and endometriosis.

b. **GnRH Antagonists:** Directly inhibit FSH and LH secretion by preventing GnRH receptor activation.

Examples include cetrorelix and ganirelix, used in ART to prevent premature ovulation.

5. Prolactin (PRL) and Its Analogues

a. **Prolactin (PRL):** Stimulates milk production in the postpartum period.

   i. **Analogues:**

     1. **No direct prolactin analogues** are used clinically, but **dopamine agonists** are used to reduce prolactin levels.

   ii. **Inhibitors:**

     1. **Dopamine Agonists:**

       a. **Cabergoline:** A potent dopamine agonist used to treat hyperprolactinemia (excess prolactin) and prolactinomas.

       b. **Bromocriptine:** Another dopamine agonist used to treat hyperprolactinemia and prolactin-secreting tumors.

THYROID HORMONES

Thyroid hormones are critical for regulating metabolism, growth, and development. They include thyroxine (T4) and triiodothyronine (T3). Here's a detailed look at the analogues and inhibitors of thyroid hormones:

1. Thyroid Hormone Analogues

a. Thyroxine (T4) Analogues:

   i. **Levothyroxine (L-T4):** The most commonly used thyroid hormone replacement therapy. It is a synthetic form of T4 and is converted to the active form, T3, in the body.

     1. **Uses:** Treats hypothyroidism and goiter, and is used as an adjunctive therapy in thyroid cancer.

     2. **Formulations:** Available in various dosages, commonly administered orally.

b. Triiodothyronine (T3) Analogues:

i. **Liothyronine (L-T3):** A synthetic form of T3, the active thyroid hormone.

   1. **Uses:** Used in cases where a more rapid onset of thyroid hormone action is needed or when patients cannot convert T4 to T3 effectively. Often used in combination with L-T4.
   2. **Formulations:** Available in oral tablets.

c. Combination Thyroid Hormones:

i. **Thyroid USP:** Contains both T4 and T3 derived from desiccated porcine thyroid gland. It is used as an alternative to synthetic hormones.

   1. **Uses:** Used for hypothyroidism in patients who may prefer natural products or when T4 alone is insufficient.
   2. **Formulations:** Available in tablet form.

2. Thyroid Hormone Inhibitors

a. Antithyroid Drugs:

i. **Thionamides:** These drugs inhibit the synthesis of thyroid hormones by blocking the enzyme thyroid peroxidase, which is involved in iodine incorporation into thyroid hormones.

   1. **Methimazole:**
      1. **Mechanism:** Inhibits thyroid peroxidase, reducing the production of T4 and T3.
      2. **Uses:** Primarily used in the treatment of hyperthyroidism and Graves' disease.
      3. **Adverse Effects:** Can include rash, agranulocytosis, and liver toxicity.
   2. **Propylthiouracil (PTU):**
      1. **Mechanism:** Inhibits thyroid peroxidase and also blocks peripheral conversion of T4 to T3.

2. **Uses:** Used for hyperthyroidism, especially in pregnant women or those who cannot tolerate methimazole.

3. **Adverse Effects:** Includes rash, agranulocytosis, and severe liver damage (hepatitis).

b. Iodine-Based Treatments:

i. **Radioactive Iodine (I-131):**

1. **Mechanism:** Radioactive iodine is taken up by the thyroid gland, where it emits radiation that destroys thyroid cells, reducing thyroid hormone production.

2. **Uses:** Effective for treating hyperthyroidism and certain types of thyroid cancer.

3. **Adverse Effects:** Can cause hypothyroidism and require lifelong thyroid hormone replacement.

ii. **Iodine Solutions (Lugol's Solution, Potassium Iodide):**

1. **Mechanism:** High doses of iodine inhibit thyroid hormone release by the Wolff-Chaikoff effect and reduce thyroid gland vascularity.

2. **Uses:** Used preoperatively to reduce thyroid gland size and vascularity, and in thyroid storm management.

3. **Adverse Effects:** Includes allergic reactions, rash, and iodine toxicity.

c. Non-Iodine Inhibitors:

i. **Lithium:**

1. **Mechanism:** Interferes with thyroid hormone release and can inhibit thyroid hormone synthesis.

2. **Uses:** Sometimes used in conjunction with other therapies for hyperthyroidism.

3. **Adverse Effects:** Can lead to hypothyroidism, especially with long-term use.

d. Other Therapies:

   i.   **Beta-Blockers (e.g., Propranolol):**

      1. **Mechanism:** While not direct inhibitors of thyroid hormone synthesis, beta-blockers can alleviate symptoms of hyperthyroidism such as tachycardia and tremors.

      2. **Uses:** Often used as adjunctive treatment in hyperthyroidism to control symptoms.

HORMONES REGULATING PLASMA CALCIUM LEVEL

Several hormones play crucial roles in regulating plasma calcium levels, including parathyroid hormone (PTH), calcitonin, vitamin D, and insulin. Here's a detailed look at each of these hormones and their pharmacological aspects:

1. Parathyroid Hormone (PTH)

  a. **Production and Regulation:**

     i.   Produced by the parathyroid glands.

     ii. Released in response to low plasma calcium levels.

    iii. Acts to increase plasma calcium through various mechanisms.

  b. **Mechanism of Action:**

     i.   **Bone:** Stimulates osteoclast activity, leading to increased bone resorption and release of calcium and phosphate into the bloodstream.

     ii. **Kidneys:** Enhances calcium reabsorption in the renal tubules and increases phosphate excretion.

    iii. **Intestines:** Indirectly increases intestinal calcium absorption by stimulating the conversion of vitamin D to its active form (calcitriol).

  c. **Pharmacological Agents:**

    i.   **Teriparatide:** A recombinant form of PTH (PTH 1-34) used to treat osteoporosis. It stimulates new bone formation and increases bone density.

        1. **Uses:** Osteoporosis, especially in patients who are at high risk of fractures.

        2. **Adverse Effects:** Potential for osteosarcoma, dizziness, and leg cramps.

    ii. **Abaloparatide:** Another PTH analogue used for osteoporosis, similar to teriparatide but with slight variations in its amino acid sequence.

        1. **Uses:** Treatment of osteoporosis in postmenopausal women.

        2. **Adverse Effects:** Similar to teriparatide, including nausea, headache, and dizziness.

2. Calcitonin

a. **Production and Regulation:**

    i.   Produced by parafollicular cells (C cells) of the thyroid gland.

    ii. Released in response to high plasma calcium levels.

b. **Mechanism of Action:**

    i.   **Bone:** Inhibits osteoclast activity, reducing bone resorption and decreasing plasma calcium levels.

    ii. **Kidneys:** Increases renal excretion of calcium and phosphate.

c. **Pharmacological Agents:**

    i.   **Calcitonin-Salmon:** A synthetic form of calcitonin derived from salmon, which has a longer half-life and greater potency than human calcitonin.

        1. **Uses:** Treatment of osteoporosis, Paget's disease, and hypercalcemia.

        2. **Adverse Effects:** Nausea, flushing, and injection site reactions.

ii. **Calcitonin (Human):** Less commonly used due to shorter duration of action and lower efficacy compared to salmon calcitonin.

3. Vitamin D

a. **Production and Regulation:**

  i. **Vitamin D3 (Cholecalciferol):** Synthesized in the skin in response to sunlight and obtained from the diet.

  ii. **Vitamin D2 (Ergocalciferol):** Obtained from dietary sources and supplements.

  iii. **Activation:** Converted to its active form, calcitriol (1,25-dihydroxyvitamin D), in the liver and kidneys.

b. **Mechanism of Action:**

  i. **Intestines:** Increases the absorption of calcium and phosphate from the gut.

  ii. **Bone:** Works with PTH to mobilize calcium from the bone.

  iii. **Kidneys:** Enhances renal reabsorption of calcium and phosphate.

c. **Pharmacological Agents:**

  i. **Calcitriol:** The active form of vitamin D used in the treatment of vitamin D deficiency and related conditions.

    1. **Uses:** Osteoporosis, rickets, and chronic kidney disease.

    2. **Adverse Effects:** Hypercalcemia, hyperphosphatemia, and gastrointestinal disturbances.

  ii. **Cholecalciferol and Ergocalciferol:** Used as vitamin D supplements to treat or prevent deficiency.

    1. **Uses:** Supplementation for vitamin D deficiency, osteoporosis, and bone health.

    2. **Adverse Effects:** Generally well-tolerated; high doses may cause hypercalcemia and hyperphosphatemia.

4. Insulin

a. **Production and Regulation:**

i. Produced by beta cells of the pancreas.

ii. Regulates blood glucose levels and indirectly influences calcium metabolism.

b. **Mechanism of Action:**

i. **Glucose Metabolism:** Promotes glucose uptake into cells, thereby lowering blood glucose levels.

ii. **Calcium Metabolism:** Although insulin primarily regulates glucose, it has secondary effects on calcium metabolism, including effects on bone mineralization.

c. **Pharmacological Agents:**

i. **Insulin Preparations:**

1. **Rapid-Acting Insulins:** Lispro, Aspart, and Glulisine. Used for postprandial glucose control.

2. **Short-Acting Insulin:** Regular insulin. Used for mealtime glucose control.

3. **Intermediate-Acting Insulin:** NPH insulin. Used for basal glucose control.

4. **Long-Acting Insulin:** Glargine, Detemir. Used for stable, long-term glucose control.

5. **Uses:** Management of diabetes mellitus to control blood glucose levels.

6. **Adverse Effects:** Hypoglycemia, weight gain, and potential effects on bone mineral density with long-term use.

ORAL HYPOGLYCEMIC AGENTS AND GLUCAGON

Managing diabetes mellitus involves various therapeutic approaches, including the use of oral hypoglycemic agents for type 2 diabetes and glucagon for emergency treatment of hypoglycemia. Here's a detailed look at these therapies:

1. Oral Hypoglycemic Agents

Oral hypoglycemic agents are used to lower blood glucose levels in patients with type 2 diabetes. They work through various mechanisms, and several classes of these drugs are available:

a. Biguanides

  i. **Metformin:**

    1. **Mechanism of Action:** Decreases hepatic glucose production, enhances insulin sensitivity, and improves peripheral glucose uptake.

    2. **Uses:** First-line treatment for type 2 diabetes. Often used in combination with other agents for better glycemic control.

    3. **Adverse Effects:** Gastrointestinal issues (e.g., nausea, diarrhea), lactic acidosis (rare but serious).

b. Sulfonylureas

  i. **Examples:** Glipizide, Glyburide, Glimepiride.

    1. **Mechanism of Action:** Stimulate insulin release from pancreatic beta cells by closing ATP-sensitive potassium channels.

    2. **Uses:** Used for type 2 diabetes to lower blood glucose levels.

    3. **Adverse Effects:** Hypoglycemia, weight gain, and possible allergic reactions.

c. Meglitinides

  i. **Examples:** Repaglinide, Nateglinide.

    1. **Mechanism of Action:** Stimulate rapid and short-lived insulin secretion from pancreatic beta cells.

    2. **Uses:** Useful for postprandial glucose control.

    3. **Adverse Effects:** Hypoglycemia, weight gain.

d. Thiazolidinediones (TZDs)

  i. **Examples:** Pioglitazone, Rosiglitazone.

1. **Mechanism of Action:** Enhance insulin sensitivity in peripheral tissues by activating peroxisome proliferator-activated receptor gamma (PPAR-γ).

2. **Uses:** Improve insulin sensitivity in type 2 diabetes.

3. **Adverse Effects:** Weight gain, edema, potential for heart failure, and increased risk of bone fractures.

e. Dipeptidyl Peptidase-4 (DPP-4) Inhibitors

i. **Examples:** Sitagliptin, Saxagliptin, Linagliptin.

1. **Mechanism of Action:** Inhibit the enzyme DPP-4, which prolongs the action of incretin hormones (e.g., GLP-1), enhancing insulin secretion and reducing glucagon levels.

2. **Uses:** Type 2 diabetes, often used in combination with other agents.

3. **Adverse Effects:** Upper respiratory infections, headache, and potential risk of pancreatitis.

f. Sodium-Glucose Co-Transporter 2 (SGLT2) Inhibitors

i. **Examples:** Canagliflozin, Dapagliflozin, Empagliflozin.

1. **Mechanism of Action:** Inhibit SGLT2 in the renal proximal tubule, reducing glucose reabsorption and increasing glucose excretion in the urine.

2. **Uses:** Type 2 diabetes, with benefits including weight loss and blood pressure reduction.

3. **Adverse Effects:** Genital infections, urinary tract infections, and risk of diabetic ketoacidosis.

g. Alpha-Glucosidase Inhibitors

i. **Examples:** Acarbose, Miglitol.

1. **Mechanism of Action:** Inhibit enzymes that break down carbohydrates in the intestines, delaying carbohydrate absorption and reducing postprandial glucose spikes.

2. **Uses:** Type 2 diabetes, particularly useful in managing postprandial hyperglycemia.

3. **Adverse Effects:** Gastrointestinal issues, such as flatulence, diarrhea, and abdominal pain.

h. Bile Acid Sequestrants

i. **Example:** Colesevelam.

1. **Mechanism of Action:** Binds bile acids in the gut, leading to increased bile acid excretion and decreased hepatic glucose production.

2. **Uses:** Type 2 diabetes, used as an adjunct therapy.

3. **Adverse Effects:** Gastrointestinal symptoms, including constipation and bloating.

2. Glucagon

a. **Production and Regulation:**

i. Produced by alpha cells of the pancreas.

ii. Released in response to low blood glucose levels to increase glucose availability.

b. **Mechanism of Action:**

i. **Liver:** Stimulates glycogenolysis and gluconeogenesis, leading to increased blood glucose levels.

ii. **Other Tissues:** Reduces glucose uptake by peripheral tissues, further contributing to increased blood glucose levels.

c. **Pharmacological Agents:**

i. **Glucagon (Injectable Form):**

1. **Uses:** Emergency treatment for severe hypoglycemia, especially in diabetic patients who cannot consume glucose orally.

2. **Administration:** Administered intramuscularly or subcutaneously.

3. **Adverse Effects:** Nausea, vomiting, and allergic reactions.

d. **Glucagon-like Peptide-1 (GLP-1) Agonists:**

    i. **Examples:** Exenatide, Liraglutide, Dulaglutide.

    ii. **Mechanism of Action:** Mimic the action of GLP-1, enhancing insulin secretion, suppressing glucagon release, and slowing gastric emptying.

    iii. **Uses:** Type 2 diabetes, often used in combination with other agents.

    iv. **Adverse Effects:** Gastrointestinal symptoms (e.g., nausea, vomiting), potential for pancreatitis.

ACTH AND CORTICOSTEROIDS

Adrenocorticotropic hormone (ACTH) and corticosteroids are crucial in regulating the adrenal cortex's production of hormones, which are vital for various physiological processes, including stress response, metabolism, and immune function. Here's a detailed overview of ACTH and corticosteroids, including their pharmacology:

1. Adrenocorticotropic Hormone (ACTH)

a. Production and Regulation:

    i. **Source:** Produced and secreted by the anterior pituitary gland.

    ii. **Regulation:** Release is stimulated by corticotropin-releasing hormone (CRH) from the hypothalamus and inhibited by cortisol through negative feedback.

b. Mechanism of Action:

    i. **Adrenal Cortex:** ACTH binds to melanocortin-2 receptors on adrenal cortex cells, stimulating the synthesis and release of corticosteroids, including cortisol, aldosterone, and androgens.

    ii. **Effects:** Increases adrenal cortex hormone levels, affecting metabolism, immune response, and stress adaptation.

c. Pharmacological Agents:

    i.   **ACTH (Cosyntropin):**

        1. **Uses:** Diagnostic tool in the ACTH stimulation test to evaluate adrenal insufficiency or Addison's disease.

        2. **Administration:** Typically administered via intramuscular injection.

        3. **Adverse Effects:** Rare, but may include hypersensitivity reactions or changes in blood glucose levels.

2. Corticosteroids

Corticosteroids are a class of steroid hormones produced by the adrenal cortex, and they have wide-ranging effects on metabolism, immune function, and stress responses. They are classified into two main types: glucocorticoids and mineralocorticoids.

a. Glucocorticoids

    i.   **Key Hormone:** Cortisol (Hydrocortisone)

        1. **Production and Regulation:** Produced by the adrenal cortex; regulated by ACTH.

        2. **Mechanism of Action:** Bind to glucocorticoid receptors in various tissues, influencing gene expression and affecting metabolism, immune response, and stress adaptation.

        3. **Effects:** Increase gluconeogenesis, decrease glucose uptake, suppress inflammation, and modulate immune responses.

    ii. **Pharmacological Agents:**

        1. **Hydrocortisone:**

            a. **Uses:** Replacement therapy for adrenal insufficiency (Addison's disease) and anti-inflammatory treatment.

            b. **Formulations:** Oral, intravenous, topical.

            c. **Adverse Effects:** Weight gain, fluid retention, hypertension, osteoporosis, and increased susceptibility to infections.

        2. **Prednisolone:**

a. **Uses:** Anti-inflammatory and immunosuppressive treatment for various conditions, including asthma, autoimmune diseases, and allergies.

b. **Formulations:** Oral, intravenous.

c. **Adverse Effects:** Similar to hydrocortisone, including gastrointestinal upset, mood changes, and adrenal suppression.

3. **Dexamethasone:**

a. **Uses:** Potent anti-inflammatory and immunosuppressive agent used in conditions like severe allergies, inflammation, and certain cancers.

b. **Formulations:** Oral, intravenous, topical.

c. **Adverse Effects:** More pronounced effects on metabolism and immune suppression compared to other glucocorticoids.

4. **Betamethasone:**

a. **Uses:** Anti-inflammatory and immunosuppressive properties; used in dermatologic conditions, and as part of preterm labor management.

b. **Formulations:** Oral, topical, intramuscular.

c. **Adverse Effects:** Similar to other glucocorticoids, with a risk of adrenal suppression and metabolic disturbances.

b. Mineralocorticoids

i. **Key Hormone:** Aldosterone

1. **Production and Regulation:** Produced by the adrenal cortex; regulated by the renin-angiotensin-aldosterone system (RAAS) and plasma potassium levels.

2. **Mechanism of Action:** Acts on the kidneys to increase sodium and water reabsorption, and potassium excretion, thereby influencing blood pressure and fluid balance.

ii. **Pharmacological Agents:**

    1. **Fludrocortisone:**

        a. **Uses:** Replacement therapy for adrenal insufficiency with mineralocorticoid deficiency (e.g., Addison's disease) and in conditions requiring mineralocorticoid activity.

        b. **Formulations:** Oral.

        c. **Adverse Effects:** Hypertension, hypokalemia, edema, and weight gain.

CLASSIFICATION:

In the context of pharmacology focusing on endocrine drugs, the classification generally encompasses hormones, hormone analogues, and inhibitors that target various endocrine glands and their hormones. Here's a detailed classification with examples for the drugs acting on the endocrine system:

1. Hormones and Their Analogues

a. **Anterior Pituitary Hormones and Analogues:**

  i. **Growth Hormone (GH) and Analogues:**

    1. **Example:** Somatropin (recombinant GH) - used to treat growth hormone deficiency.

    2. **Example:** Mecasermin - used in cases of severe primary IGF-1 deficiency.

  ii. **Adrenocorticotropic Hormone (ACTH) and Analogues:**

    1. **Example:** Cosyntropin - used for diagnostic testing of adrenal function.

  iii. **Thyroid-Stimulating Hormone (TSH) and Analogues:**

    1. **Example:** Recombinant TSH (Thyrogen) - used for diagnostic purposes in thyroid cancer.

  iv. **Luteinizing Hormone (LH) and Follicle-Stimulating Hormone (FSH) and Analogues:**

1. **Example:** Menotropins (Pergonal) - used for fertility treatments.

2. **Example:** Leuprolide (GnRH analogue) - used to suppress premature ovulation.

b. **Thyroid Hormones and Analogues:**

i. **Thyroxine (T4) and Triiodothyronine (T3):**

1. **Example:** Levothyroxine (Synthroid) - used for hypothyroidism.

2. **Example:** Liothyronine (Cytomel) - used for hypothyroidism and in cases where T3 replacement is needed.

ii. **Thyroid Hormone Inhibitors:**

1. **Example:** Methimazole - used to treat hyperthyroidism.

2. **Example:** Propylthiouracil (PTU) - also used to treat hyperthyroidism and block T4 to T3 conversion.

c. **Hormones Regulating Plasma Calcium Levels:**

i. **Parathyroid Hormone (PTH) and Analogues:**

1. **Example:** Teriparatide - used for osteoporosis treatment.

2. **Example:** Abaloparatide - used for osteoporosis.

ii. **Calcitonin and Analogues:**

1. **Example:** Calcitonin-salmon - used for osteoporosis and Paget's disease.

iii. **Vitamin D and Analogues:**

1. **Example:** Calcitriol - active form of vitamin D used to manage calcium levels.

2. **Example:** Cholecalciferol (Vitamin D3) - used for vitamin D supplementation.

iv. **Calcium- and Bone-Related Drugs:**

1. **Example:** Bisphosphonates (e.g., Alendronate) - used for osteoporosis treatment.

2. **Example:** Denosumab - used for osteoporosis and bone metastases.

d. **Insulin and Oral Hypoglycemic Agents:**

   i.   **Insulin Preparations:**

   1. **Example:** Insulin glargine (Lantus) - long-acting insulin for diabetes management.

   2. **Example:** Insulin lispro (Humalog) - rapid-acting insulin.

   ii. **Oral Hypoglycemic Agents:**

   1. **Example:** Metformin - biguanide used for type 2 diabetes.

   2. **Example:** Glipizide - sulfonylurea used for type 2 diabetes.

   3. **Example:** Canagliflozin - SGLT2 inhibitor used for type 2 diabetes.

e. **Corticosteroids:**

   i.   **Glucocorticoids:**

   1. **Example:** Hydrocortisone - used for adrenal insufficiency.

   2. **Example:** Prednisolone - used for inflammation and autoimmune conditions.

   3. **Example:** Dexamethasone - used for its potent anti-inflammatory effects.

   ii. **Mineralocorticoids:**

   1. **Example:** Fludrocortisone - used for conditions requiring mineralocorticoid activity, like Addison's disease.

f. **Sex Hormones and Their Analogues:**

   i.   **Estrogens:**

   1. **Example:** Ethinyl estradiol - used in contraceptives and hormone replacement therapy.

   2. **Example:** Estradiol - used for hormone replacement therapy.

   ii. **Progestins:**

   1. **Example:** Norgestrel - used in contraceptives.

   2. **Example:** Medroxyprogesterone acetate - used for contraception and hormone replacement therapy.

iii. **Androgens:**

    1. **Example:** Testosterone - used for testosterone replacement therapy.

    2. **Example:** Dihydrotestosterone (DHT) - used in the treatment of hair loss.

2. Inhibitors of Hormone Synthesis or Action

a. Antithyroid Agents:

i. **Example:** Methimazole - inhibits thyroid hormone synthesis.

ii. **Example:** Propylthiouracil - inhibits thyroid hormone synthesis and peripheral conversion of T4 to T3.

b. Corticosteroid Inhibitors:

i. **Example:** Ketoconazole - inhibits steroid synthesis, used in Cushing's syndrome.

ii. **Example:** Metyrapone - inhibits cortisol synthesis, used for diagnostic purposes and treatment of Cushing's syndrome.

c. Estrogen Receptor Modulators:

i. **Example:** Tamoxifen - selective estrogen receptor modulator (SERM) used in breast cancer treatment.

ii. **Example:** Raloxifene - SERM used in osteoporosis prevention.

d. Anti-Androgens:

i. **Example:** Finasteride - inhibits 5-alpha reductase, used in benign prostatic hyperplasia and androgenic alopecia.

ii. **Example:** Flutamide - androgen receptor antagonist used in prostate cancer.

A. Somatropin:

a. Mechanism of Action:

1. **Somatropin** is a recombinant form of human growth hormone (GH), which is identical to the naturally occurring GH produced by the pituitary gland.

2. **Receptor Interaction:** Somatropin binds to the growth hormone receptor on target tissues, particularly in the liver, muscle, and adipose tissue.

3. **Effect on Metabolism:** It stimulates the liver to produce insulin-like growth factor 1 (IGF-1), which mediates many of the growth-promoting effects of GH. Somatropin also promotes protein synthesis, stimulates linear bone growth, and enhances lipid metabolism by increasing lipolysis and reducing fat accumulation.

b. **Pharmacokinetics:**

1. **Absorption:** Somatropin is administered subcutaneously (SC) and is absorbed slowly.

2. **Distribution:** It is distributed throughout the body, with high concentrations in the liver.

3. **Metabolism:** It is metabolized mainly in the liver and kidneys.

4. **Excretion:** Excreted in the urine.

c. **Indications:**

1. **Growth Hormone Deficiency:** Used to treat children and adults with GH deficiency, which can result from pituitary disease or genetic conditions.

2. **Turner Syndrome:** Used in children with Turner syndrome to promote growth.

3. **Chronic Kidney Disease:** Used to improve growth in children with chronic kidney disease.

4. **Prader-Willi Syndrome:** Used to manage growth retardation in children with Prader-Willi syndrome.

d. **Dosage Forms:**

1. **Formulations:** Available as injectable solutions.

2. **Administration:** Typically administered via subcutaneous injection once daily or multiple times per week.

e. **Adverse Effects:**

1. **Common Effects:** Injection site reactions, headache, abdominal pain.

2. **Serious Effects:** Potential for increased intracranial pressure, hypothyroidism, and glucose intolerance. Long-term use may be associated with the risk of developing diabetes.

f. Contraindications and Precautions:

1. **Contraindications:** Not recommended in patients with active malignancy, acute critical illness, or severe obesity.
2. **Precautions:** Caution in patients with pre-existing diabetes or glucose intolerance. Regular monitoring is required for growth and thyroid function.

B. Mecasermin:

a. Mechanism of Action:

1. **Mecasermin** is a recombinant form of insulin-like growth factor 1 (IGF-1), which is structurally similar to endogenous IGF-1.
2. **IGF-1 Action:** IGF-1 mediates the effects of growth hormone on growth and development. It binds to IGF-1 receptors on various tissues, promoting cell growth, division, and differentiation.
3. **Effects on Growth:** It stimulates growth in children with severe primary IGF-1 deficiency who have not responded to GH therapy. Mecasermin is often used when GH therapy alone is insufficient or not effective.

b. Pharmacokinetics:

1. **Absorption:** Administered subcutaneously, with varying rates of absorption depending on the injection site.
2. **Distribution:** Distributed throughout the body, with effects on growth and metabolism seen in various tissues.
3. **Metabolism:** Metabolized by the liver and other tissues.
4. **Excretion:** Primarily excreted via the urine.

c. Indications:

1. **Primary IGF-1 Deficiency:** Used in children with severe primary IGF-1 deficiency, which is characterized by inadequate IGF-1 production despite normal or elevated levels of GH.

2. **Growth Retardation:** Used in cases where GH therapy is ineffective or inappropriate.

d. **Dosage Forms:**

1. **Formulations:** Available as injectable solutions.

2. **Administration:** Typically administered via subcutaneous injection twice daily.

e. **Adverse Effects:**

1. **Common Effects:** Hypoglycemia, injection site reactions, and headaches.

2. **Serious Effects:** Potential for increased intracranial pressure, and less commonly, signs of hypersensitivity or anaphylaxis.

f. **Contraindications and Precautions:**

1. **Contraindications:** Not recommended in patients with closed epiphyses or in those with active malignancies.

2. **Precautions:** Monitor blood glucose levels regularly due to the risk of hypoglycemia. Use with caution in patients with a history of hypoglycemia or those on medications affecting glucose metabolism.

C. Cosyntropin:

a. **Mechanism of Action:**

1. **Cosyntropin** is a synthetic analogue of adrenocorticotropic hormone (ACTH), specifically the first 24 amino acids of the ACTH molecule.

2. **ACTH Receptor Interaction:** It binds to the ACTH receptor on the adrenal cortex, stimulating the production and release of adrenal hormones, particularly cortisol.

3. **Effects:** The primary effect is the stimulation of cortisol secretion from the adrenal cortex. It is used to assess adrenal gland function by evaluating the adrenal response to ACTH stimulation.

b. **Pharmacokinetics:**

1. **Absorption:** Administered intramuscularly (IM), with rapid absorption.

2. **Distribution:** Distributed systemically after injection.

3. **Metabolism:** Metabolized in the liver and other tissues.

4. **Excretion:** Excreted in the urine.

c. **Indications:**

1. **Adrenal Insufficiency Diagnosis:** Used in the ACTH stimulation test to diagnose primary adrenal insufficiency (Addison's disease) or secondary adrenal insufficiency (due to pituitary dysfunction).

2. **Differentiation of Adrenal Disorders:** Helps differentiate between primary adrenal insufficiency (Addison's disease) and secondary adrenal insufficiency (due to pituitary gland dysfunction).

d. **Dosage Forms:**

1. **Formulations:** Available as an injectable solution.

2. **Administration:** Typically administered intramuscularly, with the dosage depending on the diagnostic test protocol.

e. **Adverse Effects:**

1. **Common Effects:** Injection site reactions, nausea, headache.

2. **Serious Effects:** Rare, but could include allergic reactions or changes in blood pressure.

f. **Contraindications and Precautions:**

1. **Contraindications:** Not recommended in patients with active malignancies, severe infections, or certain cardiovascular conditions.

2. **Precautions:** Use with caution in patients with a history of cardiovascular disease, hypertension, or severe infections.

D. Recombinant TSH (Thyrogen):

a. **Mechanism of Action:**

1. **Recombinant TSH (Thyrogen)** is a recombinant form of thyroid-stimulating hormone (TSH) produced using recombinant DNA technology.
2. **TSH Receptor Interaction:** It binds to TSH receptors on thyroid cells, stimulating thyroid hormone production and secretion.
3. **Effects:** Used to stimulate the thyroid gland in diagnostic tests, particularly in the context of thyroid cancer. It helps to assess residual or recurrent disease by increasing thyroid hormone levels without requiring the patient to stop thyroid hormone replacement therapy.

b. **Pharmacokinetics:**

1. **Absorption:** Administered intramuscularly (IM), with systemic absorption.
2. **Distribution:** Distributed throughout the body, with effects primarily on the thyroid gland.
3. **Metabolism:** Metabolized in the liver and other tissues.
4. **Excretion:** Excreted in the urine.

c. **Indications:**

1. **Thyroid Cancer Surveillance:** Used in conjunction with diagnostic imaging to evaluate for residual or recurrent thyroid cancer in patients who are on thyroid hormone replacement therapy.
2. **Thyroid Function Testing:** Helps assess thyroid function and disease status without requiring withdrawal of thyroid hormone replacement therapy.

d. **Dosage Forms:**

1. **Formulations:** Available as an injectable solution.
2. **Administration:** Administered intramuscularly, with the dosage and frequency depending on the diagnostic or therapeutic protocol.

e. **Adverse Effects:**

1. **Common Effects:** Injection site reactions, headache, nausea, and fatigue.

2. **Serious Effects:** Rare, but could include allergic reactions or changes in thyroid function tests.

E. Menotropin:

a. **Mechanism of Action:**

1. **Menotropin** is a combination of follicle-stimulating hormone (FSH) and luteinizing hormone (LH) derived from the urine of postmenopausal women.

2. **FSH and LH Activity:** Menotropin acts on the ovaries to stimulate follicular development and ovulation in women, and spermatogenesis in men.

3. **Effects:** It helps in the maturation of ovarian follicles and the production of estrogen and progesterone in women. In men, it aids in spermatogenesis and testosterone production.

b. **Pharmacokinetics:**

1. **Absorption:** Administered via intramuscular (IM) or subcutaneous (SC) injection. Absorption is generally efficient.

2. **Distribution:** Distributed throughout the body, with peak effects observed in the reproductive organs.

3. **Metabolism:** Metabolized in the liver and kidneys.

4. **Excretion:** Excreted via the urine.

c. **Indications:**

1. **Infertility Treatment:** Used in combination with human chorionic gonadotropin (hCG) to induce ovulation in women with infertility issues, such as those with hypogonadotropic hypogonadism or polycystic ovary syndrome (PCOS).

2. **Assisted Reproductive Technology (ART):** Used in protocols for in vitro fertilization (IVF) and other ART procedures.

3. **Male Infertility:** Used to treat male hypogonadism and improve sperm count.

d. **Dosage Forms:**

1. **Formulations:** Available as injectable solutions.

2. **Administration:** Typically administered intramuscularly or subcutaneously, with dosage depending on the specific fertility treatment protocol.

e. **Adverse Effects:**

1. **Common Effects:** Ovarian hyperstimulation syndrome (OHSS), abdominal pain, headache, mood swings.

2. **Serious Effects:** Risk of multiple pregnancies (e.g., twins, triplets), ovarian cysts, and allergic reactions.

f. **Contraindications and Precautions:**

1. **Contraindications:** Not recommended in women with uncontrolled thyroid or adrenal disorders, ovarian cysts, or pregnancy.

2. **Precautions:** Monitor for OHSS and multiple pregnancies. Use with caution in patients with a history of thromboembolic disorders.

F. Leuprolide:

a. **Mechanism of Action:**

1. **Leuprolide** is a synthetic analogue of gonadotropin-releasing hormone (GnRH), designed to have a prolonged action.

2. **GnRH Receptor Interaction:** Acts on the pituitary gland to initially stimulate the release of FSH and LH. However, continuous administration leads to downregulation of GnRH receptors, decreasing FSH and LH secretion, and consequently reducing testosterone and estrogen levels.

3. **Effects:** Used to suppress the production of sex hormones, which helps in the management of hormone-dependent conditions.

b. **Pharmacokinetics:**

1. **Absorption:** Administered via subcutaneous (SC) or intramuscular (IM) injection. It has a prolonged release form.

2. **Distribution:** Distributed throughout the body, with a primary effect on the pituitary gland and peripheral tissues.
3. **Metabolism:** Metabolized in the liver and kidneys.
4. **Excretion:** Excreted via the urine.

c. **Indications:**

1. **Prostate Cancer:** Used in advanced prostate cancer to reduce levels of circulating testosterone.
2. **Endometriosis:** Used to manage endometriosis by reducing estrogen levels and thereby alleviating symptoms.
3. **Precocious Puberty:** Used to treat early onset puberty in children by suppressing premature gonadotropin release.
4. **Uterine Fibroids:** Used to reduce the size of uterine fibroids and associated symptoms.

d. **Dosage Forms:**

1. **Formulations:** Available in injectable forms, including depot preparations for sustained release.
2. **Administration:** Administered via subcutaneous or intramuscular injection, with the dosing frequency varying based on the condition being treated.

e. **Adverse Effects:**

1. **Common Effects:** Hot flashes, decreased libido, erectile dysfunction, headache.
2. **Serious Effects:** Risk of osteoporosis with long-term use, mood changes, and potential for significant hormone-related effects.

f. **Contraindications and Precautions:**

1. **Contraindications:** Not recommended in patients with known hypersensitivity to leuprolide or other GnRH analogues.

2. **Precautions:** Monitor for symptoms of hormone withdrawal and bone density changes. Use with caution in patients with a history of cardiovascular disease or osteoporosis.

Multiple Choice Questions (MCQs)

1. Which hormone is directly involved in increasing plasma calcium levels by stimulating osteoclast activity?
   a) Calcitonin
   b) Parathyroid Hormone (PTH)
   c) Insulin
   d) Glucagon

2. Which drug is a recombinant form of growth hormone (GH) used to treat growth hormone deficiency?
   a) Levothyroxine
   b) Cosyntropin
   c) Somatropin
   d) Fludrocortisone

3. Which medication is used to diagnose adrenal insufficiency by stimulating cortisol production?
   a) Methimazole
   b) Cosyntropin
   c) Teriparatide
   d) Calcitonin

4. Which of the following is a selective estrogen receptor modulator (SERM) used in breast cancer treatment?
   a) Tamoxifen
   b) Estradiol
   c) Leuprolide

d) Flutamide

5. What is the primary mechanism of action of metformin in the management of type 2 diabetes?

    a) Inhibits glucose absorption in the intestines

    b) Stimulates insulin release from the pancreas

    c) Decreases hepatic glucose production

    d) Enhances glucose reabsorption in the kidneys

6. Which drug is a somatostatin analogue used to manage acromegaly?

    a) Octreotide

    b) Somatropin

    c) Levothyroxine

    d) Cosyntropin

7. Which hormone replacement therapy is commonly used to treat hypothyroidism?

    a) Liothyronine

    b) Levothyroxine

    c) Fludrocortisone

    d) Somatropin

8. Which drug is a GnRH agonist used to treat hormone-dependent prostate cancer?

    a) Finasteride

    b) Leuprolide

    c) Bromocriptine

    d) Cosyntropin

9. What is the mechanism of action of glucagon when used to treat hypoglycemia?

    a) Decreases insulin secretion

    b) Stimulates glycogenolysis and gluconeogenesis

    c) Increases glucose absorption in the intestines

d) Enhances insulin sensitivity

10. Which of the following is a mineralocorticoid used to treat adrenal insufficiency?

    a) Prednisolone

    b) Hydrocortisone

    c) Fludrocortisone

    d) Dexamethasone

11. Which oral hypoglycemic agent works by inhibiting the enzyme DPP-4?

    a) Sitagliptin

    b) Metformin

    c) Pioglitazone

    d) Acarbose

12. What is the primary adverse effect associated with the use of bisphosphonates like alendronate?

    a) Hypercalcemia

    b) Osteonecrosis of the jaw

    c) Hypoglycemia

    d) Hypertension

13. Which drug is a recombinant TSH used for thyroid cancer surveillance?

    a) Somatropin

    b) Thyrogen

    c) Fludrocortisone

    d) Levothyroxine

14. Which drug class does flutamide belong to, and what is its primary use?

    a) Antiandrogens; prostate cancer

    b) Estrogens; breast cancer

    c) Corticosteroids; inflammation

    d) Antithyroid drugs; hyperthyroidism

15. Which hormone is inhibited by octreotide in the treatment of acromegaly?

a) Thyroid-Stimulating Hormone (TSH)

b) Luteinizing Hormone (LH)

c) Growth Hormone (GH)

d) Follicle-Stimulating Hormone (FSH)

16. Which drug is used to treat osteoporosis by inhibiting bone resorption?

a) Teriparatide

b) Calcitonin-Salmon

c) Levothyroxine

d) Cosyntropin

17. Which condition is fludrocortisone primarily used to treat?

a) Hyperthyroidism

b) Adrenal insufficiency

c) Diabetes mellitus

d) Osteoporosis

18. Which of the following drugs is a biguanide used to manage type 2 diabetes?

a) Metformin

b) Glipizide

c) Canagliflozin

d) Acarbose

19. What is the primary use of menotropins in reproductive medicine?

a) Treat osteoporosis

b) Induce ovulation

c) Manage adrenal insufficiency

d) Treat prostate cancer

20. Which of the following drugs is a synthetic analogue of ACTH?

a) Cosyntropin

b) Leuprolide

c) Thyrogen

d) Teriparatide

Short Answer Questions (SAQs)

1. Explain the mechanism of action of somatropin in the treatment of growth hormone deficiency.

2. What are the primary therapeutic uses of cosyntropin in clinical practice?

3. How does levothyroxine work to treat hypothyroidism?

4. Describe the role of fludrocortisone in the management of adrenal insufficiency.

5. What is the mechanism of action of glucagon in treating severe hypoglycemia?

6. How do GnRH agonists like leuprolide work in the treatment of hormone-dependent cancers?

7. Discuss the pharmacological effects of parathyroid hormone (PTH) on calcium metabolism.

8. What are the common adverse effects associated with the use of metformin in type 2 diabetes?

9. Explain how octreotide is used in the management of acromegaly.

10. What is the role of menotropins in assisted reproductive technologies (ART)?

11. How does methimazole help in the treatment of hyperthyroidism?

12. Describe the pharmacological actions of calcitonin-salmon in the treatment of osteoporosis.

13. What is the mechanism of action of bisphosphonates in treating osteoporosis?

14. Explain the clinical significance of DPP-4 inhibitors like sitagliptin in diabetes management.

15. How does propylthiouracil (PTU) differ from methimazole in the treatment of hyperthyroidism?

16. Discuss the use of recombinant TSH (Thyrogen) in thyroid cancer management.

17. What are the primary adverse effects associated with long-term corticosteroid use?

18. Describe the mechanism by which SGLT2 inhibitors like canagliflozin lower blood glucose levels.

19. What are the primary clinical indications for the use of teriparatide?

20. Explain the role of antiandrogens like flutamide in the treatment of prostate cancer.

Long Answer Questions (LAQs)

1. Discuss the classification, mechanisms of action, and clinical applications of corticosteroids, focusing on their role in managing inflammation and adrenal insufficiency.

2. Describe the pharmacological management of osteoporosis, including the roles of bisphosphonates, calcitonin, and parathyroid hormone analogues.

3. Explain the use of hormone replacement therapy (HRT) in managing hypothyroidism, with a focus on levothyroxine and liothyronine.

4. Discuss the various pharmacological agents used in the management of diabetes mellitus, including insulin, oral hypoglycemics, and GLP-1 agonists.

5. Describe the role of GnRH analogues and antagonists in the treatment of reproductive disorders and hormone-dependent cancers.

6. Discuss the pharmacology of thyroid hormone analogues and antithyroid drugs, including their indications, mechanisms of action, and adverse effects.

7. Explain the therapeutic applications of growth hormone and its analogues in growth hormone deficiency and other related conditions.

8. Discuss the pharmacological actions, therapeutic uses, and adverse effects of antiandrogens in the management of prostate cancer.

9. Describe the mechanism of action, therapeutic indications, and adverse effects of somatostatin analogues like octreotide.

10. Discuss the role of glucocorticoids and mineralocorticoids in the management of adrenal insufficiency, including their mechanisms of action and potential side effects.

Answer Key for MCQs

1. b) Parathyroid Hormone (PTH)
2. c) Somatropin
3. b) Cosyntropin
4. a) Tamoxifen
5. c) Decreases hepatic glucose production
6. a) Octreotide
7. b) Levothyroxine
8. b) Leuprolide
9. b) Stimulates glycogenolysis and gluconeogenesis
10. c) Fludrocortisone
11. a) Sitagliptin
12. b) Osteonecrosis of the jaw
13. b) Thyrogen
14. a) Antiandrogens; prostate cancer
15. c) Growth Hormone (GH)
16. b) Calcitonin-Salmon
17. b) Adrenal insufficiency
18. a) Metformin
19. b) Induce ovulation
20. a) Cosyntropin

CHAPTER – 8

PHARMACOLOGY OF DRUGS ACTING ON ENDOCRINE SYSTEM-II

INTRODUCTION:

The **pharmacology of drugs acting on the endocrine system-II** focuses on the therapeutic agents used to modulate hormonal functions, specifically those involved in regulating metabolism, reproductive health, and related endocrine activities. This part of endocrine pharmacology typically encompasses drugs that interact with thyroid hormones, adrenal steroids, reproductive hormones, and anti-diabetic agents, among others. These drugs are designed to either mimic natural hormones or inhibit their effects, depending on the therapeutic need.

Key Areas of Focus:

1. **Thyroid and Antithyroid Drugs:**

    a. **Thyroid Hormones (L-Thyroxine, L-Triiodothyronine):** These synthetic forms of thyroid hormones are used in the treatment of hypothyroidism. They work by supplementing deficient hormone levels, thereby normalizing metabolic processes.

    b. **Antithyroid Drugs (Propylthiouracil, Methimazole):** These drugs are used to treat hyperthyroidism by inhibiting thyroid hormone synthesis. Propylthiouracil also inhibits the conversion of T4 to T3, the more active form of thyroid hormone.

2. **Adrenal Steroids:**

    a. **Corticosteroids (Cortisone, Hydrocortisone, Prednisolone, Dexamethasone, Betamethasone):** These drugs mimic the effects of cortisol, a natural hormone produced by the adrenal cortex. They are used in the treatment of inflammatory conditions, autoimmune diseases, and adrenal insufficiency. Their mechanism involves altering gene transcription to modulate immune and metabolic responses.

3. **Reproductive Hormones and Modulators:**

    a. **Estrogens and Progestins (Norgestrel, Levonorgestrel):** These are synthetic hormones used in contraception and hormone replacement therapy (HRT). They work by regulating the menstrual cycle, inhibiting ovulation, and maintaining pregnancy.

    b. **Antiprogestins (Mifepristone):** Used primarily for medical termination of pregnancy, Mifepristone works by blocking the action of progesterone, leading to the detachment of the embryo and softening of the cervix.

4. **Phosphodiesterase Inhibitors:**

    a. **Sildenafil and Tadalafil:** These drugs are used in the treatment of erectile dysfunction and pulmonary arterial hypertension. They work by inhibiting the enzyme phosphodiesterase-5 (PDE5), leading to increased levels of cyclic guanosine monophosphate (cGMP), which causes relaxation of smooth muscle in the corpus cavernosum and pulmonary vasculature.

Mechanisms of Action:

1. **Hormone Replacement:** Drugs like L-Thyroxine and L-Triiodothyronine replace deficient hormones in the body, restoring normal physiological functions.

2. **Inhibition of Hormone Synthesis:** Antithyroid drugs inhibit the production of thyroid hormones by blocking the iodination of tyrosine residues in the thyroid gland.

3. **Receptor Modulation:** Corticosteroids bind to glucocorticoid receptors, influencing gene expression and reducing inflammation. Mifepristone acts as an antagonist at progesterone receptors.

4. **Enzyme Inhibition:** Phosphodiesterase inhibitors block the breakdown of cGMP, enhancing the signaling pathways that lead to smooth muscle relaxation.

Clinical Uses:

1. **Hypothyroidism:** Treated with thyroid hormone replacements like L-Thyroxine.

2. **Hyperthyroidism:** Managed with antithyroid drugs like Methimazole or Propylthiouracil.

3. **Inflammatory and Autoimmune Diseases:** Corticosteroids are used for their potent anti-inflammatory and immunosuppressive effects.

4. **Contraception and HRT:** Estrogens, progestins, and their antagonists are used to regulate reproductive health and manage menopausal symptoms.

5. **Erectile Dysfunction:** Sildenafil and Tadalafil are prescribed to improve erectile function by enhancing blood flow to the penis.

Side Effects and Toxicity:

1. **Thyroid Hormones:** Excessive doses can lead to hyperthyroid symptoms such as palpitations, weight loss, and anxiety.

2. **Corticosteroids:** Prolonged use can cause Cushing's syndrome, characterized by weight gain, hypertension, and osteoporosis.

3. **Antithyroid Drugs:** May cause agranulocytosis, a potentially life-threatening decrease in white blood cells.

4. **Phosphodiesterase Inhibitors:** Common side effects include headache, flushing, and visual disturbances.

ANDROGENS AND ANABOLIC STEROIDS

Androgens and anabolic steroids are key components in the pharmacological treatment of conditions related to hormone deficiencies, muscle wasting, and certain types of anemia. They also play a significant role in gender-affirming hormone therapy for transgender individuals.

1. Androgens:

Androgens are male sex hormones responsible for the development and maintenance of male characteristics. The primary androgen is **testosterone**, which is produced in the testes, ovaries, and adrenal glands.

Mechanism of Action:

a. Androgens exert their effects by binding to androgen receptors (AR) in various tissues, including muscles, bones, and the reproductive system.

b. Upon binding to the AR, the hormone-receptor complex translocates to the nucleus, where it influences gene transcription, promoting the expression of genes responsible for male secondary sexual characteristics, muscle growth, and erythropoiesis.

Therapeutic Uses:

a. **Hypogonadism:** Androgens are used to treat male hypogonadism, a condition characterized by low testosterone levels, leading to symptoms like reduced libido, erectile dysfunction, and fatigue.

b. **Delayed Puberty in Males:** Testosterone can be prescribed to initiate and complete puberty in boys with delayed puberty.

c. **Gender-Affirming Therapy:** Testosterone is used in masculinizing hormone therapy for transgender men.

d. **Androgen Deficiency in Women:** Although less common, androgens may be used to treat certain conditions in women, such as low libido or menopausal symptoms, although this is controversial and less established.

Common Androgens Used:

a. **Testosterone:** Available in various forms, including injections, patches, gels, and oral formulations.

b. **Methyltestosterone:** A synthetic derivative of testosterone used primarily for androgen replacement therapy.

Side Effects:

a. **In men:** Excessive androgen use can lead to reduced sperm production, testicular atrophy, and gynecomastia (breast tissue enlargement).

b. **In women:** Can cause virilization, including deepening of the voice, hirsutism (excessive hair growth), and menstrual irregularities.

c. **In both sexes:** Androgens can cause liver dysfunction, lipid abnormalities, and an increased risk of cardiovascular disease with long-term use.

2. Anabolic Steroids:

Anabolic steroids are synthetic derivatives of testosterone designed to maximize anabolic (muscle-building) effects while minimizing androgenic (male characteristic-inducing) effects. They are often misused for performance enhancement and muscle growth.

Mechanism of Action:

a. Like natural androgens, anabolic steroids bind to androgen receptors and promote protein synthesis, leading to increased muscle mass and strength.

b. They also stimulate erythropoiesis, increasing red blood cell production, which can enhance endurance by improving oxygen delivery to muscles.

Therapeutic Uses:

a. **Cachexia and Muscle Wasting:** Used in conditions like chronic infections, cancer, and HIV/AIDS to counteract muscle wasting.

b. **Anemia:** Some anabolic steroids can stimulate erythropoiesis in patients with certain types of anemia.

c. **Osteoporosis:** Anabolic steroids may be used in postmenopausal women to increase bone density, although safer alternatives are preferred.

Common Anabolic Steroids:

a. **Oxandrolone:** Used to promote weight gain in patients recovering from severe burns or trauma.

b. **Nandrolone:** Used for anemia associated with renal failure.

c. **Stanozolol:** Used for hereditary angioedema and certain anemias.

Side Effects:

   a. **In men:** Excessive use can lead to testicular atrophy, infertility, and gynecomastia.

   b. **In women:** Can cause masculinization, including voice deepening, increased body hair, and menstrual irregularities.

   c. **General:** Anabolic steroids are associated with liver damage, cardiovascular issues, psychiatric effects like aggression ("roid rage"), and dependence.

Legal and Ethical Considerations:

   a. **Performance Enhancement:** The non-medical use of anabolic steroids for performance enhancement is illegal in many countries and banned by sports organizations.

   b. **Abuse Potential:** Anabolic steroids have a high potential for abuse, leading to severe health consequences.

ESTROGENS

Estrogens are a group of steroid hormones primarily responsible for the development and regulation of the female reproductive system and secondary sexual characteristics. They play crucial roles in various physiological processes, including menstrual cycle regulation, reproduction, bone density maintenance, and modulation of lipid metabolism. In pharmacology, estrogens are utilized for various therapeutic purposes, such as contraception, hormone replacement therapy (HRT), and treatment of certain cancers.

This detailed overview will cover the following aspects of estrogens:

1. **Types and Sources of Estrogens**
2. **Mechanism of Action**
3. **Pharmacokinetics**
4. **Therapeutic Uses**
5. **Adverse Effects**
6. **Contraindications and Precautions**

7. **Drug Interactions**

8. **Clinical Preparations of Estrogens**

1. Types and Sources of Estrogens

Estrogens can be classified based on their origin and structure into:

a. Endogenous (Natural) Estrogens

These are naturally occurring estrogens produced within the body, mainly by the ovaries, and to a lesser extent by the adrenal cortex and adipose tissue.

i. **Estradiol (E2):** The most potent and predominant estrogen during reproductive years.

ii. **Estrone (E1):** Less potent; primary estrogen post-menopause.

iii. **Estriol (E3):** Least potent; significant during pregnancy.

b. Exogenous (Synthetic) Estrogens

These are artificially synthesized compounds used for therapeutic purposes.

i. **Steroidal Synthetic Estrogens:**

  1. **Ethinylestradiol:** Commonly used in oral contraceptives; has improved oral bioavailability.

  2. **Mestranol:** Prodrug converted to ethinylestradiol in the body.

  3. **Quinestrol:** Used for hormone replacement therapy.

ii. **Non-Steroidal Synthetic Estrogens:**

  1. **Diethylstilbestrol (DES):** Previously used for various indications; now limited due to adverse effects.

  2. **Chlorotrianisene:** Used for menopausal symptoms and certain cancers.

c. Conjugated Estrogens

i. Mixtures of estrogenic substances obtained from natural sources (e.g., **Premarin**, derived from pregnant mares' urine).

ii. Contain sulfate esters of estrone and equilin; used in hormone replacement therapy.

2. Mechanism of Action

Estrogens exert their biological effects through interaction with specific estrogen receptors (ERs) and modulation of gene expression.

a. Estrogen Receptors

i. **ERα and ERβ:** Two main types of nuclear estrogen receptors distributed in various tissues.

   1. **ERα:** Predominant in reproductive tissues (uterus, vagina, ovaries), mammary glands, liver, and hypothalamus.

   2. **ERβ:** Found in ovaries, prostate, lungs, gastrointestinal tract, and central nervous system.

b. Genomic Actions

i. **Binding to ERs:**

   1. Estrogen diffuses across the cell membrane and binds to intracellular ERs.

ii. **Receptor Dimerization:**

   1. The hormone-receptor complex forms homodimers or heterodimers (ERα/ERβ).

iii. **DNA Binding:**

   1. The dimerized complex binds to estrogen response elements (EREs) on DNA.

iv. **Gene Transcription Modulation:**

   1. Recruitment of coactivators or corepressors alters transcription of target genes, leading to protein synthesis and resultant physiological effects.

c. Non-Genomic Actions

i. **Membrane-bound ERs:**

   1. Rapid actions mediated through activation of secondary messenger systems (e.g., cAMP, PI3K/Akt pathways).

   2. Contribute to vascular relaxation, neuroprotection, and modulation of immune responses.

3. Pharmacokinetics

Understanding the absorption, distribution, metabolism, and excretion of estrogens is crucial for their effective and safe therapeutic use.

a. Absorption

i. **Oral Administration:**

  1. Natural estrogens (e.g., estradiol) have poor oral bioavailability due to extensive first-pass metabolism.
  2. Synthetic estrogens (e.g., ethinylestradiol) have modifications enhancing oral potency and bioavailability.

ii. **Transdermal Patches and Topical Gels:**

  1. Bypass first-pass metabolism; provide steady systemic levels.

iii. **Parenteral Routes:**

  1. Intramuscular injections (e.g., estradiol valerate) for sustained release.

iv. **Vaginal Preparations:**

  1. Localized effect with minimal systemic absorption; used for urogenital symptoms.

b. Distribution

i. Widely distributed throughout the body.

ii. Bind extensively to plasma proteins:

  1. **Sex Hormone-Binding Globulin (SHBG):** High-affinity binding.
  2. **Albumin:** Low-affinity binding.

iii. Only unbound (free) fraction is biologically active.

c. Metabolism

i. Primarily metabolized in the **liver** via:

  1. **Phase I Reactions:** Hydroxylation by cytochrome P450 enzymes.
  2. **Phase II Reactions:** Conjugation (sulfation and glucuronidation) enhancing water solubility.

ii. Enterohepatic circulation prolongs the half-life of estrogens.

d. Excretion

    i.   Metabolites excreted via:

        1. **Bile:** Reabsorbed or eliminated in feces.

        2. **Urine:** As conjugated metabolites.

4. Therapeutic Uses

Estrogens are employed in various clinical settings to exploit their physiological effects.

a. Hormone Replacement Therapy (HRT)

    i.   **Indications:**

        1. Management of menopausal symptoms (hot flashes, night sweats, vaginal atrophy).

        2. Prevention of postmenopausal osteoporosis.

        3. Hypoestrogenism due to hypogonadism, oophorectomy, or premature ovarian failure.

    ii. **Regimens:**

        1. **Estrogen Alone (ET):** For women who have undergone hysterectomy.

        2. **Estrogen-Progestin Combination (EPT):** For women with an intact uterus to prevent endometrial hyperplasia.

b. Contraception

    i.   **Combined Oral Contraceptives (COCs):**

        1. Contain estrogen (usually ethinylestradiol) and progestin.

        2. **Mechanism:**

            1. Suppress ovulation by inhibiting gonadotropin release (FSH and LH).

            2. Alter cervical mucus and endometrial lining to prevent fertilization and implantation.

    ii. **Other Forms:**

        1. Transdermal patches, vaginal rings, and injectable formulations.

c. Treatment of Certain Cancers

   i.   **Prostate Cancer:**

      1. Estrogens used to suppress androgen production.

   ii. **Breast Cancer:**

      1. Selective estrogen receptor modulators (SERMs) and aromatase inhibitors preferred; estrogens rarely used due to potential tumor growth stimulation.

d. Osteoporosis Management

   i.   Estrogens help maintain bone density by inhibiting bone resorption.

   ii. Typically considered when other treatments are contraindicated or not tolerated.

e. Delayed Puberty in Females

   i.   Estrogen therapy initiated to induce development of secondary sexual characteristics and menstrual cycles.

f. Acne Treatment

   i.   Certain COCs approved for moderate acne management in females by decreasing androgen levels.

5. Adverse Effects

The use of estrogens is associated with several potential side effects, the risk of which varies depending on dose, duration, and individual patient factors.

a. Common Side Effects

   i.   Nausea and vomiting

   ii. Breast tenderness and enlargement

   iii. Edema and weight gain

   iv. Headaches and migraines

   v. Mood changes

b. Serious Adverse Effects

   i.   **Cardiovascular Risks:**

1. Increased risk of thromboembolic events (deep vein thrombosis, pulmonary embolism).

2. Elevated risk of myocardial infarction and stroke, especially in smokers and women over 35 years.

ii. **Cancer Risks:**

1. **Endometrial Cancer:**

1. Risk increased with unopposed estrogen use; mitigated by adding progestins.

2. **Breast Cancer:**

1. Long-term use, particularly of combined HRT, may slightly increase risk.

iii. **Gallbladder Disease:**

1. Elevated risk of cholelithiasis due to altered cholesterol metabolism.

iv. **Liver Dysfunction:**

1. Rare cases of hepatic adenomas and cholestasis.

c. Metabolic Effects

i. **Lipid Profile Alterations:**

1. Increase in HDL cholesterol and triglycerides.

2. Decrease in LDL cholesterol.

ii. **Glucose Tolerance:**

1. May impair glucose tolerance; caution in diabetic patients.

d. Other Effects

i. **Hypertension:**

1. Possible elevation in blood pressure due to sodium and water retention.

ii. **Visual Disturbances:**

1. Rare instances of retinal vascular thrombosis.

iii. **Menstrual Irregularities:**

1. Breakthrough bleeding and spotting.

6. Contraindications and Precautions

Appropriate patient selection and monitoring are essential to minimize risks associated with estrogen therapy.

a. Absolute Contraindications

i. Known or suspected pregnancy.

ii. Active or history of thromboembolic disorders.

iii. Undiagnosed abnormal genital bleeding.

iv. Known or suspected estrogen-dependent neoplasia (e.g., breast or endometrial cancer).

v. Active liver disease or dysfunction.

vi. History of cerebrovascular accidents or myocardial infarction.

vii. Hypersensitivity to estrogen preparations.

7. Drug Interactions

Estrogens can interact with various medications, affecting their efficacy and safety profiles.

a. Drugs that Decrease Estrogen Efficacy

i. **Enzyme Inducers:**

1. **Anticonvulsants:** (e.g., phenytoin, carbamazepine) induce hepatic enzymes, increasing estrogen metabolism.

2. **Rifampin:** Potent inducer leading to decreased estrogen levels.

3. **St. John's Wort:** Herbal supplement that can reduce contraceptive effectiveness.

b. Drugs Affected by Estrogens

i. **Corticosteroids:**

1. Estrogens can increase plasma concentrations, enhancing effects and potential toxicity.

ii. **Thyroid Hormones:**

1. Estrogens increase thyroid-binding globulin, necessitating dose adjustments.

iii. **Anticoagulants:**

1. Estrogens may reduce the efficacy of warfarin, increasing clotting risk.

c. Other Considerations

i. **Alcohol:**

1. May increase estrogen levels due to decreased metabolism.

ii. **Antibiotics:**

1. Certain antibiotics may alter gut flora, affecting enterohepatic recycling of estrogens.

8. Clinical Preparations of Estrogens

Various formulations are available to tailor therapy according to individual needs and indications.

a. Oral Preparations

i. **Conjugated Estrogens:** (e.g., Premarin) for HRT.

ii. **Estradiol Valerate:** Used in HRT and some contraceptives.

iii. **Ethinylestradiol:** Common in COCs.

b. Transdermal Patches

i. **Estradiol Patches:** Provide steady hormone levels with reduced hepatic effects; used in HRT.

c. Topical Gels and Creams

i. **Estradiol Gels:** Applied to the skin for systemic absorption.

ii. **Vaginal Creams:** For local treatment of atrophic vaginitis.

d. Injectable Formulations

i. **Estradiol Cypionate/Valerate:** Long-acting injections for HRT.

e. Vaginal Rings and Tablets

i. **Estradiol Rings:** Provide continuous local estrogen release for urogenital symptoms.

ii.   **Vaginal Tablets:** For local estrogen therapy.

PROGESTERONE

Progesterone is a crucial steroid hormone in the female reproductive system, primarily involved in the menstrual cycle, pregnancy, and embryogenesis. It is produced mainly by the corpus luteum in the ovaries, the placenta during pregnancy, and, to a lesser extent, the adrenal glands. In pharmacology, progesterone and its synthetic analogs, known as **progestins**, are widely used in various therapeutic applications, including contraception, hormone replacement therapy (HRT), and the management of menstrual disorders.

This detailed overview will cover the following aspects of progesterone:

1. **Types and Sources of Progesterone**
2. **Mechanism of Action**
3. **Pharmacokinetics**
4. **Therapeutic Uses**
5. **Adverse Effects**
6. **Contraindications and Precautions**
7. **Drug Interactions**
8. **Clinical Preparations of Progesterone**

1. Types and Sources of Progesterone

Progesterone can be classified based on its origin and formulation into:

a. Endogenous (Natural) Progesterone

i.   **Produced in the Body:**

1. Mainly by the corpus luteum in the ovaries during the luteal phase of the menstrual cycle.
2. By the placenta during pregnancy.
3. To a lesser extent by the adrenal cortex.

b. Exogenous Progesterone

i.   **Natural Progesterone:**

1. Micronized progesterone: Formulated to improve oral absorption and bioavailability.

c. Synthetic Progestins

i. **First-Generation Progestins:**

1. **Norethindrone, Norethindrone Acetate:** Used in oral contraceptives and HRT.

ii. **Second-Generation Progestins:**

1. **Levonorgestrel, Norgestrel:** Potent progestins used in contraceptives, including emergency contraception.

iii. **Third-Generation Progestins:**

1. **Desogestrel, Norgestimate:** Developed to reduce androgenic side effects while maintaining contraceptive efficacy.

iv. **Fourth-Generation Progestins:**

1. **Drospirenone, Dienogest:** Designed to have anti-androgenic and anti-mineralocorticoid properties.

2. Mechanism of Action

Progesterone exerts its physiological effects primarily through its interaction with specific progesterone receptors (PRs) in target tissues, modulating gene expression and cellular function.

a. Progesterone Receptors

i. **PR-A and PR-B:** Two isoforms of nuclear progesterone receptors derived from a single gene.

1. **PR-A:** Acts as a repressor of PR-B function and regulates transcriptional activity.

2. **PR-B:** Responsible for the full spectrum of progesterone's actions in reproductive tissues.

b. Genomic Actions

i. **Binding to PRs:**

1. Progesterone diffuses across the cell membrane and binds to intracellular PRs.

ii. **Receptor Dimerization:**

1. The hormone-receptor complex forms dimers (PR-A/PR-A, PR-B/PR-B, or PR-A/PR-B).

iii. **DNA Binding:**

1. The dimerized complex binds to progesterone response elements (PREs) on DNA.

iv. **Gene Transcription Modulation:**

1. Recruitment of coactivators or corepressors alters transcription of target genes, leading to protein synthesis and resultant physiological effects.

c. Non-Genomic Actions

i. **Membrane-bound PRs:**

1. Mediate rapid, non-genomic actions through secondary messenger pathways (e.g., calcium signaling).
2. Involved in processes such as sperm motility, embryo implantation, and vascular tone regulation.

3. Pharmacokinetics

The pharmacokinetics of progesterone, including its absorption, distribution, metabolism, and excretion, vary depending on the route of administration and formulation.

a. Absorption

i. **Oral Administration:**

1. Natural progesterone has poor oral bioavailability due to extensive first-pass metabolism in the liver.
2. Micronized progesterone improves absorption but still requires higher doses.

ii. **Intramuscular and Subcutaneous Injections:**

1. Provide sustained release and prolonged action.

iii. **Transdermal Patches and Gels:**

1. Bypass first-pass metabolism, delivering steady systemic levels.

iv. **Vaginal Preparations:**

1. Local administration with rapid absorption; used for luteal phase support and in assisted reproductive technologies.

b. Distribution

i. Widely distributed throughout the body, crossing the blood-brain barrier and the placenta.

ii. Binds extensively to plasma proteins, including:

1. **Albumin:** Major binding protein.

2. **Corticosteroid-Binding Globulin (CBG):** Low-affinity binding.

c. Metabolism

i. Primarily metabolized in the **liver** through reduction, hydroxylation, and conjugation processes.

ii. Major metabolites include **pregnanediol** and **pregnanolone**.

iii. Metabolites are excreted in the urine as glucuronide and sulfate conjugates.

d. Excretion

i. Excreted primarily via the **kidneys** as conjugated metabolites.

ii. A small proportion is excreted in bile and feces.

4. Therapeutic Uses

Progesterone and its synthetic analogs are used in various clinical settings, reflecting their diverse physiological roles.

a. Contraception

i. **Combined Oral Contraceptives (COCs):**

1. Contain estrogen and progestin; inhibit ovulation and alter cervical mucus and endometrial lining.

ii. **Progestin-Only Contraceptives:**

    1. **Mini-Pills:** Progestin-only pills that thicken cervical mucus and alter the endometrium to prevent implantation.

    2. **Injectables (e.g., Depo-Provera):** Long-acting progestins that provide sustained contraceptive effects.

    3. **Implants (e.g., Nexplanon):** Subdermal progestin implants that provide long-term contraception.

    4. **Intrauterine Devices (IUDs) (e.g., Mirena):** Release progestin locally to prevent fertilization and implantation.

b. Hormone Replacement Therapy (HRT)

i. **For Menopausal Symptoms:**

    1. Used in combination with estrogen in women with an intact uterus to prevent endometrial hyperplasia and reduce the risk of endometrial cancer.

ii. **In Premature Ovarian Insufficiency:**

    1. Provides necessary hormonal support to prevent symptoms of estrogen deficiency and maintain bone density.

c. Management of Menstrual Disorders

i. **Dysmenorrhea:** Progestins reduce menstrual cramps by decreasing prostaglandin production.

ii. **Menorrhagia:** Progestins reduce heavy menstrual bleeding by stabilizing the endometrial lining.

iii. **Amenorrhea:** Progestin therapy induces withdrawal bleeding in women with secondary amenorrhea.

d. Support in Assisted Reproductive Technologies

i. **Luteal Phase Support:**

    1. Administered to enhance endometrial receptivity and support early pregnancy in assisted reproductive technologies (ART) like in vitro fertilization (IVF).

e. Endometriosis Management

i. Progestins are used to reduce endometrial growth and alleviate pain associated with endometriosis by inducing a hypoestrogenic state.

f. Prevention of Preterm Birth

i. **Progesterone Therapy:**

1. Used to reduce the risk of preterm birth in women with a history of spontaneous preterm delivery or those with a short cervix during pregnancy.

g. Treatment of Endometrial Hyperplasia and Cancer

i. **Progestins:**

1. Used to treat endometrial hyperplasia (without atypia) and certain cases of early-stage endometrial cancer by inducing differentiation and apoptosis of endometrial cells.

5. Adverse Effects

While progesterone and progestins are generally well-tolerated, they can cause a range of side effects, particularly with prolonged use or high doses.

a. Common Side Effects

i. Weight gain

ii. Fluid retention and edema

iii. Breast tenderness

iv. Mood swings and depression

v. Acne and hirsutism (with androgenic progestins)

vi. Irregular menstrual bleeding

b. Serious Adverse Effects

i. **Thromboembolic Events:**

1. Increased risk of deep vein thrombosis (DVT) and pulmonary embolism, particularly in combination with estrogen.

ii. **Cardiovascular Risks:**

1. May increase the risk of hypertension and cardiovascular disease, especially in smokers or older women.

iii. **Liver Dysfunction:**

1. Rare cases of hepatic adenomas and cholestatic jaundice.

iv. **Bone Density Loss:**

1. Long-term use of injectable progestins (e.g., Depo-Provera) may lead to decreased bone mineral density, increasing the risk of osteoporosis.

c. Metabolic Effects

i. **Glucose Tolerance:**

1. May impair glucose tolerance, requiring monitoring in diabetic patients.

ii. **Lipid Profile Alterations:**

1. Some progestins can adversely affect lipid profiles by decreasing HDL cholesterol and increasing LDL cholesterol.

d. Other Effects

i. **Allergic Reactions:**

1. Rare instances of hypersensitivity reactions, including rash, itching, and anaphylaxis.

ii. **Visual Disturbances:**

1. Rarely, progestins may cause visual disturbances due to retinal vascular changes.

6. Contraindications and Precautions

Progesterone therapy is contraindicated in certain conditions, and precautions should be taken in others to minimize risks.

a. Absolute Contraindications

i. **Active Thromboembolic Disorders:**

1. History of or current deep vein thrombosis (DVT), pulmonary embolism (PE), or stroke.

ii. **Liver Disease:**

1. Active liver disease or hepatic dysfunction.

iii. **Breast Cancer:**

1. Known or suspected breast cancer or other hormone-dependent malignancies.

iv. **Undiagnosed Vaginal Bleeding:**

1. Any unexplained vaginal bleeding requires investigation before starting progesterone therapy.

b. Relative Contraindications

i. **Cardiovascular Disease:**

1. Use with caution in patients with a history of cardiovascular disease or risk factors such as hypertension or hyperlipidemia.

ii. **Diabetes Mellitus:**

1. Monitor glucose levels closely in diabetic patients receiving progesterone therapy.

iii. **Migraine:**

1. Patients with a history of migraines, particularly those with aura, should be monitored closely due to an increased risk of stroke.

7. Drug Interactions

Progesterone may interact with various medications, affecting their efficacy or leading to adverse effects.

a. CYP450 Enzyme Inducers and Inhibitors

i. **Inducers (e.g., Rifampin, Phenytoin, Carbamazepine):**

1. Increase progesterone metabolism, potentially reducing its effectiveness.

ii. **Inhibitors (e.g., Ketoconazole, Erythromycin):**

1. Decrease progesterone metabolism, potentially increasing the risk of side effects.

b. Anticoagulants

i. **Warfarin:**

1. Progesterone may reduce the anticoagulant effect of warfarin, requiring dose adjustments and close monitoring of INR.

c. Antihypertensives

i. **Spironolactone:**

1. Drospirenone-containing progestins have anti-mineralocorticoid activity, which may enhance the hypotensive effect of spironolactone.

d. Diabetes Medications

i. **Insulin and Oral Hypoglycemics:**

1. Progesterone may impair glucose tolerance, necessitating adjustments in the dosage of diabetes medications.

8. Clinical Preparations of Progesterone

Progesterone is available in various formulations to meet different therapeutic needs.

a. Oral Preparations

i. **Micronized Progesterone Capsules (e.g., Prometrium):**

1. Used in hormone replacement therapy, luteal phase support, and for the treatment of menstrual disorders.

b. Injectable Preparations

i. **Progesterone in Oil:**

1. Administered intramuscularly for luteal phase support in assisted reproductive technologies.

c. Transdermal Preparations

i. **Progesterone Creams and Gels (e.g., Crinone):**

1. Used for hormone replacement therapy and luteal phase support.

d. Vaginal Preparations

i. **Vaginal Progesterone Gel (e.g., Crinone):**

1. Used for luteal phase support and in assisted reproductive technologies.

ii. **Vaginal Suppositories:**

1. Provide local administration for luteal phase support and the treatment of menstrual disorders.

ORAL CONTRACEPTIVES

Oral contraceptives (OCs) are a widely used method of hormonal birth control that prevent pregnancy primarily by inhibiting ovulation. They are a key component of pharmacology within the endocrine system due to their profound effects on hormonal regulation. OCs are typically categorized into two main types: **combined oral contraceptives (COCs),** which contain both an estrogen and a progestin, and **progestin-only pills (POPs),** which contain only a progestin. The choice of contraceptive type, formulation, and dosage is often tailored to the individual needs of the patient, considering factors such as efficacy, side effects, and underlying health conditions.

This comprehensive overview covers:

1. **Types of Oral Contraceptives**
2. **Mechanism of Action**
3. **Pharmacokinetics**
4. **Therapeutic Uses**
5. **Adverse Effects**
6. **Contraindications and Precautions**
7. **Drug Interactions**
8. **Clinical Preparations**

1. Types of Oral Contraceptives

Oral contraceptives are categorized based on their hormonal composition.

a. Combined Oral Contraceptives (COCs)

COCs contain both an estrogen and a progestin component. They are the most commonly used type of oral contraceptive and are available in various formulations:

i. **Monophasic Pills:**

1. Contain a fixed dose of estrogen and progestin in each active pill.
2. Examples: Ethinylestradiol + Levonorgestrel, Ethinylestradiol + Norethindrone.

ii. **Biphasic and Triphasic Pills:**

1. Contain varying doses of hormones throughout the cycle to more closely mimic the natural menstrual cycle.
2. Examples: Ethinylestradiol + Desogestrel (biphasic), Ethinylestradiol + Norgestimate (triphasic).

iii. **Extended-Cycle Pills:**

1. Designed to reduce the frequency of menstruation, with 84 active pills followed by 7 placebo pills or low-dose estrogen pills.
2. Examples: Ethinylestradiol + Levonorgestrel (Seasonale, Seasonique).

b. Progestin-Only Pills (POPs)

POPs, also known as "mini-pills," contain only a progestin and no estrogen. They are often recommended for women who cannot take estrogen due to contraindications:

i. **Low-Dose Progestin:**

1. Example: Norethindrone (Micronor).

ii. **Newer Progestins:**

1. Example: Drospirenone (Slynd).

2. Mechanism of Action

Oral contraceptives prevent pregnancy through several mechanisms that involve the suppression of the hypothalamic-pituitary-ovarian axis and alterations in the reproductive tract.

a. Inhibition of Ovulation

i. Estrogen Component:

1. Inhibits the release of follicle-stimulating hormone (FSH) from the anterior pituitary, preventing the development of the ovarian follicle.

ii. Progestin Component:

1. Suppresses luteinizing hormone (LH) surge, which is necessary for ovulation. By maintaining high levels of exogenous progestin, LH secretion is inhibited, and ovulation is effectively prevented.

b. Alteration of Cervical Mucus

i. Progestin Effect:

1. Increases the viscosity of cervical mucus, making it difficult for sperm to penetrate and reach the egg.

c. Endometrial Changes

i. Progestin Effect:

1. Induces a thin, atrophic endometrium, which is less receptive to implantation even if fertilization occurs.

d. Alteration of Tubal Motility

i. Both Estrogen and Progestin:

1. May affect the motility and secretion of the fallopian tubes, reducing the likelihood of sperm and egg meeting.

3. Pharmacokinetics

The pharmacokinetics of oral contraceptives vary depending on the specific formulation and the individual's metabolic profile.

a. Absorption

i. Oral Bioavailability:

1. Both estrogen and progestin components are well absorbed from the gastrointestinal tract. Ethinylestradiol, a common estrogen,

undperundergoes significant first-pass metabolism in the liver, which reduces its bioavailability.

b. Distribution

i. **Plasma Protein Binding:**

1. Both estrogen and progestins are extensively bound to plasma proteins. Estrogens primarily bind to sex hormone-binding globulin (SHBG), while progestins bind to SHBG and albumin.

c. Metabolism

i. **Hepatic Metabolism:**

1. Ethinylestradiol and progestins are metabolized by the liver, primarily through the cytochrome P450 enzyme system (CYP3A4). Metabolites are generally inactive but contribute to the enterohepatic circulation of these hormones, which can influence their overall activity.

d. Excretion

i. **Renal and Fecal Excretion:**

1. Metabolites of both estrogen and progestins are excreted via the kidneys and in the feces.

4. Therapeutic Uses

Oral contraceptives have multiple clinical applications beyond contraception.

a. Contraception

i. **Primary Use:**

1. Prevention of pregnancy through the mechanisms described above. Combined oral contraceptives are more commonly prescribed due to their high efficacy and additional benefits.

b. Management of Menstrual Disorders

i. **Dysmenorrhea:**

1. COCs reduce menstrual pain by decreasing the production of prostaglandins in the endometrium.

ii. **Menorrhagia:**

1. OCs reduce excessive menstrual bleeding by thinning the endometrial lining.

iii. **Amenorrhea:**

1. Hormonal therapy with OCs can help induce regular menstrual cycles.

c. Acne and Hirsutism

i. **Anti-Androgenic Effect:**

1. Certain COCs, particularly those containing newer progestins like drospirenone, reduce androgen levels, leading to improvement in acne and hirsutism.

d. Premenstrual Dysphoric Disorder (PMDD)

i. **Mood Regulation:**

1. Some OCs, especially those containing drospirenone, are effective in managing the symptoms of PMDD due to their anti-androgenic and mood-stabilizing effects.

e. Polycystic Ovary Syndrome (PCOS)

i. **Regulation of Menstrual Cycles:**

1. OCs help regulate menstrual cycles, reduce androgen levels, and improve symptoms associated with PCOS, such as acne and hirsutism.

f. Endometriosis

i. **Symptom Management:**

1. OCs suppress ovulation and reduce the proliferation of endometrial tissue, helping to manage the pain associated with endometriosis.

g. Reduction of Ovarian and Endometrial Cancer Risk

i. **Long-Term Use:**

1. Long-term use of COCs has been associated with a reduced risk of ovarian and endometrial cancers.

5. Adverse Effects

While oral contraceptives are generally safe, they can be associated with various side effects, some of which may be severe.

a. Common Side Effects

i.   Nausea

ii.   Breast tenderness

iii.   Headaches

iv.   Weight gain

v.   Mood changes

vi.   Breakthrough bleeding

b. Serious Adverse Effects

i.   **Thromboembolic Events:**

    1. Increased risk of deep vein thrombosis (DVT), pulmonary embolism (PE), and stroke, particularly in women who smoke or are over the age of 35.

ii.   **Cardiovascular Risks:**

    1. Elevated risk of myocardial infarction, especially in smokers and women with pre-existing cardiovascular conditions.

iii.   **Hypertension:**

    1. Long-term use may contribute to the development of hypertension.

c. Metabolic Effects

i.   **Glucose Tolerance:**

    1. OCs may impair glucose tolerance, which is particularly important in women with diabetes or at risk for diabetes.

ii.   **Lipid Profile Alterations:**

    1. Some progestins can adversely affect lipid profiles by increasing LDL cholesterol and decreasing HDL cholesterol.

d. Other Effects

i.   **Cholelithiasis:**

1. Increased risk of gallstone formation due to estrogen-induced changes in bile composition.

ii.   **Hepatic Effects:**

1. Rare cases of hepatic adenomas and other liver dysfunctions.

6. Contraindications and Precautions

Oral contraceptives are contraindicated in certain conditions, and precautions should be taken to minimize risks.

a. Absolute Contraindications

i.   **Active Thromboembolic Disorders:**

1. History or current deep vein thrombosis (DVT), pulmonary embolism (PE), or cerebrovascular disease.

ii.   **Cardiovascular Disease:**

1. Known or suspected ischemic heart disease or stroke.

iii.   **Breast Cancer:**

1. Current or history of hormone-sensitive cancers.

iv.   **Liver Disease:**

1. Active liver disease or hepatic dysfunction.

v.   **Uncontrolled Hypertension:**

1. Blood pressure above 160/100 mmHg.

7. Drug Interactions

Oral contraceptives may interact with various medications, leading to decreased efficacy or increased risk of adverse effects.

a. CYP450 Enzyme Inducers and Inhibitors

i.   **Inducers (e.g., Rifampin, Phenytoin, Carbamazepine):**

1. Increase metabolism of OCs, reducing contraceptive efficacy and increasing the risk of breakthrough bleeding and unintended pregnancy.

ii.   **Inhibitors (e.g., Ketoconazole, Erythromycin):**

1. Decrease metabolism of OCs, potentially increasing the risk of side effects like nausea and venous thromboembolism.

b. Antibiotics

i.   **Broad-Spectrum Antibiotics:**

1. Some antibiotics, particularly those affecting gut flora, may reduce the enterohepatic circulation of estrogens, potentially decreasing contraceptive efficacy.

c. Anticoagulants

i.   **Warfarin:**

1. OCs may decrease the anticoagulant effect of warfarin, necessitating dose adjustments and careful monitoring of INR.

d. Anti-Hypertensives

i.   **Spironolactone:**

1. Drospirenone-containing OCs have anti-mineralocorticoid activity, which may enhance the hypotensive effect of spironolactone.

e. Diabetes Medications

i.   **Insulin and Oral Hypoglycemics:**

1. OCs may impair glucose tolerance, necessitating adjustments in the dosage of diabetes medications.

8. Clinical Preparations

Oral contraceptives are available in various formulations to meet different therapeutic needs.

a. Monophasic Pills

i.   **Fixed-Dose Formulations:**

1. Example: Ethinylestradiol + Levonorgestrel.

b. Multiphasic Pills

i.   **Varying Dose Formulations:**

1. Examples: Biphasic or triphasic formulations, which vary the dose of hormones throughout the cycle.

c. Extended-Cycle Pills

   i.   **Reducing Frequency of Menstruation:**

      1. Example: Ethinylestradiol + Levonorgestrel (Seasonale).

d. Progestin-Only Pills (POPs)

   i.   **Progestin-Only Formulations:**

      1. Example: Norethindrone (Micronor).

DRUGS ACTING ON THE UTERUS

Drugs acting on the uterus are integral in the management of various obstetric and gynecological conditions. These drugs can either stimulate or relax uterine muscles, making them essential in managing labor, inducing abortion, controlling postpartum hemorrhage, and treating conditions like dysmenorrhea. The primary classes of drugs include **uterotonics** (which stimulate uterine contractions), **tocolytics** (which inhibit uterine contractions), and other drugs that affect uterine function by modulating hormonal influences.

This overview includes:

1. **Uterotonics**
2. **Tocolytics**
3. **Antiprogestins**
4. **Prostaglandins**
5. **Selective Estrogen Receptor Modulators (SERMs)**
6. **Clinical Applications**
7. **Adverse Effects**
8. **Contraindications and Precautions**
9. **Drug Interactions**

1. Uterotonics

Uterotonics are drugs that enhance uterine muscle contractions. They are primarily used in obstetric practice to induce labor, manage postpartum hemorrhage, and facilitate uterine involution after delivery.

a. Oxytocin

i. **Mechanism of Action:**

1. Oxytocin binds to oxytocin receptors on the uterine myometrium, causing an increase in intracellular calcium levels and stimulating uterine contractions. The sensitivity of the uterus to oxytocin increases during pregnancy, especially near term.

ii. **Therapeutic Uses:**

1. Induction and augmentation of labor.
2. Control of postpartum hemorrhage.
3. Facilitation of uterine involution.

iii. **Adverse Effects:**

1. Hyperstimulation of the uterus leading to fetal distress.
2. Water intoxication due to its antidiuretic effect.

b. Ergometrine (Ergonovine)

i. **Mechanism of Action:**

1. Ergometrine induces sustained uterine contractions by direct action on smooth muscle. It also has vasoconstrictive properties.

ii. **Therapeutic Uses:**

1. Prevention and treatment of postpartum and post-abortion hemorrhage.

iii. **Adverse Effects:**

1. Nausea, vomiting, hypertension, and possible risk of coronary artery spasm.

c. Prostaglandins (e.g., Dinoprostone, Misoprostol)

i. **Mechanism of Action:**

1. Prostaglandins stimulate uterine contractions by binding to specific prostaglandin receptors on the myometrium, leading to increased calcium levels and muscle contraction.

ii. **Therapeutic Uses:**

1. Induction of labor (Dinoprostone).

2. Medical abortion (Misoprostol).

3. Management of postpartum hemorrhage.

iii. **Adverse Effects:**

1. Gastrointestinal discomfort, uterine hyperstimulation, fever.

2. Tocolytics

Tocolytics are drugs that inhibit uterine contractions, primarily used to delay preterm labor.

a. Beta-2 Adrenergic Agonists (e.g., Terbutaline)

i. **Mechanism of Action:**

1. These drugs relax the uterine smooth muscle by activating beta-2 adrenergic receptors, which leads to an increase in cyclic AMP and a subsequent decrease in intracellular calcium levels.

ii. **Therapeutic Uses:**

1. Short-term management of preterm labor.

iii. **Adverse Effects:**

1. Tachycardia, palpitations, hyperglycemia, and tremors.

b. Calcium Channel Blockers (e.g., Nifedipine)

i. **Mechanism of Action:**

1. Nifedipine inhibits calcium influx through voltage-gated calcium channels, reducing uterine contractions.

ii. **Therapeutic Uses:**

1. Delay of preterm labor.

iii. **Adverse Effects:**

1. Hypotension, dizziness, and headache.

c. Magnesium Sulfate

i. **Mechanism of Action:**

1. Magnesium sulfate acts as a calcium antagonist, competing with calcium for entry into the cells and thereby reducing uterine contractions.

ii. **Therapeutic Uses:**

1. Neuroprotection in preterm labor.

2. Prevention of eclampsia.

iii. **Adverse Effects:**

1. Respiratory depression, hypotonia, and hypocalcemia in the neonate.

d. Oxytocin Receptor Antagonists (e.g., Atosiban)

i. **Mechanism of Action:**

1. Atosiban directly inhibits oxytocin receptors, reducing uterine contractions.

ii. **Therapeutic Uses:**

1. Management of preterm labor.

iii. **Adverse Effects:**

1. Nausea, vomiting, headache.

3. Antiprogestins

Antiprogestins block the action of progesterone, which is crucial for maintaining pregnancy.

a. Mifepristone (RU-486)

i. **Mechanism of Action:**

1. Mifepristone is a progesterone receptor antagonist that disrupts the maintenance of the uterine lining, leading to detachment of the pregnancy and cervical softening.

ii. **Therapeutic Uses:**

1. Medical termination of pregnancy in combination with a prostaglandin analogue (e.g., Misoprostol).

2. Management of missed or incomplete abortion.

3. Treatment of Cushing's syndrome (off-label).

iii. **Adverse Effects:**

1. Vaginal bleeding, cramping, nausea, and risk of infection.

4. Prostaglandins

Prostaglandins play a significant role in reproductive physiology by modulating uterine contractions.

a. Dinoprostone (PGE2)

   i.   **Mechanism of Action:**

       1. Dinoprostone, a natural prostaglandin E2, induces uterine contractions and cervical ripening.

   ii.   **Therapeutic Uses:**

       1. Induction of labor.

       2. Cervical ripening before surgical procedures.

   iii.   **Adverse Effects:**

       1. Nausea, vomiting, diarrhea, uterine hyperstimulation.

b. Misoprostol (PGE1)

   i.   **Mechanism of Action:**

       1. Misoprostol binds to prostaglandin receptors, leading to increased uterine tone and contractions.

   ii.   **Therapeutic Uses:**

       1. Medical abortion.

       2. Management of postpartum hemorrhage.

       3. Induction of labor.

   iii.   **Adverse Effects:**

       1. Uterine hyperstimulation, gastrointestinal disturbances.

5. Selective Estrogen Receptor Modulators (SERMs)

SERMs modulate estrogen receptors with tissue-specific effects on the uterus.

a. Tamoxifen

   i.   **Mechanism of Action:**

       1. Tamoxifen acts as an estrogen receptor antagonist in the breast but can have partial agonist effects on the uterus, potentially leading to endometrial hyperplasia.

ii. **Therapeutic Uses:**

    1. Treatment of estrogen receptor-positive breast cancer.

    2. Prevention of breast cancer in high-risk individuals.

iii. **Adverse Effects:**

    1. Risk of endometrial cancer, thromboembolic events, and hot flashes.

b. Raloxifene

i. **Mechanism of Action:**

    1. Raloxifene acts as an estrogen agonist in bone but an antagonist in the uterus and breast.

ii. **Therapeutic Uses:**

    1. Prevention and treatment of osteoporosis in postmenopausal women.

    2. Reduction of breast cancer risk in postmenopausal women.

iii. **Adverse Effects:**

    1. Risk of venous thromboembolism, leg cramps, hot flashes.

6. Clinical Applications

a. Labor Induction

i. **Drugs:**

    1. Oxytocin, Dinoprostone, Misoprostol.

ii. **Application:**

    1. Induction of labor in cases of post-term pregnancy or when early delivery is medically indicated.

b. Medical Abortion

i. **Drugs:**

    1. Mifepristone, Misoprostol.

ii. **Application:**

    1. Termination of early pregnancy, often up to 9 weeks of gestation.

c. Management of Preterm Labor

i. **Drugs:**

1. Tocolytics such as Terbutaline, Nifedipine, and Magnesium Sulfate.

ii. **Application:**

1. Delay of preterm birth to allow for fetal lung maturity.

d. Postpartum Hemorrhage Control

i. **Drugs:**

1. Oxytocin, Ergometrine, Misoprostol.

ii. **Application:**

1. Prevention and treatment of postpartum hemorrhage, which is a leading cause of maternal mortality.

e. Management of Menstrual Disorders

i. **Drugs:**

1. NSAIDs, hormonal therapies.

ii. **Application:**

1. Management of dysmenorrhea, menorrhagia, and other uterine-related menstrual disorders.

7. Adverse Effects

a. Uterotonics

i. **Adverse Effects:**

1. Uterine hyperstimulation, hypotension, water intoxication (Oxytocin).
2. Nausea, vomiting, hypertension (Ergometrine).

b. Tocolytics

i. **Adverse Effects:**

1. Tachycardia, hypotension, pulmonary edema (Beta-2 agonists).
2. Hypotension, dizziness (Nifedipine).

c. Prostaglandins

i. **Adverse Effects:**

1. Uterine rupture, gastrointestinal upset, hyperthermia (Misoprostol).

8. Contraindications and Precautions

a. Uterotonics

i. **Contraindications:**

1. Hypersensitivity, conditions with a high risk of uterine rupture.

b. Tocolytics

i. **Contraindications:**

1. Severe preeclampsia, intrauterine infection, placental abruption.

c. Prostaglandins

i. **Contraindications:**

1. Known hypersensitivity, previous cesarean section (caution with Misoprostol).

9. Drug Interactions

a. Oxytocin

i. **Interactions:**

1. Combined use with other uterotonics may increase the risk of uterine rupture.

b. Tocolytics

i. **Interactions:**

1. Concurrent use with corticosteroids may increase the risk of pulmonary edema.

c. Prostaglandins

i. **Interactions:**

1. NSAIDs may reduce the efficacy of prostaglandins.

Multiple Choice Questions (MCQs)

1. Which of the following drugs is used to treat hypothyroidism?

   a) Methimazole

b) L-Thyroxine

c) Propylthiouracil

d) Cortisone

2. What is the mechanism of action of antithyroid drugs like Methimazole?

   a) Inhibition of thyroid hormone synthesis

   b) Stimulation of thyroid hormone release

   c) Replacement of deficient thyroid hormones

   d) Blocking thyroid hormone receptors

3. Which of the following is a common side effect of corticosteroid use?

   a) Agranulocytosis

   b) Osteoporosis

   c) Hypothyroidism

   d) Hyperthyroidism

4. Which drug is used primarily for the medical termination of pregnancy?

   a) Mifepristone

   b) Levonorgestrel

   c) Ethinylestradiol

   d) Cortisone

5. Which of the following drugs is a phosphodiesterase inhibitor used to treat erectile dysfunction?

   a) Sildenafil

   b) Oxandrolone

   c) Methimazole

   d) Hydrocortisone

6. What is the primary therapeutic use of L-Thyroxine?

   a) Treatment of hyperthyroidism

   b) Treatment of hypothyroidism

   c) Treatment of Cushing's syndrome

   d) Treatment of Addison's disease

7. Which hormone is primarily replaced in hormone replacement therapy (HRT) for postmenopausal women?

   a) Progesterone

   b) Estrogen

   c) Testosterone

   d) Oxytocin

8. What is the mechanism of action of androgens like testosterone?

   a) Inhibition of protein synthesis

   b) Stimulation of androgen receptors

   c) Inhibition of androgen receptors

   d) Blocking estrogen receptors

9. Which of the following drugs is a synthetic estrogen commonly used in oral contraceptives?

   a) Norgestrel

   b) Mestranol

   c) Levonorgestrel

   d) Progesterone

10. Which of the following is a side effect of excessive androgen use in men?

   a) Virilization

   b) Gynecomastia

   c) Hirsutism

   d) Testicular atrophy

11. What class of drugs does Mifepristone belong to?

   a) Progestins

   b) Antiprogestins

   c) Estrogens

   d) Androgens

12. Which drug is used in the treatment of cachexia and muscle wasting?

   a) Spironolactone

b) Oxandrolone

c) Sildenafil

d) Levonorgestrel

13. Which hormone is commonly targeted by drugs like Methimazole and Propylthiouracil?

a) Insulin

b) Cortisol

c) Thyroid hormone

d) Estrogen

14. What is the primary action of Phosphodiesterase-5 inhibitors like Sildenafil?

a) Increase blood glucose levels

b) Relax smooth muscle in the corpus cavernosum

c) Stimulate androgen receptors

d) Inhibit thyroid hormone synthesis

15. Which of the following is a potential side effect of long-term corticosteroid use?

a) Cushing's syndrome

b) Hypothyroidism

c) Hypercalcemia

d) Hypoglycemia

16. Which drug is used to treat male hypogonadism?

a) Estrogen

b) Testosterone

c) Mifepristone

d) Propylthiouracil

17. Which of the following drugs is a non-steroidal synthetic estrogen?

a) Mestranol

b) Diethylstilbestrol (DES)

c) Progesterone

d) Norethindrone

18. Which of the following is a contraindication for estrogen therapy?

    a) Active liver disease

    b) Hypothyroidism

    c) Anemia

    d) Hyperthyroidism

19. What is the primary clinical use of antithyroid drugs like Propylthiouracil?

    a) Treatment of hypothyroidism

    b) Treatment of hyperthyroidism

    c) Treatment of Addison's disease

    d) Treatment of Cushing's syndrome

20. Which of the following drugs is an anabolic steroid?

    a) Oxandrolone

    b) Mifepristone

    c) Levonorgestrel

    d) Ethinylestradiol

Short Answer Questions (SAQs)

1. Explain the mechanism of action of corticosteroids in reducing inflammation.

2. What are the clinical uses of Phosphodiesterase-5 inhibitors like Sildenafil?

3. Describe the role of androgens in the treatment of male hypogonadism.

4. What are the potential side effects of long-term use of corticosteroids?

5. How do antithyroid drugs like Methimazole and Propylthiouracil work in the treatment of hyperthyroidism?

6. What is the clinical significance of using Mifepristone in medical termination of pregnancy?

7. Explain the mechanism of action and therapeutic uses of L-Thyroxine.

8. What are the primary therapeutic applications of estrogens in clinical practice?

9. Discuss the side effects associated with the use of synthetic androgens.

10. How does Sildenafil work to treat erectile dysfunction?

11. Describe the pharmacological actions of testosterone in the body.

12. What are the contraindications for the use of estrogen therapy?

13. How does Methimazole differ from Propylthiouracil in the treatment of hyperthyroidism?

14. What are the side effects of phosphodiesterase inhibitors like Sildenafil?

15. Explain the role of progesterone in hormone replacement therapy.

16. How are anabolic steroids used in the management of muscle wasting conditions?

17. What are the clinical uses of synthetic estrogens like Ethinylestradiol?

18. Discuss the potential adverse effects of Mifepristone in medical abortion.

19. How do corticosteroids affect glucose metabolism?

20. Explain the importance of monitoring thyroid hormone levels in patients receiving antithyroid drugs.

Long Answer Questions (LAQs)

1. Discuss the pharmacology, clinical uses, and side effects of corticosteroids in the treatment of inflammatory and autoimmune diseases.

2. Describe the role of androgens and anabolic steroids in clinical medicine, including their mechanisms of action, therapeutic uses, and potential side effects.

3. Explain the pharmacology, therapeutic applications, and side effects of estrogens in hormone replacement therapy and contraception.

4. Discuss the mechanism of action, clinical uses, and potential side effects of phosphodiesterase inhibitors like Sildenafil and Tadalafil.

5. Compare and contrast the use of Methimazole and Propylthiouracil in the management of hyperthyroidism, including their mechanisms, side effects, and clinical considerations.

6. Explain the pharmacological management of hypothyroidism, focusing on the use of L-Thyroxine and L-Triiodothyronine.

7. Describe the role of antiprogestins like Mifepristone in reproductive health, including their mechanisms, clinical uses, and potential risks.

8. Discuss the clinical applications and safety concerns of using oral contraceptives, including combined oral contraceptives and progestin-only pills.

9. Explain the mechanism of action and clinical applications of drugs acting on the uterus, including uterotonics and tocolytics.

10. Discuss the role of synthetic hormones in the management of endocrine disorders, focusing on their mechanisms, clinical applications, and potential side effects.

Answer Key for MCQs

1. b) L-Thyroxine
2. a) Inhibition of thyroid hormone synthesis
3. b) Osteoporosis
4. a) Mifepristone
5. a) Sildenafil
6. b) Treatment of hypothyroidism
7. b) Estrogen
8. b) Stimulation of androgen receptors
9. b) Mestranol
10. d) Testicular atrophy
11. b) Antiprogestins
12. b) Oxandrolone

13.c) Thyroid hormone

14.b) Relax smooth muscle in the corpus cavernosum

15.a) Cushing's syndrome

16.b) Testosterone

17.b) Diethylstilbestrol (DES)

18.a) Active liver disease

19.b) Treatment of hyperthyroidism

20.a) Oxandrolone

CHAPTER – 9

BIOASSAY

INTRODUCTION:

A bioassay is a type of scientific experiment that measures the effects of a substance on living organisms, tissues, or cells. It is a crucial tool in pharmacology, toxicology, and environmental science, used to assess the potency, concentration, and biological activity of a substance, such as a drug, chemical, or toxin.

Key Concepts in Bioassay:

1. **Purpose:**

    a. The primary aim of a bioassay is to determine the concentration or potency of a substance by observing its effect on living systems. This helps in understanding the therapeutic, toxic, or environmental impact of a substance.

2. **Types of Bioassays:**

    a. **Quantitative Bioassay**: Measures the exact amount of a substance required to produce a specific biological effect. It involves comparing the response produced by the test substance to that produced by a standard reference substance.

    b. **Qualitative Bioassay**: Provides a general assessment of the biological effect of a substance but does not measure the exact concentration. It's more about the presence or absence of an effect.

3. **Methods:**

    a. **Direct Method**: The substance is applied directly to the test organism or tissue, and the response is measured. For example, applying a drug to an isolated muscle and measuring its contraction.

b. **Indirect Method**: Involves measuring the effect of a substance on a biological system that then affects another system. For instance, measuring the blood pressure response in animals after administering a drug.

4. **Applications:**

   a. **Pharmacology**: To determine the effective dose and therapeutic index of new drugs.

   b. **Toxicology**: To assess the toxicity of chemicals, pollutants, and other environmental agents.

   c. **Environmental Science**: To evaluate the impact of pollutants on ecosystems by testing their effects on specific organisms.

5. **Common Test Systems:**

   a. **In Vivo Bioassays**: Performed on whole living organisms, such as animals or plants. Example: LD50 (lethal dose 50%) testing in animals.

   b. **In Vitro Bioassays**: Conducted on isolated cells, tissues, or organs. Example: Cell culture assays to test the cytotoxicity of a substance.

   c. **In Silico Bioassays**: Use computational models to predict the biological effects of a substance based on its chemical structure and known data.

6. **Standardization and Controls:**

   a. Bioassays require strict standardization to ensure accuracy and reproducibility. This includes the use of control groups, standard reference substances, and consistent test conditions.

7. **Limitations:**

   a. While bioassays provide valuable information, they can have limitations such as variability in biological responses, ethical concerns (especially with in vivo assays), and the need for complex setups and controls.

Principles and applications of bioassay

Bioassays are designed to evaluate the biological activity of a substance by measuring its effect on a living organism, tissue, or cell. The core principles governing bioassays include specificity, sensitivity, reproducibility, and quantifiability. Below are the key principles:

1. **Specificity**:
    a. The bioassay should measure the specific effect of the substance being tested without interference from other factors. This means the chosen biological system (organism, tissue, or cell) should respond specifically to the test substance.

2. **Sensitivity**:
    a. The assay system must be sensitive enough to detect even small quantities of the substance and produce measurable effects. This ensures that the assay can accurately determine the potency and concentration of the substance.

3. **Reproducibility**:
    a. The bioassay must yield consistent and reproducible results across different experiments. Standardization of procedures, conditions, and materials is critical to achieving reproducibility.

4. **Quantifiability**:
    a. A bioassay should allow for the quantification of the substance's effect, typically by generating a dose-response curve. This involves plotting the biological response against varying concentrations of the substance to determine its potency and efficacy.

5. **Control and Standardization**:
    a. Proper controls and standard reference materials are essential to validate the results of a bioassay. Negative controls (no effect) and positive controls (known effect) help in interpreting the results accurately.

6. **Statistical Analysis**:
   a. Bioassay data are typically analyzed using statistical methods to ensure that the observed effects are significant and not due to random variation. Common methods include probit analysis, regression analysis, and analysis of variance (ANOVA).

Applications of Bioassay

Bioassays have broad applications in various fields, including pharmacology, toxicology, environmental science, and biotechnology. Some of the major applications are:

1. **Drug Development**:
   a. **Potency Testing**: Bioassays are used to determine the potency of new drugs by comparing their effects with a standard reference drug.
   b. **Efficacy Testing**: Bioassays help in assessing the therapeutic efficacy of drugs in preclinical and clinical trials.
   c. **Dose-Response Studies**: Bioassays are used to establish dose-response relationships, which are crucial for determining the effective dose (ED50) and lethal dose (LD50) of drugs.

2. **Toxicology**:
   a. **Toxicity Testing**: Bioassays are essential for evaluating the toxicity of chemicals, pollutants, and other hazardous substances on living organisms. They help in determining the safe exposure levels and the potential health risks associated with these substances.
   b. **Environmental Monitoring**: Bioassays are employed to assess the impact of environmental pollutants on ecosystems by testing their effects on indicator species (e.g., fish, algae, or invertebrates).

3. **Quality Control in Manufacturing**:
   a. **Biological Product Testing**: Bioassays are used in the quality control of biological products, such as vaccines, hormones, and enzymes, to ensure their potency and safety.
   b. **Standardization of Herbal Products**: In the pharmaceutical industry, bioassays are used to standardize herbal products by measuring their biological activity.
4. **Agriculture**:
   a. **Pesticide Testing**: Bioassays are utilized to evaluate the efficacy and safety of pesticides, herbicides, and other agricultural chemicals on target pests and non-target organisms.
   b. **Plant Growth Regulation**: Bioassays help in testing plant growth regulators and fertilizers to optimize their use in agriculture.
5. **Environmental Toxicology**:
   a. **Biomonitoring**: Bioassays are used in biomonitoring programs to detect and quantify the presence of toxic substances in water, soil, and air. This helps in assessing the environmental impact of industrial and agricultural activities.
   b. **Ecotoxicology Studies**: Bioassays help in studying the toxic effects of pollutants on different trophic levels in ecosystems, providing valuable data for environmental protection and conservation efforts.
6. **Medical Research**:
   a. **Cancer Research**: Bioassays are used to screen potential anti-cancer agents by testing their effects on cancer cell lines.
   b. **Endocrine Disruptor Testing**: Bioassays help in identifying chemicals that disrupt the endocrine system by mimicking or blocking hormones in the body.

TYPES OF BIOASSAY

Bioassays can be categorized into various types based on their purpose, methodology, and the biological system used. Here are the primary types of bioassays:

1. Quantitative Bioassay

Quantitative bioassays measure the concentration or potency of a substance by comparing its biological effect to that of a standard reference substance. The results are typically expressed in terms of the dose or concentration required to produce a specific response.

Types of Quantitative Bioassay:

a. **Direct Comparison Assay:**

   i. Involves a direct comparison of the effect of the test substance with that of a standard substance. For example, the response (e.g., contraction of muscle, blood pressure change) is measured for both the test and standard substances, and their relative potencies are calculated.

b. **Graded Dose-Response Assay:**

   i. In this assay, varying doses of the test substance are administered, and the magnitude of the biological response is measured. A dose-response curve is plotted, and the effective dose (ED50) or lethal dose (LD50) is determined.

c. **Parallel Line Assay:**

   i. This method involves comparing the effects of different doses of the test substance and a standard substance, with the results plotted on a graph as parallel lines. The assay is particularly useful in determining the potency of hormones, vitamins, and other biologically active substances.

d. **Quantal Bioassay:**

    i.   A quantal bioassay measures the proportion of a population that responds to different doses of the substance. The response is binary (e.g., death/no death, occurrence/non-occurrence of a specific effect). The median effective dose (ED50) or lethal dose (LD50) is calculated from the dose-response curve.

2. Qualitative Bioassay

Qualitative bioassays provide a general assessment of the biological activity of a substance without determining its exact concentration or potency. These assays are typically used for screening purposes.

Types of Qualitative Bioassay:

a. **Yes/No Assay:**

    i.   This is a simple test that determines whether a substance produces a specific biological effect or not. It's commonly used in initial screening of compounds to identify potential biological activity.

b. **Threshold Assay:**

    i.   This assay determines the minimum concentration of a substance required to produce a detectable biological effect. It is often used in toxicity testing to identify the lowest observed effect level (LOEL).

3. In Vivo Bioassay

In vivo bioassays are conducted on whole living organisms, such as animals, plants, or humans. These assays provide comprehensive information on the biological effects of a substance, including its absorption, distribution, metabolism, and excretion.

Examples of In Vivo Bioassay:

a. **Animal Testing:**

    i.   Used to evaluate the safety, toxicity, and efficacy of drugs and chemicals. Common assays include the LD50 test (to determine the lethal dose for 50% of the population), and the Draize test (for skin and eye irritation).

b. **Plant Bioassays:**

    i.   Used in agriculture to test the effects of pesticides, herbicides, and fertilizers on plant growth and development.

4. In Vitro Bioassay

In vitro bioassays are performed outside of a living organism, typically in a controlled laboratory environment using isolated cells, tissues, or organs. These assays are widely used in drug discovery, toxicology, and research.

Examples of In Vitro Bioassay:

a. **Cell Culture Assays:**

    i.   Involve growing cells in a controlled environment and exposing them to test substances to measure effects like cell viability, proliferation, and apoptosis. Examples include the MTT assay (to assess cell viability) and the comet assay (to detect DNA damage).

b. **Tissue/Organ Assays:**

    i.   These assays use isolated tissues or organs to study the effects of substances on specific biological functions. For instance, isolated heart tissue can be used to test the effects of drugs on cardiac contractility.

5. In Silico Bioassay

In silico bioassays utilize computer models and simulations to predict the biological activity of a substance based on its chemical structure and known data. This type of bioassay is increasingly used in drug discovery and environmental toxicology due to its efficiency and cost-effectiveness.

Examples of In Silico Bioassay:

a. **Molecular Docking:**

i. A computational technique used to predict the interaction between a drug and its target protein, helping to identify potential therapeutic effects.

b. **Quantitative Structure-Activity Relationship (QSAR) Models:**

i. Use mathematical models to predict the biological activity of a substance based on its chemical structure. QSAR models are widely used in the early stages of drug development and environmental risk assessment.

6. Microbial Bioassay

Microbial bioassays utilize microorganisms, such as bacteria, yeast, or fungi, to test the effects of substances on microbial growth, metabolism, or genetic expression.

Examples of Microbial Bioassay:

a. **Antibiotic Testing:**

i. Used to determine the potency of antibiotics by measuring their effect on bacterial growth. The Kirby-Bauer disk diffusion test is a common example.

b. **Ames Test:**

i. A widely used assay that assesses the mutagenic potential of chemicals by observing their effect on the mutation rate in bacteria.

7. Biochemical Bioassay

Biochemical bioassays measure the effects of substances on specific biochemical processes, such as enzyme activity, receptor binding, or metabolic pathways.

Examples of Biochemical Bioassay:

a. **Enzyme Assays:**

i. Test the effect of substances on enzyme activity, which can provide insights into their mechanism of action. For example, an enzyme inhibition assay can be used to study how a drug inhibits a specific enzyme.

   b. **Receptor Binding Assays:**

      i. Measure the binding of a substance to a specific receptor, often used in pharmacology to assess the affinity and efficacy of drugs.

BIOASSAY OF INSULIN

Insulin is a vital hormone used in the treatment of diabetes, and its bioassay is essential to determine its potency, efficacy, and safety. The bioassay of insulin involves measuring its ability to lower blood glucose levels in vivo (in animals) or in vitro (in isolated tissues or cells). Given the critical nature of insulin's function in glucose metabolism, its bioassay is crucial in ensuring the consistent quality of insulin preparations.

Principles of Insulin Bioassay

1. **Glucose Lowering Effect**:

   a. The primary effect of insulin is to lower blood glucose levels by promoting glucose uptake in tissues like muscle and fat, and by inhibiting glucose production in the liver. The bioassay of insulin is based on this hypoglycemic effect.

2. **Standardization**:

   a. A reference standard of insulin with known potency is used in the bioassay to compare the activity of the test insulin preparation. The potency of the test sample is calculated relative to this standard.

3. **Dose-Response Relationship**:

   a. The bioassay typically involves administering different doses of insulin and measuring the corresponding biological response (e.g., reduction in blood glucose levels). A dose-response curve is plotted to determine the potency of the insulin sample.

Methods of Insulin Bioassay

1. In Vivo Bioassays

a. Rabbit Blood Glucose Method:

i.   **Procedure**:

1. The rabbit blood glucose method is a classical bioassay for insulin. In this method, rabbits are fasted for a certain period to stabilize their blood glucose levels.

2. Insulin is then administered intravenously or subcutaneously in different doses to different groups of rabbits.

3. Blood samples are taken at regular intervals to measure the blood glucose levels.

4. The hypoglycemic effect is determined by the reduction in blood glucose levels after insulin administration.

ii.   **Evaluation**:

1. The results are plotted to create a dose-response curve, and the potency of the test insulin is compared to a standard insulin preparation. The relative potency is expressed as a percentage of the standard.

b. Mouse Convulsion Method:

i.   **Procedure**:

1. This method is based on the observation that high doses of insulin induce convulsions in mice due to hypoglycemia.

2. Mice are injected with different doses of the test insulin preparation, and the time taken for convulsions to occur is recorded.

3. The shorter the time to convulsion, the more potent the insulin preparation.

ii.   **Evaluation**:

1. The potency of the test sample is determined by comparing the convulsion time with that of a standard insulin preparation.

c. Rat Blood Glucose Method:

i. **Procedure**:

1. Similar to the rabbit method, this involves fasting rats and administering insulin in varying doses.

2. Blood glucose levels are measured at different time points after insulin administration.

ii. **Evaluation**:

1. A dose-response curve is plotted, and the potency of the test insulin is determined relative to a standard preparation.

2. In Vitro Bioassays

a. Rat Diaphragm Assay:

i. **Procedure**:

1. This in vitro method involves isolating the diaphragm muscle from rats and incubating it with the test insulin preparation and a glucose solution.

2. The uptake of glucose by the diaphragm muscle in response to insulin is measured by determining the amount of glucose remaining in the incubation medium.

ii. **Evaluation**:

1. The glucose uptake is compared to that induced by a standard insulin preparation. The potency of the test insulin is calculated based on the glucose uptake.

b. Adipose Tissue Assay:

i. **Procedure**:

1. Adipose tissue (fat) from rats is isolated and incubated with the test insulin preparation.

2. The incorporation of glucose into lipids (fatty acids) in the adipose tissue is measured.

ii. **Evaluation**:

1. The ability of the test insulin to promote glucose incorporation into lipids is compared with that of a standard insulin. The potency of the test insulin is then determined.

Applications of Insulin Bioassay

1. **Quality Control**:
   a. Insulin bioassays are crucial in the pharmaceutical industry for quality control. They ensure that insulin preparations meet the required potency and efficacy standards before they are released for clinical use.

2. **Research and Development**:
   a. During the development of new insulin formulations, bioassays are used to assess their biological activity and compare them with existing products.

3. **Standardization**:
   a. Regulatory agencies require standardized bioassays to ensure consistency in insulin potency across different batches and manufacturers.

4. **Biosimilar Insulins**:
   a. Bioassays are also used in the development and approval of biosimilar insulins, ensuring they have the same biological activity as the original product.

BIOASSAY OF OXYTOCIN

Oxytocin is a peptide hormone and medication widely used to induce labor, control postpartum hemorrhage, and promote milk ejection during breastfeeding. The bioassay of oxytocin is crucial to determine its biological activity and potency. Since oxytocin exerts its effects primarily on the uterine muscles and mammary glands, the bioassay focuses on these tissues to evaluate its efficacy.

Principles of Oxytocin Bioassay

1. **Uterotonic Effect**:

   a. The primary action of oxytocin is to stimulate uterine contractions. The bioassay measures the strength and frequency of these contractions in response to oxytocin.

2. **Milk Ejection**:

   a. Oxytocin also stimulates the myoepithelial cells around the mammary alveoli, leading to milk ejection. This effect can be measured in specific bioassays.

Methods of Oxytocin Bioassay

1. In Vivo Bioassays

a. Rat Uterus Bioassay (In Situ or Isolated Uterus)

   i. **Procedure**:

      1. The rat uterus bioassay is one of the most common methods used to determine oxytocin's potency. The uterus from an estrogen-treated rat is isolated and placed in an organ bath containing a physiological solution.

      2. The uterus is then exposed to different concentrations of oxytocin, and the resulting contractions are measured using a force transducer connected to a recording device.

      3. The amplitude and frequency of contractions are recorded and compared to those induced by a standard oxytocin preparation.

   ii. **Evaluation**:

      1. A dose-response curve is generated by plotting the contractile response against the log of the oxytocin concentration. The potency of the test sample is determined by comparing its dose-response curve to that of the standard.

b. Rabbit Uterus Bioassay (In Vivo)

   i. **Procedure**:

1. In this method, the bioassay is performed on a living rabbit. Oxytocin is administered intravenously, and the resulting uterine contractions are recorded.

2. The uterus is exposed to increasing doses of oxytocin, and the contractile response is measured.

ii. **Evaluation**:

1. The intensity of uterine contractions is compared to those produced by a standard oxytocin preparation. The potency of the test oxytocin is calculated based on the response.

c. **Milk Ejection Assay in Lactating Rats or Rabbits**

i. **Procedure**:

1. This bioassay measures oxytocin's ability to induce milk ejection in lactating animals. The lactating animal is injected with oxytocin, and the amount of milk ejected from the mammary glands is measured.

2. The test oxytocin preparation is compared with a standard preparation to determine its efficacy.

ii. **Evaluation**:

1. The amount of milk ejected in response to the test oxytocin is compared to that ejected in response to a standard preparation. The potency of the test sample is calculated accordingly.

2. In Vitro Bioassays

a. **Isolated Guinea Pig Uterus Assay**

i. **Procedure**:

1. The isolated uterus of a guinea pig, pre-treated with estrogen, is used to measure the contractile response to oxytocin.

2. The uterus is mounted in an organ bath, and different concentrations of oxytocin are added. The contractions are recorded using a force transducer.

ii. **Evaluation**:

1. A dose-response curve is plotted, and the test sample's potency is compared to a standard oxytocin preparation.

b. **Isolated Rabbit Mammary Gland Assay**

i. **Procedure**:

1. This method assesses the oxytocin-induced milk ejection by isolating the mammary gland tissue from a lactating rabbit.
2. The tissue is placed in an organ bath, and the amount of milk ejected in response to oxytocin is measured.

ii. **Evaluation**:

1. The test sample's ability to induce milk ejection is compared to that of a standard oxytocin preparation, and its potency is calculated.

Applications of Oxytocin Bioassay

1. **Quality Control**:

a. Bioassays are essential in the pharmaceutical industry to ensure that oxytocin preparations meet the required standards of potency and efficacy before they are released for clinical use.

2. **Research and Development**:

a. In the development of new oxytocin analogs or formulations, bioassays are used to assess their biological activity and compare them to existing products.

3. **Regulatory Compliance**:

a. Regulatory agencies require standardized bioassays to ensure consistency in oxytocin potency across different batches and manufacturers.

4. **Biosimilar Development**:

a. Bioassays are also used in the development and approval of biosimilar oxytocin preparations to ensure they have the same biological activity as the original product.

BIOASSAY OF VASOPRESSIN

Vasopressin, also known as antidiuretic hormone (ADH), is a peptide hormone that plays a key role in regulating water balance in the body by increasing water reabsorption in the kidneys. Additionally, vasopressin causes vasoconstriction, which can increase blood pressure. The bioassay of vasopressin is crucial to assess its potency and effectiveness, particularly in its role in water retention and vasoconstriction.

Principles of Vasopressin Bioassay

1. **Antidiuretic Effect:**
   a. Vasopressin promotes water reabsorption in the kidneys by acting on the collecting ducts, reducing urine output. Bioassays often measure this effect to evaluate vasopressin's potency.

2. **Vasoconstrictive Effect:**
   a. Vasopressin causes constriction of blood vessels, leading to an increase in blood pressure. Some bioassays measure this effect to assess vasopressin's activity.

3. **Standardization:**
   a. A standard reference preparation of vasopressin with known activity is used for comparison. The biological activity of the test sample is expressed relative to this standard.

Methods of Vasopressin Bioassay

1. In Vivo Bioassays

a. **Rat Pressor Assay**

   i. **Procedure:**

      1. The rat pressor assay is a classical method for assessing vasopressin's vasoconstrictive effects. The test involves anesthetizing a rat and monitoring its blood pressure.

      2. Different doses of vasopressin are administered intravenously, and the resulting increase in blood pressure is recorded.

ii. **Evaluation**:

    1. The dose of vasopressin required to produce a specified increase in blood pressure is determined. A dose-response curve is plotted, and the potency of the test vasopressin is compared to a standard preparation.

b. **Rat Antidiuretic Assay**

  i. **Procedure**:

    1. In this method, rats are deprived of water to induce a state of diuresis (increased urine production). Vasopressin is then administered, and the reduction in urine output is measured.

    2. The amount of urine produced over a set period is collected and measured.

  ii. **Evaluation**:

    1. The antidiuretic effect of the test vasopressin is compared to that of a standard preparation by measuring the reduction in urine output. The potency of the test sample is determined by comparing the results to those obtained with the standard.

c. **Dog Antidiuretic Assay**

  i. **Procedure**:

    1. This assay is similar to the rat antidiuretic assay but is conducted in dogs. Dogs are deprived of water, and vasopressin is administered.

    2. The reduction in urine output is measured to assess the antidiuretic effect.

  ii. **Evaluation**:

    1. The potency of the test vasopressin is determined by comparing its effect on urine output to that of a standard vasopressin preparation.

2. In Vitro Bioassays

a. **Isolated Rat Kidney Assay**

  i. **Procedure**:

1. This in vitro method involves isolating the kidney from a rat and perfusing it with a solution containing vasopressin.

2. The effect of vasopressin on water reabsorption is measured by analyzing the composition of the urine produced by the isolated kidney.

ii. **Evaluation**:

1. The antidiuretic activity of the test vasopressin is compared to a standard preparation by measuring the water reabsorption in the kidney. The potency is calculated based on the response.

b. **Isolated Blood Vessel Assay**

i. **Procedure**:

1. This assay measures vasopressin's vasoconstrictive effect on isolated blood vessels. Blood vessels, such as the aorta or mesenteric arteries, are isolated from rats and placed in an organ bath.

2. The vessels are exposed to different concentrations of vasopressin, and the contractile response is measured using a force transducer.

ii. **Evaluation**:

1. A dose-response curve is plotted, and the contractile response to the test vasopressin is compared to that of a standard preparation. The potency is determined based on the vasoconstrictive effect.

Applications of Vasopressin Bioassay

1. **Quality Control**:

a. Bioassays are essential in the pharmaceutical industry to ensure that vasopressin preparations meet the required standards of potency and efficacy before they are released for clinical use.

2. **Research and Development**:

a. In the development of new vasopressin analogs or formulations, bioassays are used to assess their biological activity and compare them to existing products.

3. **Regulatory Compliance**:

   a. Regulatory agencies require standardized bioassays to ensure consistency in vasopressin potency across different batches and manufacturers.

4. **Biosimilar Development**:

   a. Bioassays are used in the development and approval of biosimilar vasopressin preparations, ensuring they have the same biological activity as the original product.

BIOASSAY OF ACTH

Adrenocorticotropic hormone (ACTH) is a peptide hormone produced by the anterior pituitary gland that stimulates the adrenal cortex to secrete glucocorticoids, primarily cortisol. The bioassay of ACTH is important for evaluating its biological activity and potency, particularly in its ability to stimulate adrenal steroidogenesis.

Principles of ACTH Bioassay

1. **Stimulation of Cortisol Production**:

   a. The primary action of ACTH is to stimulate the adrenal cortex to produce cortisol. Bioassays measure the increase in cortisol or other corticosteroids in response to ACTH administration.

2. **Standardization**:

   a. A standard reference preparation of ACTH is used to compare the biological activity of the test sample. The potency of the test ACTH is expressed relative to this standard.

Methods of ACTH Bioassay

1. In Vivo Bioassays

a. Rat Adrenal Gland Bioassay

i. **Procedure**:

1. This bioassay involves injecting ACTH into rats and measuring the subsequent increase in corticosteroid levels in the blood. Rats are used because their adrenal glands respond well to ACTH stimulation.

2. Blood samples are taken at intervals after ACTH administration, and the levels of cortisol or corticosterone are measured using a suitable assay, such as radioimmunoassay (RIA) or enzyme-linked immunosorbent assay (ELISA).

ii. **Evaluation**:

1. The corticosteroid levels in response to the test ACTH are compared to those produced by a standard ACTH preparation. A dose-response curve is generated, and the potency of the test sample is calculated by comparing it to the standard.

b. **Dog Adrenal Gland Bioassay**

i. **Procedure**:

1. This method is similar to the rat adrenal gland bioassay but is conducted in dogs. ACTH is administered, and the resulting increase in blood corticosteroid levels is measured.

ii. **Evaluation**:

1. The increase in corticosteroid levels in response to the test ACTH is compared to that produced by a standard preparation. The potency of the test sample is determined based on the response.

2. In Vitro Bioassays

a. **Isolated Rat Adrenal Cell Bioassay**

i. **Procedure**:

1. This in vitro method uses isolated adrenal cells from rats to measure the production of corticosteroids in response to ACTH.

The adrenal cells are incubated with different concentrations of ACTH.

2. The amount of corticosteroid (usually corticosterone or cortisol) released into the culture medium is measured using a suitable assay (RIA, ELISA).

ii. **Evaluation**:

1. The corticosteroid production by the adrenal cells in response to the test ACTH is compared to that of a standard ACTH preparation. A dose-response curve is plotted, and the potency of the test sample is calculated.

b. **Adrenal Cortex Slice Bioassay**

i. **Procedure**:

1. Slices of adrenal cortex tissue are used in this assay to measure corticosteroid production in response to ACTH. The tissue slices are incubated with ACTH, and the corticosteroid levels in the medium are measured.

ii. **Evaluation**:

1. The corticosteroid production is compared to that produced by a standard ACTH preparation. The potency of the test sample is determined based on the response curve.

c. **Isolated Perfused Adrenal Gland Bioassay**

i. **Procedure**:

1. This bioassay involves perfusing an isolated adrenal gland with a physiological solution and measuring corticosteroid production in response to ACTH.

2. The gland is perfused with different concentrations of ACTH, and the corticosteroid output is measured.

ii. **Evaluation**:

1. The corticosteroid production in response to the test ACTH is compared to that of a standard preparation. The potency of the test sample is calculated from the dose-response curve.

Applications of ACTH Bioassay

1. **Quality Control**:
   a. Bioassays are used to ensure that ACTH preparations meet the required potency standards before they are released for clinical use.

2. **Research and Development**:
   a. Bioassays are employed in the development of new ACTH analogs or formulations, as well as in the study of adrenal function and the regulation of corticosteroid production.

3. **Regulatory Compliance**:
   a. Regulatory agencies require standardized bioassays to ensure consistency in ACTH potency across different batches and manufacturers.

4. **Biosimilar Development**:
   a. Bioassays are essential in the development and approval of biosimilar ACTH preparations, ensuring they have the same biological activity as the original product.

BIOASSAY OF D-TUBOCURARINE

d-Tubocurarine is a naturally occurring alkaloid that acts as a non-depolarizing neuromuscular blocking agent. It is commonly used in clinical settings as a muscle relaxant during anesthesia. The bioassay of d-tubocurarine is essential to determine its potency and efficacy in blocking neuromuscular transmission.

Principles of d-Tubocurarine Bioassay

1. **Neuromuscular Blocking Effect**:
   a. d-Tubocurarine competes with acetylcholine at nicotinic receptors in the neuromuscular junction, preventing depolarization and

causing muscle relaxation. Bioassays measure this effect by evaluating muscle contraction or relaxation.

2. **Standardization**:

a. A standard reference preparation of d-tubocurarine with known activity is used for comparison. The biological activity of the test sample is expressed relative to this standard.

Methods of d-Tubocurarine Bioassay

1. In Vivo Bioassays

a. **Rabbit Head Drop Assay**

   i. **Procedure**:

      1. The rabbit head drop assay is one of the classical methods used to assess the neuromuscular blocking activity of d-tubocurarine.

      2. Rabbits are injected intravenously with different doses of d-tubocurarine. The onset of muscle paralysis is observed, particularly the point at which the rabbit is no longer able to hold its head up (the "head drop" point).

   ii. **Evaluation**:

      1. The dose of d-tubocurarine required to produce the head drop in 50% of the animals (ED50) is determined. A dose-response curve is plotted, and the potency of the test d-tubocurarine is compared to that of a standard preparation.

b. **Mouse Diaphragm Assay**

   i. **Procedure**:

      1. Mice are injected with d-tubocurarine, and the effect on their diaphragm muscle is observed. The diaphragm is the primary muscle involved in respiration, and its paralysis leads to respiratory failure.

      2. The time taken for respiratory arrest or the degree of diaphragm muscle relaxation is recorded.

ii. **Evaluation**:

> 1. The potency of the test d-tubocurarine is determined by comparing the degree of diaphragm muscle relaxation or the time to respiratory arrest with that produced by a standard preparation.

2. In Vitro Bioassays

a. Isolated Rat Phrenic Nerve-Diaphragm Preparation

i. **Procedure**:

> 1. This in vitro bioassay involves isolating the phrenic nerve and diaphragm muscle from a rat. The preparation is placed in an organ bath containing a physiological solution.
> 2. The phrenic nerve is electrically stimulated, causing the diaphragm to contract. d-Tubocurarine is added to the bath, and its effect on the muscle contractions is observed.

ii. **Evaluation**:

> 1. The reduction in the amplitude of muscle contractions in response to d-tubocurarine is measured. A dose-response curve is generated, and the potency of the test d-tubocurarine is compared to that of a standard preparation.

b. Isolated Frog Rectus Abdominis Muscle Assay

i. **Procedure**:

> 1. The rectus abdominis muscle is isolated from a frog and placed in an organ bath containing a physiological solution.
> 2. The muscle is exposed to d-tubocurarine, and the effect on muscle contraction is observed. The muscle can be stimulated either electrically or by adding acetylcholine to the bath.

ii. **Evaluation**:

> 1. The degree of muscle relaxation in response to d-tubocurarine is measured. The potency of the test d-tubocurarine is determined by

comparing the results with those obtained using a standard preparation.

c. Isolated Guinea Pig Ileum Assay

  i. **Procedure**:

    1. This method involves using the isolated ileum (a portion of the small intestine) from a guinea pig. The ileum is suspended in an organ bath and is exposed to d-tubocurarine.

    2. The effect of d-tubocurarine on the contractions of the ileum, which are typically induced by acetylcholine, is observed.

  ii. **Evaluation**:

    1. The inhibition of acetylcholine-induced contractions is measured. A dose-response curve is plotted, and the potency of the test d-tubocurarine is compared to that of a standard preparation.

Applications of d-Tubocurarine Bioassay

  1. **Quality Control**:

    a. Bioassays are used to ensure that d-tubocurarine preparations meet the required potency standards before they are released for clinical use.

  2. **Research and Development**:

    a. Bioassays are employed in the development of new neuromuscular blocking agents and in the study of neuromuscular transmission.

  3. **Regulatory Compliance**:

    a. Regulatory agencies require standardized bioassays to ensure consistency in d-tubocurarine potency across different batches and manufacturers.

  4. **Toxicology Studies**:

    a. Bioassays can be used in toxicology studies to determine the safety and appropriate dosing of d-tubocurarine and related compounds.

BIOASSAY OF DIGITALIS

Digitalis is a group of compounds derived from the foxglove plant, commonly used in the treatment of heart failure and atrial arrhythmias. The most notable compounds include digoxin and digitoxin, which exert their effects by inhibiting the Na^+/K^+-ATPase pump, leading to increased intracellular calcium and enhanced cardiac contractility. The bioassay of digitalis is crucial to assess its potency and therapeutic efficacy.

Principles of Digitalis Bioassay

1. **Cardiac Effects**:
    a. Digitalis compounds increase the force of cardiac contractions (positive inotropic effect) and slow the heart rate (negative chronotropic effect). Bioassays measure these effects to determine the potency of the digitalis preparation.

2. **Standardization**:
    a. A standard reference preparation of digitalis with known activity is used to compare the biological activity of the test sample.

Methods of Digitalis Bioassay

1. In Vivo Bioassays

a. **Pigeon Method (Cumulative Method)**

  i. **Procedure**:

    1. This method involves administering increasing doses of digitalis to pigeons until signs of toxicity or death occur, typically through intravenous or intramuscular injection.

    2. Pigeons are sensitive to the toxic effects of digitalis, and the endpoint of the bioassay is the dose that causes cardiac arrest or death in 50% of the birds (LD50).

  ii. **Evaluation**:

1. The LD50 value of the test digitalis is compared to that of a standard preparation. A dose-response curve is plotted, and the potency of the test sample is determined relative to the standard.

b. Cat Method

   i. **Procedure**:

1. Cats are anesthetized and the effects of digitalis on the heart are monitored. The drug is administered intravenously, and parameters such as heart rate, contractility, and blood pressure are recorded.
2. The cat's response to the test digitalis is compared to that of a standard preparation. The endpoint is usually the onset of arrhythmias or cardiac arrest.

   ii. **Evaluation**:

1. The potency of the test digitalis is calculated by comparing the response curve with that obtained using a standard digitalis preparation.

c. Frog Method

   i. **Procedure**:

1. Frogs are injected with digitalis, and their heart rate and contractility are observed. The response is typically assessed by examining the frog's heart under a microscope.
2. The endpoint is the dose of digitalis that causes cardiac arrest in the frog.

   ii. **Evaluation**:

1. The dose required to cause cardiac arrest in 50% of the frogs (LD50) is determined, and the potency of the test digitalis is compared to that of a standard preparation.

2. In Vitro Bioassays

a. Isolated Guinea Pig Heart Method (Langendorff Preparation)

   i. **Procedure**:

1. The isolated heart from a guinea pig is perfused with a physiological solution using the Langendorff apparatus. Digitalis is added to the perfusion fluid, and the effects on heart rate and contractility are observed.
2. The heart's response to increasing concentrations of digitalis is recorded, typically focusing on the force of contraction and the development of arrhythmias.

ii. **Evaluation**:

1. The potency of the test digitalis is determined by comparing the dose-response curve with that obtained using a standard digitalis preparation.

b. **Isolated Frog Heart Assay**

i. **Procedure**:

1. The isolated heart of a frog is suspended in a physiological solution and stimulated to contract. Digitalis is added, and its effects on the heart's contractions are observed.
2. The endpoint is typically the concentration of digitalis that leads to a marked decrease in heart rate or contractility.

ii. **Evaluation**:

1. The potency of the test digitalis is assessed by comparing the effects on the frog heart with those of a standard preparation.

c. **Isolated Rabbit Heart Assay**

i. **Procedure**:

1. The isolated rabbit heart is perfused with a physiological solution, and digitalis is introduced into the perfusion medium. The heart's contractile force and rhythm are monitored.
2. The endpoint may be the dose that causes arrhythmias or a significant decrease in heart rate.

ii. **Evaluation**:

    1. The potency of the test digitalis is calculated by comparing the response to that produced by a standard digitalis preparation.

Applications of Digitalis Bioassay

1. **Quality Control**:

    a. Bioassays are used to ensure that digitalis preparations meet potency standards before they are released for therapeutic use.

2. **Therapeutic Monitoring**:

    a. Bioassays help in determining appropriate dosing regimens for patients to avoid toxicity while ensuring efficacy.

3. **Pharmaceutical Development**:

    a. Bioassays are employed in the development of new cardiac glycosides or analogs and in the study of their pharmacodynamics.

4. **Regulatory Compliance**:

    a. Standardized bioassays are required by regulatory agencies to ensure the consistency of digitalis potency across different batches and manufacturers.

BIOASSAY OF HISTAMINE

Histamine is a biologically active amine involved in various physiological processes, including allergic responses, gastric acid secretion, and neurotransmission. The bioassay of histamine is essential for determining its potency, especially in pharmaceutical preparations and research settings.

Principles of Histamine Bioassay

1. **Smooth Muscle Contraction**:

    a. Histamine causes contraction of smooth muscles in various tissues, such as the guinea pig ileum, rabbit duodenum, and guinea pig trachea. This contraction is mediated by histamine receptors, primarily the H1 receptor. Bioassays measure this contractile effect to determine histamine's potency.

2. **Vasodilation and Increased Vascular Permeability**:

   a. Histamine can cause vasodilation and increase vascular permeability, leading to hypotension and edema. These effects can also be used to assess histamine activity.

3. **Standardization**:

   a. A standard reference preparation of histamine with known activity is used for comparison. The biological activity of the test sample is expressed relative to this standard.

Methods of Histamine Bioassay

1. In Vivo Bioassays

a. Guinea Pig Bronchoconstriction Assay

   i. **Procedure**:

      1. Histamine is administered to guinea pigs, typically via inhalation or intravenous injection, to induce bronchoconstriction (narrowing of the airways).

      2. The degree of bronchoconstriction is measured, usually by assessing the changes in airway resistance or by observing the respiratory distress in the animal.

   ii. **Evaluation**:

      1. The dose of histamine required to cause a 50% reduction in respiratory function (ED50) is determined. The potency of the test histamine is compared to that of a standard preparation.

b. Cat Hypotension Assay

   i. **Procedure**:

      1. Cats are anesthetized, and histamine is injected intravenously. The resulting drop in blood pressure (hypotension) is monitored.

      2. The magnitude and duration of the hypotensive response are recorded.

ii. **Evaluation**:

    1. The dose of histamine that produces a 50% reduction in blood pressure (ED50) is determined. The potency of the test histamine is compared to that of a standard preparation.

c. **Mouse Paw Edema Assay**

  i. **Procedure**:

    1. Histamine is injected subcutaneously into the paw of a mouse, causing localized edema (swelling) due to increased vascular permeability.

    2. The degree of edema is measured, usually by comparing the weight or volume of the treated paw to that of the untreated paw.

  ii. **Evaluation**:

    1. The dose of histamine that causes a significant increase in paw volume is determined. The potency of the test histamine is compared to that of a standard preparation.

2. In Vitro Bioassays

a. Guinea Pig Ileum Assay

  i. **Procedure**:

    1. The guinea pig ileum (a portion of the small intestine) is isolated and suspended in an organ bath containing a physiological solution. The ileum is subjected to electrical stimulation to induce contractions.

    2. Histamine is added to the bath, and its effect on the contractile response of the ileum is observed.

  ii. **Evaluation**:

    1. The increase in the amplitude of contractions in response to histamine is measured. A dose-response curve is generated, and the potency of the test histamine is compared to that of a standard preparation.

b. **Rabbit Duodenum Assay**

   i.   **Procedure**:

      1. The rabbit duodenum (part of the small intestine) is isolated and suspended in an organ bath. Histamine is added to the bath, and its effect on the contractile activity of the duodenum is observed.

      2. The response is recorded as an increase in muscle contraction.

   ii.   **Evaluation**:

      1. The potency of the test histamine is determined by comparing the response curve to that obtained using a standard histamine preparation.

c. **Guinea Pig Trachea Assay**

   i.   **Procedure**:

      1. The trachea of a guinea pig is isolated and suspended in an organ bath. Histamine is added to induce contraction of the tracheal smooth muscle.

      2. The contractile response is measured, typically as a change in the tracheal ring's tension.

   ii.   **Evaluation**:

      1. The potency of the test histamine is determined by comparing the contraction induced by the test sample to that induced by a standard histamine preparation.

Applications of Histamine Bioassay

   1. **Pharmaceutical Quality Control**:

      a. Bioassays are used to ensure that histamine preparations used in pharmaceuticals have the correct potency.

   2. **Research and Development**:

      a. Bioassays help in studying the effects of histamine on various tissues and in the development of histamine antagonists or other related compounds.

3. **Toxicology Studies**:

   a. Bioassays are used to assess the toxic effects of histamine and related compounds in animal models.

4. **Regulatory Compliance**:

   a. Standardized bioassays are required by regulatory agencies to ensure the consistency and safety of histamine preparations.

BIOASSAY OF 5-HT

5-Hydroxytryptamine (5-HT), commonly known as serotonin, is a neurotransmitter with various physiological roles, including regulation of mood, appetite, and sleep, as well as influencing gastrointestinal motility and cardiovascular function. The bioassay of 5-HT is important for evaluating its potency and understanding its biological effects in research and pharmaceutical applications.

Principles of 5-HT Bioassay

1. **Smooth Muscle Contraction**:

   a. 5-HT affects smooth muscle contraction in various tissues, such as the gastrointestinal tract and blood vessels. These effects are mediated primarily through 5-HT receptors, including 5-HT1, 5-HT2, and 5-HT3 subtypes.

2. **Standardization**:

   a. A standard reference preparation of 5-HT with known activity is used to compare the biological activity of the test sample.

Methods of 5-HT Bioassay

1. In Vivo Bioassays

a. Gastrointestinal Motility Assay (e.g., Rat or Mouse)

i. **Procedure**:

   1. 5-HT is administered to animals, and its effects on gastrointestinal motility are observed. This can be done by measuring the rate of gastric emptying or the contraction of the intestinal smooth muscle.

2. For example, 5-HT can be injected intraperitoneally (IP), and the effects on gastrointestinal transit are recorded.

ii. **Evaluation:**

1. The potency of 5-HT is assessed by measuring changes in gastrointestinal motility and comparing it to a standard 5-HT preparation.

b. **Rat or Mouse Blood Pressure Assay**

i. **Procedure:**

1. 5-HT is administered to rats or mice, and its effects on blood pressure are monitored. This involves measuring changes in systolic and diastolic blood pressure after 5-HT injection.

ii. **Evaluation:**

1. The dose required to produce a 50% change in blood pressure (ED50) is determined, and the potency of the test 5-HT is compared to that of a standard preparation.

c. **Mouse Ear Vasodilation Assay**

i. **Procedure:**

1. 5-HT is applied topically or injected into the ear of a mouse. The degree of vasodilation is observed as an increase in ear blood flow or a visible reddening of the ear.

ii. **Evaluation:**

1. The dose required to produce a significant vasodilation response is determined and compared to that of a standard 5-HT preparation.

2. In Vitro Bioassays

a. **Isolated Guinea Pig Ileum Assay**

i. **Procedure:**

1. The guinea pig ileum is isolated and suspended in an organ bath containing a physiological solution. 5-HT is added to the bath, and its effect on the contraction of the ileum is observed.

ii. **Evaluation:**

1. The increase in the amplitude of ileum contractions in response to 5-HT is measured. A dose-response curve is generated, and the potency of the test 5-HT is compared to that of a standard preparation.

b. **Isolated Rat Aorta Assay**

i. **Procedure:**

1. The isolated rat aorta is placed in an organ bath, and its contraction in response to 5-HT is observed. The tissue is pre-contracted with a vasoconstrictor to measure the relaxation effect.

ii. **Evaluation:**

1. The potency of 5-HT is assessed by measuring the degree of relaxation or contraction of the aorta compared to the standard preparation.

c. **Isolated Frog Rectus Abdominis Muscle Assay**

i. **Procedure:**

1. The isolated rectus abdominis muscle of a frog is placed in an organ bath. 5-HT is added, and its effect on muscle contraction is observed.

ii. **Evaluation:**

1. The potency of 5-HT is determined by comparing the degree of muscle contraction induced by the test sample to that induced by a standard preparation.

d. **Isolated Rabbit Heart Assay**

i. **Procedure:**

1. The isolated rabbit heart is perfused with a physiological solution, and the effects of 5-HT on heart rate and contractility are monitored.

ii. **Evaluation:**

1. The potency of 5-HT is determined by comparing the effects on heart rate and contractility with those of a standard preparation.

Applications of 5-HT Bioassay

1. **Pharmaceutical Development**:
   a. Bioassays are used to develop and evaluate drugs that target serotonin receptors, such as antidepressants and antiemetics.

2. **Research**:
   a. Bioassays help in studying the physiological and pharmacological roles of serotonin and in understanding its interactions with various receptors and systems.

3. **Quality Control**:
   a. Bioassays are employed to ensure the potency and consistency of serotonin preparations used in research and clinical settings.

4. **Regulatory Compliance**:
   a. Standardized bioassays are required by regulatory agencies to ensure the reliability and safety of serotonin-related pharmaceuticals.

Multiple Choice Questions (MCQs)

1. What is the primary purpose of a bioassay?
   a) To determine the color of a substance
   b) To measure the effects of a substance on living organisms
   c) To identify the physical properties of a substance
   d) To calculate the melting point of a substance

2. Which type of bioassay measures the exact amount of a substance required to produce a specific biological effect?
   a) Qualitative Bioassay
   b) Quantitative Bioassay

c) In Vivo Bioassay

d) In Vitro Bioassay

3. Which of the following is NOT an application of bioassays?

a) Drug development

b) Environmental monitoring

c) Determining molecular weight

d) Quality control in manufacturing

4. What does the term "ED50" refer to in a bioassay?

a) The dose that produces a toxic effect in 50% of the population

b) The effective dose that produces a response in 50% of the population

c) The dose that produces no effect

d) The dose that cures 50% of diseases

5. In the bioassay of insulin, which method involves measuring the reduction in blood glucose levels in rabbits?

a) Rat Diaphragm Assay

b) Rabbit Blood Glucose Method

c) Mouse Convulsion Method

d) Isolated Guinea Pig Uterus Assay

6. Which type of bioassay is used to assess the potency of oxytocin by measuring uterine contractions?

a) Rat Blood Glucose Method

b) Guinea Pig Ileum Assay

c) Rat Uterus Bioassay

d) Rabbit Duodenum Assay

7. What is the primary action of vasopressin that is measured in its bioassay?

a) Hypoglycemic effect

b) Antidiuretic effect

c) Muscle relaxation

d) Blood glucose reduction

8. The bioassay of d-tubocurarine typically measures its ability to:

    a) Increase blood pressure

    b) Relax muscles

    c) Stimulate uterine contractions

    d) Induce milk ejection

9. Which of the following is a common method used to assess the bioactivity of digitalis?

    a) Rabbit Head Drop Assay

    b) Isolated Frog Heart Assay

    c) Rat Pressor Assay

    d) Mouse Paw Edema Assay

10. In the bioassay of histamine, the guinea pig ileum assay is used to measure:

    a) Blood pressure

    b) Bronchoconstriction

    c) Muscle contraction

    d) Blood glucose levels

11. The in vitro bioassay of 5-HT can be conducted using:

    a) Isolated Rat Phrenic Nerve-Diaphragm Preparation

    b) Isolated Frog Rectus Abdominis Muscle Assay

    c) Rabbit Uterus Bioassay

    d) Rat Antidiuretic Assay

12. What is the principle behind the bioassay of ACTH?

    a) Inhibition of glucose uptake

    b) Stimulation of cortisol production

    c) Relaxation of bronchial muscles

    d) Reduction of urine output

13. In which bioassay method is the "head drop" in rabbits used as an endpoint?

    a) Mouse Convulsion Method

b) Rabbit Head Drop Assay

c) Isolated Rat Kidney Assay

d) Rat Adrenal Gland Bioassay

14. Which of the following bioassays is used to evaluate the milk ejection effect of oxytocin?

a) Rabbit Uterus Bioassay

b) Milk Ejection Assay in Lactating Rats

c) Rat Diaphragm Assay

d) Frog Method

15. The antidiuretic assay of vasopressin is typically performed in:

a) Dogs

b) Rabbits

c) Guinea pigs

d) Mice

16. What does the isolated rat phrenic nerve-diaphragm preparation assess in the bioassay of d-tubocurarine?

a) Contraction of the uterus

b) Reduction in blood glucose

c) Muscle relaxation

d) Increase in blood pressure

17. Which bioassay is used to assess the ability of histamine to induce bronchoconstriction?

a) Guinea Pig Ileum Assay

b) Guinea Pig Bronchoconstriction Assay

c) Mouse Paw Edema Assay

d) Rabbit Duodenum Assay

18. The bioassay of digitalis using the Langendorff preparation involves:

a) Isolated frog heart

b) Isolated rabbit heart

c) Isolated guinea pig heart

d) Isolated mouse heart

19. Which of the following is an example of an in silico bioassay?

a) Molecular Docking

b) Isolated Guinea Pig Uterus Assay

c) Pigeon Method

d) Rat Adrenal Gland Bioassay

20. The Ames Test is a type of:

a) Microbial Bioassay

b) In Vivo Bioassay

c) In Vitro Bioassay

d) In Silico Bioassay

Short Answer Questions (SAQs)

1. Define bioassay and explain its primary purpose.

2. Differentiate between quantitative and qualitative bioassays.

3. What is the significance of dose-response curves in bioassays?

4. Describe the Rabbit Blood Glucose Method for insulin bioassay.

5. Explain the principle behind the Rat Uterus Bioassay for oxytocin.

6. How is the antidiuretic effect of vasopressin measured in a bioassay?

7. What are the primary applications of bioassays in pharmacology?

8. Discuss the role of standard reference substances in bioassays.

9. Describe the Guinea Pig Ileum Assay for histamine bioassay.

10. What is the significance of the "head drop" endpoint in the Rabbit Head Drop Assay?

11. Explain the method used for the bioassay of 5-HT in isolated frog rectus abdominis muscle.

12. How is the potency of digitalis determined using the pigeon method?

13. Describe the Milk Ejection Assay used for oxytocin bioassay.

14. What is the role of bioassays in quality control of pharmaceuticals?

15. Explain the use of molecular docking in in silico bioassays.

16. How is the isolated rat phrenic nerve-diaphragm preparation used to assess d-tubocurarine?

17. Describe the method of the Langendorff preparation in digitalis bioassay.

18. What are the key differences between in vivo and in vitro bioassays?

19. Discuss the significance of microbial bioassays in assessing antibiotic potency.

20. What are the limitations of bioassays, and how can they be addressed?

Long Answer Questions (LAQs)

1. Discuss the principles, methods, and applications of bioassays, providing examples from pharmacology and toxicology.

2. Describe the types of bioassays used for insulin, including both in vivo and in vitro methods. Discuss the advantages and limitations of each.

3. Explain the bioassay methods used for oxytocin, focusing on uterotonic and milk ejection effects. Compare the efficacy of different bioassay models.

4. Discuss the role of bioassays in the quality control of pharmaceutical products, with specific examples related to vasopressin and d-tubocurarine.

5. Describe the bioassay techniques used to evaluate the potency of digitalis. How do these methods contribute to ensuring safe and effective therapeutic use?

6. Explain the importance of histamine bioassays in research and clinical settings. Discuss the various methods used and their respective applications.

7. Discuss the principles, methods, and significance of 5-HT bioassays in pharmaceutical development and research.

8. Explain the importance of bioassays in the development and approval of biosimilar products, providing examples of ACTH and oxytocin.

9. Compare and contrast in vivo and in vitro bioassays, discussing their respective advantages, limitations, and applications.

10.Discuss the application of in silico bioassays in modern drug discovery and environmental toxicology. How do these methods complement traditional bioassays?

Answer Key for MCQs

1. b) To measure the effects of a substance on living organisms

2. b) Quantitative Bioassay

3. c) Determining molecular weight

4. b) The effective dose that produces a response in 50% of the population

5. b) Rabbit Blood Glucose Method

6. c) Rat Uterus Bioassay

7. b) Antidiuretic effect

8. b) Relax muscles

9. b) Isolated Frog Heart Assay

10.c) Muscle contraction

11.b) Isolated Frog Rectus Abdominis Muscle Assay

12.b) Stimulation of cortisol production

13.b) Rabbit Head Drop Assay

14.b) Milk Ejection Assay in Lactating Rats

15.a) Dogs

16.c) Muscle relaxation

17.b) Guinea Pig Bronchoconstriction Assay

18.c) Isolated guinea pig heart

19.a) Molecular Docking

20.a) Microbial Bioassay